Amartya Sen

Amartya Sen was awarded the Nobel M("for his contributions to welfare economi appointments have been mostly in econor theorist and philosopher. His work on soc   _ ...inal, and his writings on poverty, famine, and development, as well as his contributions to moral and political philosophy, are important and influential. Sen's views about the nature and primacy of liberty also make him a major contemporary liberal thinker.

This volume of essays on aspects of Sen's work is aimed at a broad audience of readers interested in social theory, political philosophy, ethics, public policy, welfare economics, the theory of rational choice, poverty, and development. Written by a team of well-known experts, each chapter provides an overview of Sen's work in a particular area and a critical assessment of his contributions to the field.

Christopher W. Morris is professor of philosophy at the University of Maryland, College Park. He is the author of *An Essay on the Modern State* and coeditor, with Arthur Ripstein, of *Practical Rationality and Preference: Essays for David Gauthier.*

Contemporary Philosophy in Focus

Contemporary Philosophy in Focus offers a series of introductory volumes to many of the dominant philosophical thinkers of the current age. Each volume consists of newly commissioned essays that cover major contributions of a preeminent philosopher in a systematic and accessible manner. Comparable in scope and rationale to the highly successful series **Cambridge Companions to Philosophy**, the volumes do not presuppose that readers are already intimately familiar with the details of each philosopher's work. They thus combine exposition and critical analysis in a manner that will appeal to students of philosophy and to professionals, as well as to students across the humanities and social sciences.

VOLUMES IN THE SERIES:

Amartya Sen

Edited by

CHRISTOPHER W. MORRIS
University of Maryland, College Park

CAMBRIDGE
UNIVERSITY PRESS

CAMBRIDGE UNIVERSITY PRESS
Cambridge, New York, Melbourne, Madrid, Cape Town, Singapore,
São Paulo, Delhi, Dubai, Tokyo

Cambridge University Press
32 Avenue of the Americas, New York, NY 10013-2473, USA

www.cambridge.org
Information on this title: www.cambridge.org/9780521618069

First published 2010

Printed in the United States of America

A catalog record for this publication is available from the British Library.

Library of Congress Cataloging in Publication data

Amartya Sen / edited by Christopher Morris. – 1st ed.
   p.   cm. – (Contemporary philosophy in focus)
Includes bibliographical references and index.
ISBN 978-0-521-85291-3 (hardback) – ISBN 978-0-521-61806-9 (pbk.)
1. Sen, Amartya, 1933–   2. Social sciences – Philosophy.   3. Economics.
I. Morris, Christopher W.   II. Title.   III. Series.
H61.15.A43   2009
300.1–dc22   2009010913

ISBN   978-0-521-85291-3 Hardback
ISBN   978-0-521-61806-9 Paperback

For Terence Moore, in memoriam

Contents

Contributors

SABINA ALKIRE directs the Oxford Poverty and Human Development Initiative at the University of Oxford. Her publications include *Valuing Freedoms: Sen's Capability Approach and Poverty Reduction* (Oxford University Press, 2002) and numerous articles. She is the secretary of the Human Development and Capability Association (HDCA) and holds a DPhil in economics from Oxford (Magdalen College).

DAVID A. CROCKER is a senior research scholar at the Institute for Philosophy and Public Policy and the School of Public Policy at the University of Maryland. He directs the school's specialization in international development and the undergraduate College Park Scholars program in public leadership. Crocker specializes in sociopolitical philosophy, international development ethics, transitional justice, and democratic theory. He was twice a Fulbright Scholar at the University of Costa Rica and held the UNESCO Chair in Development at the University of Valencia. He is the author of *Ethics of Global Development: Agency, Capability, and Deliberative Democracy* (Cambridge University Press, 2008).

SHATAKSHEE DHONGDE is an assistant professor of economics at the Rochester Institute of Technology in Rochester, New York. She received her PhD from the University of California, Riverside, where she won the best graduate research award. Her research interests are in the fields of microeconomics and development economics and include topics such as inequality, growth, trade liberalization, poverty, and segregation. She has contributed essays to *Spatial Disparities in Human Development* (United Nations University Press, 2006) and *International Studies Association Compendium on Global Development* (Blackwell, forthcoming).

CHRISTOPHER W. MORRIS is a professor of philosophy at the University of Maryland, College Park. He is the author of "The Trouble with Justice" in *Morality and Self-Interest*, edited by Paul Bloomfield (Oxford University Press, 2008); "The Very Idea of Popular Sovereignty: 'We the People'

Reconsidered," in *Social Philosophy & Policy* (2000); and *An Essay on the Modern State* (Cambridge University Press, 1998) and coeditor, with Arthur Ripstein, of *Practical Rationality and Preference: Essays for David Gauthier* (Cambridge University Press, 2001).

PRASANTA K. PATTANAIK is an emeritus professor of economics at the University of California, Riverside, and is currently working on welfare economics and the theory of social choice, the measurement of deprivation and living standards, and the theory of stochastic preference and choice. Some of his recent publications are "On the Mean of Squared Deprivation Gaps" (with A. Chakraborty and Y. Xu) in *Economic Theory* (2008); "Minimal Relativism, Dominance, and Standard of Living Comparisons Based on Functionings" (with Y. Xu) in *Oxford Economic Papers* (2007); and "'Regular Choice' and the Weak Axiom of Stochastic Revealed Preference" (with I. Dasgupta) in *Economic Theory* (2007). He is a Fellow of the Econometric Society and of the Public Choice Society.

PHILIP PETTIT teaches political theory and philosophy at Princeton University, where he is the L. S. Rockefeller University Professor of Politics and Human Values. He is a Fellow of the American Academy of Arts and Sciences and holds fellowships in the Humanities and Social Sciences Academies in Australia. Among his books are *Republicanism* (Oxford University Press, 1997); *A Theory of Freedom* (Polity, 2001); *Rules, Reasons and Norms* (Oxford University Press, 2004); and *Made with Words: Hobbes on Language, Mind and Politics* (Princeton University Press, 2007). He has also coauthored a number of books, including *Mind, Morality and Explanation* with F. Jackson and M. Smith (Oxford University Press, 2004) and *The Economy of Esteem* with G. Brennan (Oxford University Press, 2004). A volume of essays on his work has appeared under the title *Common Minds: Themes from the Philosophy of Philip Pettit* (Oxford University Press, 2007).

KEVIN ROBERTS is the Sir John Hicks Professor of Economics at Oxford University and a Fellow of Nuffield College. He has previously taught at the London School of Economics and Political Science, MIT, and Warwick University. His main research interests are in microeconomic theory, broadly conceived, and he has a particular interest in the theoretical foundations of welfare and public economics, including social choice theory. He is a Fellow of the British Academy and of the Econometric Society.

INGRID ROBEYNS is a professor of practical philosophy at Erasmus University in Rotterdam, Netherlands. She studied philosophy and economics and received her doctorate from Cambridge University for a dissertation on gender inequality and the capability approach. In 2006, she was awarded a prestigious five-year Vidi grant for research on theories of justice by the Netherlands Organisation for Scientific Research. She coedited *Amartya Sen's Work and Ideas: A Gender Perspective* with Bina Agarwal and Jane Humphries (Routledge, 2005) and *Measuring Justice: Primary Goods and Capabilities* with Harry Brighouse (Cambridge University Press, forthcoming).

STEVEN SCALET is an associate professor of philosophy and economics and director of the Program in Philosophy, Politics, and Law at Binghamton University, State University of New York. He is currently writing a book about the ethics of markets and economics for Prentice Hall and has authored articles in business ethics and corporate responsibility. He is also the coeditor with John Arthur of *Morality and Moral Controversies* (8th ed., Prentice Hall, 2009).

DAVID SCHMIDTZ is the Kendrick Professor of Philosophy, joint professor of economics, and director of the Program in Philosophy of Freedom at the University of Arizona, and recently has taught property law at Florida State University College of Law. He is the author of *Rational Choice and Moral Agency* (Princeton University Press, 1995); *Elements of Justice* (Cambridge University Press, 2006); and *Person, Polis, Planet* (Oxford University Press, 2008) and coauthor with Robert Goodin of *Social Welfare and Individual Responsibility* (Cambridge University Press, 1998). He and Jason Brennan are working on a history of liberty for Blackwell's Brief History series.

PETER VALLENTYNE is the Florence G. Kline Professor of Philosophy at the University of Missouri, Columbia. He writes on issues of liberty and equality – and left-libertarianism in particular. He edited *Equality and Justice* (6 vols., Routledge, 2003) and *Contractarianism and Rational Choice: Essays on David Gauthier's "Morals by Agreement"* (Cambridge University Press, 1991), and he coedited, with Hillel Steiner, *The Origins of Left Libertarianism: An Anthology of Historical Writings* (Palgrave, 2000) and *Left-Libertarianism and Its Critics: The Contemporary Debate* (Palgrave, 2000). He was coeditor of *Economics and Philosophy* from 2003 to 2008.

Preface

The Cambridge University Press series *Contemporary Philosophy in Focus*, founded by my late editor Terence Moore, is meant to provide an introduction to the work of important living philosophers. The volumes in this series are to be, in good part, expository, as well as accessible to nonspecialists and to readers outside of philosophy. Terence invited me to put together a volume on the work of Amartya Sen, the 1998 Nobel laureate in economics. An economist by training, Sen is an important social and political theorist, and his work is very influential in contemporary moral and political philosophy.

My own interest in Sen's work initially was limited to social choice theory, to which I was introduced by Howard Sobel and David Gauthier while in graduate school in philosophy. In the early eighties, while a visiting assistant professor in government at the University of Texas at Austin, I sat in on Thomas Schwartz's eye-opening seminar on social choice theory and came to appreciate the importance of the field for the study of political institutions, as well as for moral theory. In the fall of 1986, I sat in on Sen's masterful (and breathless) lectures on social choice at Oxford and gained a broader appreciation of the field. Sen's critical thoughts about the theory of rational choice influenced me later. Sen's well-known studies of famine also interested me for a number of reasons, one being the revelation of an unambiguous virtue of democracy. Having absorbed a number of the pessimistic lessons about democratic institutions taught by contemporary political science and public choice theory, I was cheered by Sen's account of the importance of democracy for famine relief. And, much later, in part through the influence of David Crocker, I became interested in Sen's and Martha Nussbaum's accounts of capabilities and well-being.

Many people have offered me advice. I owe special thanks to Philippe Mongin early on and to Ingrid Robeyns for numerous matters along the way. A number of anonymous readers have offered helpful suggestions at different stages.

I am grateful to Terence Moore for the opportunity to work on this volume and to think more systematically about Sen's work. As can happen, it took longer to complete than anticipated, and Terence did not live to see the volume completed. Beatrice Rehl took over the project, and I am grateful for her patience and support.

With Terence's passing we have lost one of the great academic editors of our time. This volume is dedicated to his memory.

C.W.M.

Introduction

CHRISTOPHER W. MORRIS

Amartya Sen was awarded the 1998 Nobel Memorial Prize in Economics "for his contributions to welfare economics." Although his primary academic appointments have been mostly in economics, Sen is an important and influential social theorist. His work on social choice theory is seminal, as well as the first introduction many political philosophers have to the field. His books on poverty, famine, and development are well-known and influential. The primacy he places on liberty and its expansion is attractive to many. And, he has made many other contributions to moral and political philosophy.

One of the aims of this collection is to present some of Sen's work to a wider audience than that of scholars already familiar with it. To this end, the chapters devote a certain amount of space to presenting and summarizing Sen's writings on particular topics. There is some overlap between the chapters, as Sen's work on different topics is continuous and reflects concerns that underlie what otherwise may seem like different fields. There are some omissions, including some of Sen's most recent work, mainly because of constraints of space. This introduction is meant principally to highlight some of Sen's most important ideas and achievements, especially for those who are either unfamiliar with his work or familiar with only parts of it.

Amartya Sen was born in 1933 in Santiniketan in West Bengal, India. He spent much of his childhood in Dhaka in what is now Bangladesh. Following partition in 1947, his family moved to India. Sen studied in the school established by the Nobel laureate poet Rabindranath Tagore in Santiniketan and at Presidency College in Calcutta, where he earned a BA in economics. He moved to Cambridge University, where he obtained a second BA and a PhD. Winning a competitive Prize Fellowship at Trinity College, Cambridge, gave Sen "four years of freedom to do anything I liked (no questions asked), and I took the radical decision of studying philosophy in that period. I had always been interested in logic and in epistemology, but soon got involved in moral and political philosophy as well" (Sen 1998a). Sen's main academic appointments have been at Jadavpur University (Calcutta), Trinity College

(Cambridge), the University of Delhi, the London School of Economics, Oxford University, and Harvard University.

Sen's life has been an academic one, lived mostly in university settings. As he says in his autobiographical essay, "I was born in a University campus and seem to have lived all my life in one campus or another.... I have not had any serious non-academic job" (Sen 1998a). But, his life's work, even when mathematical and abstract, has been devoted to recognizably practical questions and interests.

Sen's Nobel Prize was, as we noted, awarded "for his contributions to welfare economics." Sen's writings range over many domains not normally grouped under welfare economics, but the term may serve as an umbrella for his work. He chose to devote his Nobel lecture to social choice theory, the study of the decisions or choices of groups of people, from small committees to large societies. There he says that

> if there is a central question that can be seen as the motivating issue that inspires social choice theory, it is this: how can it be possible to arrive at cogent aggregative judgments about the society (for example, about "social welfare," or "the public interest," or "aggregate poverty"), given the diversity of preferences, concerns, and predicaments of the different individuals *within* the society? How can we find any rational basis for making such aggregative judgements as "the society prefers this to that," or "the society should choose this over that," or "this is socially right?" Is reasonable social choice at all possible ... ? (Sen 1998b)

Social choice theory in its contemporary form was established by Kenneth Arrow. Sen is known for his development of Arrow's seminal work as well as for his appreciation of the breadth of the field or domain. As he says in his Nobel lecture,

> Social choice theory is a very broad discipline, covering a variety of distinct questions, and it may be useful to mention a few of the problems as illustrations of its subject matter (on many of which I have been privileged to work). When would *majority rule* yield unambiguous and consistent decisions? How can we judge how well a *society as a whole* is doing in the light of the disparate interests of its different members? How do we measure *aggregate poverty* in view of the varying predicaments and miseries of the diverse people that make up the society? How can we accommodate *rights and liberties* of persons while giving adequate recognition to their preferences? How do we appraise social valuations of public goods such as the *natural environment, or epidemiological security*? Also, some investigations, while not directly a part of social choice theory, have been helped by the

understanding generated by the study of group decisions (such as the causation and prevention of *famines and hunger*, or the forms and consequences of *gender inequality*, or the demands of *individual freedom* seen as a "social commitment"). The reach and relevance of social choice theory can be very extensive indeed. (Sen 1998b)

Arrow founded contemporary social choice theory in 1951 with a remarkable "impossibility theorem." He showed that no social choice procedure could satisfy all of a small number of conditions. The significance of the result is in no small part because of the fact that all of these conditions, at least at first glance, are reasonable to impose on most of the social choice mechanisms we know. Assuming that a social choice procedure[1] has to produce an ordering of alternatives,[2] it should also apply to any domain, that is, to any set of individual preferences (unrestricted domain). Next, it has to satisfy a technical but seemingly compelling condition requiring that social choice over any set of alternatives has to depend on preferences *only* over those alternatives (independence). Arrow showed that none could also satisfy two very weak and reasonable conditions, the Pareto principle and nondictatorship. The first of these requires that if everyone in a society prefers one alternative to another, the social choice procedure must as well; the nondictatorship condition rules out the possibility of a "dictator," someone whose preference for one alternative over another would dictate social choice regardless of how everyone else ranked the alternatives.[3]

Arrow's surprising result was initially viewed as destroying the possibility of social choice. The conditions seemed eminently reasonable, and the theorem so simple and robust, that it was hard not to be impressed. Considerable work was done attempting to avoid the impossibility result, but much of it merely deepened the pessimistic conclusions that were drawn from the initial theorem. Only abandoning or weakening one of the conditions would undermine the result. But, all of the conditions seemed plausible. One certainly would not want social choice mechanisms to allow for a "dictator." Our democratic political constitutions, for instance, are meant to prevent just that. And, it seems unacceptable to reject the weak Pareto principle. What are we to do?

Arrow's theorem spawned a body of research on voting systems of different kinds. Much of this has shown how voting procedures are subject

---

[1] Technically, a social welfare function.
[2] An ordering here is a set of binary relations that are reflexive, transitive, and complete.
[3] Additional conditions are that there are at least two individuals (and not infinitely many) and at least three alternatives. For further details and more formal statements, see Chapter 5.

to intransitivities of preference familiar to scholars (and politicians) at least since Condorcet's voting paradox.[4] Actual voting mechanisms respond to transitivities by relaxing one or more of Arrow's conditions. (For instance, in most elections and athletic contests, candidates or contestants may win without competing against and beating all others.)

Sen focused our attention especially on the so-called independence condition and on the ways in which it and other conditions effectively restrict the kinds of information that social choice mechanisms can use. Voting systems typically register information about how many voters prefer one alternative to another. Other information – for example, the intensity or urgency of their preferences, the identity of participants, ownership patterns, and other rights – is not to be taken into account. This makes sense for the formal study of many electoral systems. But, it make less sense for the formal study of a variety of questions about the condition of a group or society, about poverty, about opportunities, and the like. A study of certain kinds of evaluative and distributive questions requires taking into account more information.

Some of the Arrovian conditions, then, rule out choice mechanisms that use more or different information than voting rules do. This is not accidental. Economists early in the last century became skeptical of the possibility of comparing the preference satisfaction or well-being of one person to another. Preference satisfaction, welfare, and the like are often measured by utility functions, and the manner in which the latter are normally defined does not allow for comparisons between persons. Economists boldly declared interpersonal comparisons of utility to be "impossible." Certainly, if utility functions are understood to measure choices or preferences (understood in certain ways), then it is hard to see how they can be compared. However, it is hard to believe that all interpersonal comparisons are impossible. For instance, when one helps someone in a difficult spot, it is often with the thought that one's trouble benefits the other more than it burdens one. Similarly, Sen notes that Nero's gain in burning Rome surely was less than the loss of the other inhabitants of the city (Sen 1970a: 99). Some interpersonal comparisons surely can be made.[5]

Much of Sen's work in social choice theory has been in exploring mechanisms for judgment and choice that make use of more information than

---

[4] Condorcet (1785) showed how a preference cycle could occur with three voters and three alternatives – for instance, in a contest between three candidates, a majority of voters might prefer A to B, another majority B to C, and yet another majority C to A, suggesting that no outcome is stable.

[5] Some philosophers have argued that the very ascription of beliefs and desires to others presupposes such comparison (Davidson 1986).

permitted by the Arrovian framework (see Chapter 5 of this volume). His approach may be dubbed one of "informational enrichment." Not only may we for some purposes use information about interpersonal comparisons of utility, we should also use some information that is not represented by ordinary utility measures, even if interpersonally comparable. Sen has argued that preference satisfaction and other attitudes are not all that is important for the evaluation of social states. He has long been a critic of what he calls "welfarism," the view that evaluations of outcomes or alternatives are to consider only utility information. Sen argues that information about the satisfaction of needs and basic interests, opportunities and freedoms, and rights and duties must also be included for many purposes. His work in social choice theory and related fields is thus devoted to a broadening of the established framework for understanding social evaluation and choice.

Sen has long been interested in poverty and especially famine. His work here is very important. Not surprisingly, given his competencies in measurement theory and his sensitivities to questions about aggregation and distribution, Sen's work has been pioneering. He may be best known for his work on famine. He discovered, for instance, that famines can occur without any significant decline in food production in a country or region. The phenomenon of famine, he argues, is better understood as one of entitlement. For reasons having to do with income and relative prices, a group of people may be unable to secure an adequate amount of food to survive, even if enough is available where they live. Specifically, he discovered that famines have never occurred in democracies, no matter how poor. The explanation is simply that democratic pressures on government will lead to measures to prevent famines.[6]

Sen's interests in poverty and development have led him to be interested in the measurement of poverty. Difficult questions about measurement require thinking about the nature of poverty, and Sen is critical of influential characterizations of poverty. Levels of income are often used to measure poverty, understandably for many reasons, one of which being the relative availability of data about income. Some even say that poverty *is* lack of money. But, Sen argues that concentrating on income is inadequate in many contexts. Income is instrumentally significant, of course, but other factors may merit more attention than they are often given – for example, age, gender, health, location. Information about income may not tell the full story about the deprivations that many suffer. It also may not point in the

---

[6] A short introduction to Sen's views on famine is chapter 7 of Sen 1999. See also Chapter 7 of this volume. For Sen's work on development generally, see Chapter 8.

right directions for solutions. Sen has long urged that we concentrate our attentions on the substantive freedoms that people have to live their lives. In contrast to the influential utilitarian tradition in ethics, which would have us look at utility measures of well-being, and in contrast to the different proposals of some other theorists, such as John Rawls, Sen thinks we should be concerned with the real opportunities people have to pursue their objectives. This means that the concept of "functionings," what a person can do or be, is central to the analysis of poverty or deprivation. Functionings such as being adequately nourished or healthy are important, but so is being able to take part in the life of the community. A person's "capability set" is the different combinations of functionings that are feasible for him or her to achieve. "Capability is thus a kind of freedom: the substantive freedom to achieve alternative functioning combinations (or, less formally put, the freedom to achieve various lifestyles)" (Sen 1999: 75). An example that Sen frequently uses contrasts two people who are not eating enough. One is starving because he is destitute, the other one fasting while affluent. The two are equally hungry but have different capability sets or substantive freedoms. The "capability approach" to judgments about the development of a society and associated questions about policy can focus on what people are able to do, their realized functionings, or on their real opportunities, the capability sets of alternatives available to them.

Sen's focus on functionings and capabilities allows us to see what is wrong with understanding poverty solely in terms of low income. The latter is of course important and can be incorporated in his approach. But, the important insight lies in understanding that low income is but one deprivation of capability and that poverty generally is the deprivation of basic capabilities. (See especially Chapter 3 of this volume.)

Capabilities are a kind of freedom, the substantive freedom "to choose a life one has reason to value" (Sen 1999: 285). Sen is a liberal thinker in the broad, old-fashioned sense, that is, a political thinker for whom the value of liberty is primary. Sen thinks of the expansion of freedom as the primary end and means of development: "Development consists of the removal of various types of unfreedoms that leave people with little choice and little opportunity of exercising their reasoned agency" (1999: xii). Development, he argues, "requires the removal of major sources of unfreedom: poverty as well as tyranny, poor economic opportunities as well as systematic social deprivation, neglect of public facilities as well as intolerance or overactivity of repressive states" (1999: 3).

Sen's development of the capability approach to social evaluation and policy is central to his liberalism. Capabilities are a kind of freedom. But,

Sen's analysis of liberty is also a significant contribution to political thought. In 1970, he published an impossibility result with multiple implications for liberalism (1970a: chapters 6 and 6*; 1970b). The theorem, often dubbed the "paradox of the Paretian liberal," is very simple. Liberalism requires that people be allowed to make a number of choices undisturbed by others. Some of the least controversial would be "personal" choices, such as the decision to read *Lady Chatterley's Lover* (Sen's original example, now quite dated!). Sen shows that no social decision rule or procedure[7] exists that would provide a complete ordering of alternatives, would apply to any set of individual preferences (unrestricted domain), and would also satisfy the weak Pareto principle and a liberalism condition saying that each person is decisive over at least one pair of alternatives.

The theorem is very interesting and has given rise to much discussion and a huge literature. Some critical discussions raised questions as to how the notion of "decisiveness" should be understood, an important concern for our understanding of liberty and of rights. Many also worried that the social choice theoretic representation of freedom is misleading. Two different conceptions of freedom, direct and indirect, need to be distinguished. The first would have someone be decisive insofar as his or her choices determine which of two alternatives is to prevail; the second requires either actual or hypothetical choice. The distinction needs to be developed with some care (see Chapter 4 of this volume). Sen understands indirect freedom as a kind of liberty, and this has important implications for democracy and, in general, for understanding how institutions can sustain our liberty.

The significance that Sen attributes to freedom also helps to explain his capabilities approach to evaluation and policy. Sen thinks that in a number of contexts, especially policy ones, we should care about people's capabilities and not merely their functionings: "quality of life is to be assessed in terms of the capability to achieve valuable functionings" (Sen 1993: 31). Capabilities may enhance one's prospects (of functioning), but the value of the former are not exhausted by their consequences. Capabilities are a kind of freedom that may also have intrinsic importance.[8]

Sen is by training an economist – he may prefer the classical label, a "political economist." Economics is associated with an account of humans conceived as rational agents of a certain kind. One of the large lessons

---

[7] Technically a social decision function.

[8] This a quick summary of some very complex discussions, some initiated by G. A. Cohen's (1993) criticism of Sen and the latter's response, and some important clarifications made by Pettit. See Chapter 4 of this volume, as well as Pettit 2001 and Sen's reply (2001).

learned from classical economics is that much economic activity could be understood as motivated largely by the self-interested concerns of people. In neoclassical economics, the model of human action becomes that of utility maximization, permitting the development of more precise and mathematical economic models. More recently the (expected) utility-maximizing model has influenced much of social science as "rational choice theory." Sen is suitably impressed by the explanatory power of economic models, but he has always been worried about the narrow interpretations many economists place on "rational choice." For Sen, rationality generally is the "the discipline of subjecting one's choices – of actions as well as of objectives, values and priorities – to reasoned scrutiny" (2002: 4). But, economists usually think of rationality more narrowly. And, Sen has long been a critic of many of the different ways in which rational choice has been understood, especially the emphasis on self-interested behavior. His concern here has been in part to leave room for the ways in which people are not always self-interested in their thought and action, especially when they cooperate with others. The rational agents of economic theory are often, in his words, "rational fools" (Sen 1977).[9]

Sen's research is rarely divorced from his ethical and political concerns. From his abstract studies of social choice theory to his work on the measurement of poverty, his interests are broadly moral. Part of his extraordinary influence has been to restore "an ethical dimension to economics and related disciplines" (Nobel Committee 1998). 'Restoration' is the appropriate term, as Adam Smith and other classical economists did not accept the divorce between economics and ethics (and politics) influential in the twentieth century. Sen's work has also contributed enormous clarity to different parts of moral philosophy, in particular the theory of justice. He has analyzed in very helpful ways the differences and relations between different kinds of principles of justice. (See Chapter 6 of this volume.)

Sen has been concerned with the ways in which certain understandings of rational choice are inimical to ethics. (See Chapter 2 of this volume.) For instance, if people are understood largely as self-interested in certain ways, it is hard to find much room for a number of moral concerns, especially values of justice. Sen has as well made a number of contributions to moral theory more narrowly understood. He has written extensively about human rights and has questioned attacks on their universality, especially from the standpoint of "Asian values." He has written a number of papers

---

[9] See Chapter 1 in this volume.

on the theory of justice and is now working on a statement of his views on justice.

As noted, we do not propose to cover all of Sen's major areas of interest in this volume. He has many publications about India, and, aside from some of his studies of poverty, we have left this large topic to the side. We also have left out many topics of interest primarily to economists working in different subfields of the discipline. More recently, Sen has published *Identity and Violence: The Illusion of Destiny* (2006), a work already translated into eight languages. Sen's lifelong interests in identity and commitment are treated only as part of other topics. In his autobiographical essay, he notes that he was impressed early on by the cultural diversity of India, as well as by the ease with which people's identities gave rise to murderous violence. One particular story is striking:

> I had to observe, as a young child, some of that mindless violence. One afternoon in Dhaka, a man came through the gate screaming pitifully and bleeding profusely. The wounded person, who had been knifed in the back, was a Muslim daily labourer, called Kader Mia. He had come for some work in a neighbouring house – for a tiny reward – and had been knifed on the street by some communal thugs in our largely Hindu area. As he was being taken to the hospital by my father, he went on saying that his wife had told him not to go into a hostile area during the communal riots. But he had to go out in search of work and earning because his family had nothing to eat. The penalty of that economic unfreedom turned out to be death, which occurred later on in the hospital. The experience was devastating for me, and suddenly made me aware of the dangers of narrowly defined identities, and also of the divisiveness that can lie buried in communitarian politics. It also alerted me to the remarkable fact that economic unfreedom, in the form of extreme poverty, can make a person a helpless prey in the violation of other kinds of freedom: Kader Mia need not have come to a hostile area in search of income in those troubled times if his family could have managed without it. (Sen 1998a)

This incident also shows how Sen's experiences have fed his more abstract theoretical concerns.

A volume as slim as this one cannot cover all of Sen's work, but it should provide a good introduction. Readers who know little about Sen's work or who merely know something about one of his many areas of research might welcome further guidance. Someone interested in learning about Sen's work could read the chapters of this volume in order. But, some of the essays (especially Chapters 1, 5, and 6) may be difficult for readers who are not accustomed to the abstract styles of philosophers and economists or who are unfamiliar with elementary formal logic or set theory. Much of Sen's work is more formal or mathematical than that of most of the other thinkers represented in the Contemporary Philosophy in Focus series. Some familiarity with economics or rational choice theory will be useful for parts of many of the chapters. So, depending on the particular interests of readers, the chapters may be read in different orders.

The first four chapters cover topics familiar to philosophers and social theorists: the nature of rational choice, the relation between ethics and rationality, well-being and agency, and freedom. The second group of four chapters focuses more on societies and institutions: social choice theory, principles of distributive justice, famine and poverty, and the theory of development. Readers most interested in Sen's "political" work might start with these chapters.

The theory of rational choice that dominates economics and Sen's important criticisms of it are the topic of the opening chapter by Shatak-shee Dhongde and Prasanta K. Pattanaik. It may be difficult reading for the uninitiated, although the formalisms are not very complex. The dominant account of rationality in economics is also influential in the other social sciences as well as in philosophy. Sen's critical concerns are of great import to social theory in general. The second chapter, by Christopher W. Morris, focuses on the relation between economics and ethics, specifically the kinds of skepticism of ethics that have come from economics. This chapter follows naturally from the first, but may be read independently.

Although most economists and most social theorists know something about Sen's work, many others have come to it through his account of human well-being or, rather, his theory of capabilities and functionings. This is the topic of the chapter by David A. Crocker and Ingrid Robeyns. Readers interested especially in this part of Sen's work may start with this chapter and then turn to the next chapter on freedom and the last one on development. In Chapter 4, on freedom, Philip Pettit examines Sen's important analyses of human freedom and proposes some extensions of these.

As we have noted, Sen chose social choice theory as the topic for his Nobel Prize address. His distinctive approach to social choice theory is explained in Chapter 5 by Kevin Roberts. This is the work of Sen's that first attracted the attention of many economists and philosophers, and it is of great importance to social theory, as well as to moral theory. Chapter 6, by Peter Vallentyne, focuses on Sen's study of principles of justice, a topic closely related to his work on social choice theory. This chapter may be of special interest to political philosophers.

The last two chapters focus on a number of questions about poverty, development, and famine that Sen has addressed. Chapter 7, by Steven Scalet and David Schmidtz, examines Sen's influential writings on famine, and Chapter 8, by Sabina Alkire, offers a critical survey of his large body of work on human development. Some readers, perhaps neither economists nor philosophers, may wish to start with these essays and then move to the earlier ones.

There are, then, many different ways of approaching the chapters of this book. It is hoped that the essays will be useful to the different audiences that share interests with Sen. Sen's own writings are typically clear and well written, and they often offer the best introduction to his own work and to the field in question. The only difficulty for those who do not know his work well is its quantity. A short bibliography of Sen's writings is provided at the end of the volume, in addition to the reference lists accompanying each chapter.[10]

References

Caritat, M. J. A. N. de, Marquis de Condorcet (1785). *Essay on the Application of Analysis to the Probability of Majority Decisions*.

Cohen, G. A. (1993). "Equality of What? On Welfare, Goods, and Capabilities," in Nussbaum and Sen (eds.), *The Quality of Life* (Oxford: Clarendon Press).

Davidson, D. (1986). "Judging Interpersonal Interests," in Elster and Hylland (eds.), *Foundations of Social Choice Theory* (Cambridge: Cambridge University Press).

Nobel Committee (1998). Statement of the award of the 1998 Nobel Memorial Prize in Economics, Press Release (Background Information). http://nobelprize.org/ nobel_prizes/economics/laureates/1998/ecoback98.pdf.

Pettit, P. (2001). "Capabilities and Freedom: A Defense of Sen," *Economics & Philosophy*, 17, 1–20.

Sen, A. K. (1970a). *Collective Choice and Social Welfare* (San Francisco: Holden-Day; republished, Amsterdam: North-Holland, 1979).

Sen, A. K. (1970b). "The Impossibility of a Paretian Liberal," *Journal of Political Economy*, 78, 152–7.

Sen, A. K. (1977). "Rational Fools: A Critique of the Behavioral Foundations of Economic Theory," *Philosophy & Public Affairs*, 6, 317–44.

Sen, A. K. (1993). "Capabilities and Well-Being," in Nussbaum and Sen (eds.), *The Quality of Life* (Oxford: Clarendon Press).

Sen, A. K. (1998a). "Autobiography." http://nobelprize.org/nobel_prizes/economics/ laureates/1998/sen-autobio.html.

---

[10] A complete list of Sen's publications may be found on his Web site (http://www.economics. harvard.edu/faculty/sen).

Sen, A. K. (1998b). "The Possibility of Social Choice." http://nobelprize.org/nobel_prizes/economics/laureates/1998/sen-lecture.html.

Sen, A. K. (1999). *Development as Freedom* (New York: Knopf).

Sen, A. K. (2001). "Reply [to Anderson, Pettit, and Scanlon]," *Economics & Philosophy*, 17, 51–66.

Sen, A. K. (2002). *Rationality and Freedom* (Cambridge, MA: Harvard University Press).

1 Preference, Choice, and Rationality
Amartya Sen's Critique of the Theory of Rational Choice in Economics

SHATAKSHEE DHONGDE AND PRASANTA K. PATTANAIK

1. INTRODUCTION

The theory of preference and rational choice of individuals constitutes the foundation of much of positive economic theory. It is also intimately linked to normative economics, especially the part of normative economics that studies welfare properties of the competitive market mechanism.[1] It is not, therefore, surprising that the theory of individual preference and rational choice has engaged some of the leading economic theorists of our time, such as Kenneth J. Arrow (1958, 1959, 1971), J. R. Hicks (1939, 1956), P. Samuelson (1938, 1947), and A. K. Sen (1969, 1971, 1973, 1974, 1977a, 1977b, 1981, 1986a, 1986b, 1989, 1991, 1993, 1994, 1995). The role of Sen in this foundational area of economic theory has been somewhat different from that of many other prominent theorists. Although, in some of his earlier works (see Sen 1969, 1971, 1977a), Sen has made important contributions to the traditional economic theory of rational choice and preference, several aspects of this theory have come under searching criticism by him. He has repeatedly asked probing questions about the intuitive significance and realism of various elements in the mainstream economic theory of rational choice and drawn attention to many limitations of the theory. The purpose of this chapter is to review Sen's contributions to the theory of rational choice by individuals, especially his contributions as a critic of the conventional economic theory of rational choice.

The plan of the chapter is as follows. In section 2, we briefly recapitulate some features of the theory of rational choice as it has developed in mainstream economics. Whereas economists may like to skip this section, noneconomists, who may not be familiar with the standard theory of

---

[1] The two "fundamental theorems of welfare economics" are classic examples of the close connection that exists between the economists' theory of rational choice and the welfare properties of competitive market equilibria. For rigorous statements and proofs of these theorems, see Arrow (1951), Debreu (1959), and Koopmans (1957), among others.

rational choice in economics, may find it helpful as a background for Sen's ideas. Sections 3 and 4 are devoted to Sen's critical analysis of two different branches of the theory of rational choice. Section 3 deals with Sen's critique of the so-called revealed preference approach to the issue of rational choice, where the primitive concept of the theory is choice rather than preference. In section 4, we consider Sen's thoughts on the preference-based theory of rational choice in economics. We conclude in section 5.

2. SOME SALIENT FEATURES OF THE ECONOMIC THEORY OF RATIONAL CHOICE UNDER PERFECT CERTAINTY

The theory of rational choice in economics is not entirely homogeneous in nature.

It takes somewhat different forms depending on the nature of the problem. For our purpose, it may be worthwhile to distinguish three distinct types of situations where an agent may have to make choices.

First, we have a broad category of choice problems where there is no uncertainty involved. The agent chooses from a given set of mutually exclusive feasible "outcomes." He or she knows (or, at least, thinks that he or she knows) what each of the outcomes represents; and he or she knows that he or she will get any of the outcomes that he or she chooses. In contrast to this problem of choice under certainty, there are two other types of choice problems. First, there is the problem of choice under nonstrategic uncertainty, where the agent chooses an "action" from a given set of mutually exclusive actions, but the outcome of an action may depend on the state of nature.[2] Secondly, there is the problem of choice under strategic uncertainty where the outcome for the agent may depend on the actions of other individuals as well as his or her own action. Much of Sen's analysis focuses on the problem of choice under certainty, although some of his arguments also use elements of the theory of choice under strategic uncertainty. Therefore, we start with an outline of some basic features of the classical economic theory of rational choice under certainty.

2.1. Some Notation and Basic Concepts

Let the set of all outcomes or alternatives that the agent may conceivably face be denoted by X. We call this set the universal set. In the economic

---

[2] For some alternative approaches to the theory of choice under nonstrategic uncertainty, see, among others, Savage (1954), Fishburn (1970), Arrow and Hurwicz (1972), Kannai and Peleg (1984), and Kreps (1988).

theory of consumers' behavior, the universal set is often assumed to be the set of all possible consumption bundles. At any given time, the set of all feasible alternatives before the agent will be a nonempty subset of X. The set of feasible options, of course, can be different in different situations.

When an agent is assumed to have preferences over the outcomes in X, these preferences are represented by a binary weak preference relation R ("at least as good as") defined over X. For all outcomes x and y in X, xRy denotes that x is at least as good as y for the agent. A binary weak preference relation R is said to be an ordering if and only if it is reflexive (for all x in X, xRx, that is, every alternative is as good as itself), connected (for all distinct x and y in X, xRy or yRx, that is, the agent can compare every pair of distinct alternatives), and transitive (for all x, y, and z in X, $[xRy$ and $yRz]$ implies xRz, that is, if x is at least as good as y and y is at least as good as z, then x is at least as good as z). Given a feasible set of alternatives, H, let $B(H, R)$ denote the set of all alternatives x in H such that xRy for all y in H. Thus, $B(H,R)$ is the set of best alternatives in H, when "best" is defined in terms of R; note that there may be more than one such best alternative in H. When $B(H, R)$ has more than one element, the interpretation of $B(H, R)$ is that an agent choosing on the basis of the preference ordering R can choose any one of the alternatives in $B(H, R)$.

When discussing the agent's choice behavior, we shall assume that for every set, H, of feasible alternatives that the agent may face in some situation, we have for the agent a (nonempty) set of alternatives that he or she will choose from H. This gives us the formal notion of an agent's choice function.

Definition 2.1. The agent's choice function is a function, C, which, for every set of feasible alternatives, H, specifies exactly one nonempty subset $C(H)$ of H.

Intuitively, the function C can be regarded as giving a description of how the agent will choose from the different sets of feasible alternatives that may confront him or her in different situations. $C(H)$ can be interpreted as the set of alternatives that the agent chooses from the set H. If $C(H)$ contains exactly one element, then that element has the straightforward interpretation as the unique alternative chosen by the agent from H. However, a considerable amount of the literature (see, for example, the classic papers of Arrow [1959] and Richter [1966]) does not assume that the chosen element is necessarily unique. Because the alternatives in H are assumed to be mutually exclusive and the agent can "ultimately" have only one of these alternatives, an interpretational issue arises when $C(H)$ is permitted to have more than one element; we discuss this issue in section 4.1.

2.2. The Economic Theory of Rational Choice under Certainty: The Preference-Based Framework

The economic theory of rational choice in the absence of uncertainty has two distinct strands. First, we have the preference-based theory of rational choice under certainty, where one starts with the agent's preferences and rational choice is typically defined to be choice generated by a preference ordering defined over X. We shall call this type of theory the *preference-based theory of rational choice under certainty*. The main features of the theory are as follows.

(i) The theory starts by specifying a universal set of alternatives, X. The interpretation of the universal set depends on the specific context.

(ii) It is then assumed that the agent has a binary weak preference relation R over X. Further, it is assumed that the agent's choices are generated by R in the sense that the agent will choose a feasible alternative that is at least as good as every feasible alternative in terms of the ordering R. Thus, given any set, H, of feasible alternatives, $B(H, R)$ will emerge as the set, $C(H)$, of alternatives chosen by the agent from the set H. This is what makes the agent's choices "preference-based" in this framework.

(iii) R is typically assumed to be an ordering. In fact, the notion of rationality of preferences is often treated as being synonymous with the requirement that R be an ordering. Thus, in this framework, rational choice is simply choice generated by "rational" preferences, that is, by a preference ordering over X.

(iv) Finally, the theory explores, possibly with additional assumptions, the implications, for the agent's choice behavior, with the assumption that the agent's choices are generated by a preference ordering.

Several points may be noted here. First, the set of outcomes may have different interpretations in different contexts. Thus, in the theory of consumers' behavior, the universal set of outcomes for a consumer is the consumption set or the set of commodity bundles that the consumer can possibly consume. On the other hand, for a political leader who has an ideological commitment to social reform, and is, at the same time, interested in electoral success, the alternatives may be the different possible combinations of social reform and political support that the leader can garner. Second, as should be clear from these examples, the agent's preference ordering may be based on a variety of considerations, from pure self-interest to ideological commitments. At an abstract level, the economic theory of rational choice does not put any restrictions on the range of motives and concerns that may enter the agent's preference ordering. However, in specific applications, economists typically assume that the agent's preference ordering is based on his or her self-interest. Third, although in much of the economic literature choice on the basis of a preference ordering is taken to be the hallmark of rationality, there exists a significant literature that explores weaker notions of rational choice, such as the choice of a best feasible alternative defined in terms of a binary weak preference relation that satisfies, in addition to reflexivity and connectedness, certain weaker versions of the requirement of transitivity.[3] Finally, the assumption that the agent's choices are generated by his or her preference ordering over X has direct implications for these choices. For example, it can be shown that, if the agent has a preference ordering R over the universal set and if this preference ordering generates his or her choices, then the agent's choices will satisfy the familiar Weak Axiom of Revealed Preference, which may be stated as follows.

Definition 2.2. The agent's choices satisfy the Weak Axiom of Revealed Preference (WARP) if, and only if, for all possible sets, H and K, of feasible alternatives, and for all alternatives x and y belonging to both H and K, if x belongs to $C(H)$ and y belongs to $H - C(H)$, then y does not belong to $C(K)$.[4]

WARP says that, if, given a set of feasible alternatives, H, which contains alternatives x and y, the agent chooses x and rejects y, then, given any other feasible set of alternatives, K, containing x and y, the agent does not choose y. WARP, in turn, implies a much weaker property, which was first introduced by Chernoff (1954) and was later called Condition α by Sen (1970, 1971).

Definition 2.3. The agent's choices satisfy Condition α if, and only if, for all possible sets, H and K, of feasible alternatives, and for all $x \in X$, if H is a subset of K and x belongs to $H - C(H)$, then x belongs to $K - C(K)$.

Condition α stipulates that, if a person rejects x when choosing from a given set of feasible alternatives, then he or she should not choose x when the set of feasible alternatives is expanded by adding to the set some new alternatives.

2.3. The Theory of Rational Choice under Certainty: The Choice-Based Framework

As we noted, the starting point of the preference-based theory of rational choice is the agent's preferences over a given universal set of options. In

---

[3] See, for example, Sen (1969, 1971, 1977a) and Herzberger (1973).
[4] The definition of WARP given here is an adaptation of the axiom as originally introduced by Samuelson (1938).

contrast, in the choice-based theory of rational choice that originated in Samuelson (1938), and subsequently developed by several writers including Houthakker (1950), Little (1949, 1957), Arrow (1959), and Richter (1966), the notions of a universal set of options and the agent's choice function, which tells us how the consumer chooses from different sets of alternatives, constitute the primitive concepts of the theory. The theory starts with the agent's choice function rather than with the agent's preferences. The agent's preference is either not introduced or, if it is introduced at all, then it is defined in terms of the agent's choices.[5] The concept of rationality of choice is embodied in restrictions imposed on the agent's choice function. These restrictions typically stipulate that, if the agent chooses in a certain fashion from some sets of options, then he or she must or must not choose in a certain fashion from some other sets of options. Thus, typically they are conditions of "internal consistency" of choices, that is, conditions of "consistency" between the agent's choices from different sets of options. There are numerous such restrictions (e.g., WARP and Condition α) on the agent's choice function that have been discussed in the literature (see, among others, Samuelson [1938], Arrow [1959], Richter [1966], Sen [1970, 1971], and Herzberger [1973]). It is open to the theorist to decide which of these restrictions he or she would take to be the defining features of rationality of choice. However, some restrictions on the choice function, such as Condition α and WARP, have been widely considered essential properties of rational choice. The main features of the economists' choice-based theory of rational choice may be summarized as follows.

(i) Like the preference-based theory of rational choice, the choice-based theory also starts by specifying a universal set of alternatives, which can have different interpretations in different contexts.

(ii) The agent's choice behavior is introduced through the notion of a choice function, which constitutes the central concept in the theory.

(iii) Rationality of choice is conceived as restrictions on the choice function, which stipulate how choices from different sets of feasible alternatives should be related to each other.

(iv) It is assumed that the agent's choices are rational in the sense explained in the previous examples.

---

[5] For example, given the agent's choice function, C, one can define a weak preference relation R over the universal set, X, as follows: for all $x, y \in X$, xRy if, and only if $x \in C(\{x, y\})$ (i.e., if, and only if x is a chosen element when the set of feasible alternatives has only two options, x and y).

(v) Given the assumption that the agent's choices are rational in the stip-
ulated sense, the theorist infers, possibly with the help of additional
assumptions, further restrictions on the choice function. These restrictions on the choice function deduced by the theorist constitute the
testable conclusions of the theoretical structure.

A famous illustration of these different aspects of the choice-based theory of rational behavior can be found in Samuelson (1938). Samuelson
(1938) considers competitive consumers whose choice functions are defined
with reference to a universal set of consumption bundles and who are rational in the sense that their choice functions (i.e., market demand functions)
satisfy WARP. Samuelson then deduces certain restrictions on the demand
behavior of consumers, which constitute the testable conclusions of his
theory.

3. SEN ON THE CHOICE-BASED THEORY OF RATIONAL CHOICE

In a series of papers over more than two decades, Sen (1973, 1977b, 1986a,
1986b, 1989, 1993, and 1994) offers a searching critique of the choice-
based theory of rational choice. Can one really construct a theory of rational
choice exclusively in terms of the agent's choices and consistency conditions
imposed on such choices without interpreting the agent's choices in terms
of his or her preferences or motivations? Sen has repeatedly asked this
question, and, contrary to the position that sometimes seems to have been
taken by several writers (see, for example, Samuelson [1938, 1947] and
Little [1949, 1957]), Sen is skeptical about formulations of the theory of
rational behavior exclusively in terms of choice and internal consistency of
choice without any reference to underlying preferences. In this section, we
examine his views relating to this issue.

3.1. Internal Consistency Conditions for Choice and the Notion of Inconsistency

Recall that rationality of choice in the choice framework is defined in terms
of the fulfillment of various "internal consistency conditions," such as the
Weak Axiom of Revealed Preference or Condition α by the agent's choice
function. Sen (1973: 243) questions this use of the term "consistency":

> Preferring x to y is inconsistent with preferring y to x, but if it is asserted
> that choice has nothing to do with preference, then choosing x rather than

y in one case and y rather than x in another need not necessarily be at all inconsistent.

The point is elaborated further by Sen (1993), where he calls it a "foundational" problem involved in the use of the idea of internal consistency of choice without any *external* reference to preferences, objectives, and motivations of the agent. Sen (1993: 499) writes,

> Statements A and *not-A* are contradictory in a way that choosing x from $\{x, y\}$ and y from $\{x, y, z\}$ cannot be. If the latter pair of choices were to entail respectively the statement (1) x is a better alternative than y, and (2) y is a better alternative than x, then there would indeed be a contradiction here (assuming that the content of "being better than requires asymmetry"). But those choices do not, *in themselves*, entail any such statements.

3.2. Conditions of Internal Consistency of Choice as Testable Empirical Hypotheses

One possible interpretation of internal consistency conditions for choice is that they are testable hypotheses about the agent's behavior, but Sen does not agree with this interpretation. There are several strands in Sen's reasoning here. First, consider the case of a competitive consumer, where WARP was first introduced and studied. The class of budget sets that may conceivably confront such a consumer is an infinite class, whereas the number of budget situations where the consumer's choices can be observed in principle is limited. Secondly, not only is it infeasible in principle to observe the consumer's choices in all possible budget situations, but the amount of empirical evidence actually collected by economists about the validity of consistency conditions for consumers' choices is very limited. On both these grounds, Sen is reluctant to accept the status of internal consistency conditions for choice as a testable empirical hypothesis. Sen (1973: 243) writes,

> To check whether the Weak Axiom holds for the entire field of market choices, we have to observe the person's choices under infinitely many price-income configurations. In contrast, the number of actual choices that can be studied is extremely limited. Not only is the ratio of observations to potential choices equal to zero, but moreover the absolute number of cases investigated is also fairly small.

Thus, Sen (1993) rejects the claim of WARP, Condition α, and other such conditions as empirical hypotheses. He claims that the economists' faith in these conditions really has its origin in the intuitive reasonableness of these conditions when interpreted in terms of preferences.

3.3. The Plausibility of Consistency Condition When Divorced from Considerations of the Agent's Preferences and Motivations

If the axioms of "revealed preference" are not to be accepted either as primitive requirements of consistency or as testable hypotheses and are to be judged in terms of their intuitive reasonableness instead, can such reasonableness be assessed without reference to the motivations and preferences of the agent? Sen (1993) does not think so. He gives several examples to argue that the mechanical applications of the consistency conditions, without reference to the agent's motivations and preferences, may lead the agent to be branded as irrational in situations where, from an intuitive point of view, there may not be anything irrational about the agent's choices. The two examples that follow are essentially taken from Sen (1993).

Example 3.1. Consider a guest, *i*, at a party. Suppose *i* faces a choice between having the last remaining apple in the fruit basket and having nothing instead. He or she decides to behave decently and picks nothing. If, instead, the basket had contained two apples and *i* had a choice between having nothing, having one apple, and having the other apple, he or she would choose one apple. *Prima facie, i*'s choice in the two situations seems to violate the Weak Axiom of Revealed Preference; in fact, it seems to violate even the weaker rationality condition α. Yet, there does not seem to be anything odd about *i*'s behavior. Most polite persons avoid picking up the only apple in a fruit tray if there are other guests who are going to choose after them.

Example 3.2. Consider a man and a woman, who have met each other only a short while ago. At the end of the day, the man suggests that they could perhaps go for a cup of tea. The woman has the option of either accepting the invitation to tea or going back to her hotel. The woman accepts the invitation. However, now suppose that the man offers the woman another option: he can take her to have a cup of tea or, if she would like it, he can also take her somewhere to have some cocaine. So the woman now has three options: she can go back to her hotel, she can go for a cup of tea with the man, or she can go with the man and have cocaine. Given this expanded set of options, the woman now chooses to go back to her hotel. Again, the agent's behavior seems to violate Condition α. However, the woman's behavior does not seem to be odd in any way.

Consider what happens in examples 3.1 and 3.2. In example 3.1, the person is trying to be polite by not picking from the fruit tray the only remaining fruit. However, what constitutes polite choice depends on the "menu" represented by the contents of the fruit tray. Thus, the value for the agent of his or her choice depends on the menu. It is this "menu-dependence" of the value of a particular choice that is at the root of the observed violation of WARP or Condition α. The intuition here is similar to the intuition of an example given by Luce and Raiffa (1957: 133, 288). In their discussion of the plausibility of Nash's (1950) condition of "independence of irrelevant alternatives,"[6] which constitutes a version of Condition α, Luce and Raiffa (1957: 133) give a counterexample to show how this condition may be violated by "reasonable" people. The structure of the counterexample of Luce and Raiffa (1957: 133) is based exactly on the type of "menu-dependence" that underlies Sen's example.

The structure of example 3.2 is somewhat different. The woman is clearly uncertain about the character of the man. The extra option of having cocaine that the man offers her gives her more information about the man's character. Consequently, the act of having tea with the man, which was previously chosen over going back to the hotel, is not an optimal act in the expanded menu of available acts. Here, also, we have a type of menu-dependence, but the nature of menu-dependence is different from the menu-dependence in example 3.1. Here, the menu is not linked to the criteria by which the agent judges the actions. Instead, in example 3.2, the menu influences the choice of an action by changing the nature of the information available to the woman. If one likes, one can interpret the example in terms of Bayesian updating of probabilities. Assume that, originally, the woman's subjective probability that the man is a "nice" person is p and her subjective probability that the man is not a nice person is $1 - p$. So, the act of going for tea with the man is really a lottery L that assigns probability p to having tea with a nice man and probability $1 - p$ to having tea with a non-nice person. The woman prefers this lottery to the perfect certainty of spending time by herself in her hotel. However, when the man gives her the option of having cocaine with him, she revises her subjective probabilities to q for the man being nice and $1 - q$ to the man being nasty. Accordingly, the act of going for tea with the man is now a lottery L' that assigns probability q $(q < p)$ to having tea with a nice man and $1 - q$ to having tea with a nasty man. Going to smoke cocaine with the man can be considered to

---

[6] Note that Nash's "independence of irrelevant alternatives" is very different from Arrow's condition with the same name.

be a lottery L'' with probability q of smoking cocaine with a nice person and probability $1 - q$ of smoking cocaine with a nasty person. The woman strictly prefers the perfect certainty of spending time alone in her hotel room to lottery L' as well as to lottery L''. The important point is that it is the change in the menu that leads to the updating of the probabilities, and that, once the woman is visualized as choosing from alternative lotteries, there is no violation of Condition α. The situation here is similar to the situation in a counterexample that Luce and Raiffa (1957: 288) give to show how a "reasonable agent" may violate the axiom that "If an act is non-optimal [for a decision problem under uncertainty], it cannot be made optimal by adding new acts to the problem."

Whereas Luce and Raiffa (1957: 133, 288) intended their examples as counterexamples to specific axioms, Sen (1993) uses his examples to argue more generally that the reasonableness of the consistency conditions cannot be judged in isolation from the motivations of the agent. After all, the two agents in examples 3.1 and 3.2, whose choices violate some basic internal consistency conditions for choice, seem to behave perfectly rationally from an intuitive point of view when we take into account their goals and motivations.

3.4. An Assessment of Sen's Criticisms of the Choice-Based Theory of Rational Choice

We now present an assessment of some of the arguments of Sen outlined in sections 3.1, 3.2, and 3.3.

Consider first Sen's (1993) objection to calling Condition α, WARP, and so forth conditions of internal consistency of choice. As he points out, there is clearly no logical inconsistency or contradiction involved if, given the set $\{x, y\}$, the agent chooses x and rejects y, and, given the set $\{x, y, z\}$, he chooses y and rejects x and z. The use of the term "inconsistency" to describe violations of these conditions is rather loose insofar as the term "inconsistency" has a precise meaning in logic. However, it may be worth noting two distinct points. First, although economists have generally referred to conditions such as Condition α and WARP as internal consistency conditions for choice, it is not clear that they have considered violations of these conditions as logical contradictions. Nor is the use of the term confined to choice-based theories. Thus, a popular undergraduate textbook (Frank 2003: 71) has the following comment on the property of transitivity of preferences: "Transitivity is a simple consistency property...." The use of the term "consistency" in this fashion is certainly loose, but very few economists, and certainly very few economic theorists, have thought of violations of "internal consistency conditions" for choice as instances of logical contradiction. Secondly, Sen seems to argue that, although there is no logical contradiction involved in choosing x rather than y from $\{x, y\}$ and choosing y from $\{x, y, z\}$, there is a logical contradiction in preferring x to y and preferring y to x (assuming that strict preference is asymmetric). The contrast that Sen draws between choice and preference here may be somewhat sharper than warranted. Thus, the agent does not seem to be involved in any *logical* contradiction if he or she tells us that he or she prefers x to y when the set of feasible alternatives is $\{x, y\}$, but prefers y to x when the set of feasible alternatives is $\{x, y, z\}$. These expressed preferences become logically contradictory when we assume that they are all embedded in a single binary weak preference relation defined over the universal set of alternatives, but such an assumption is not a logical necessity. Just as choices can be menu-dependent, preferences also can be menu-dependent, and, however odd such menu-dependent preferences may seem to be, they do not represent a logical contradiction.

It seems to us that the core of Sen's critique of the revealed preference framework lies in his claim that it is impossible to construct an interesting theory of rational choice exclusively in terms of choice and restrictions on choice without any reference to the agent's preferences and motivations. The argument here is simple but fundamental. Before one can judge the intuitive reasonableness of various restrictions postulated for choice, and, indeed, before one can even introduce these restrictions, one needs to specify the space with references to which the agent's choices are defined. The reasonableness of various rationality properties for choice cannot be judged independently of how the objects of choice are specified. Take the textbook case of a consumer and his or her choices of commodity bundles in the market. Suppose the consumer really buys commodity bundles containing quantities of bread, milk, and meat, but suppose the economist specifies the choice space as consisting of bundles of only bread and milk. It is then easy to see that even when the consumer's choices in the "true" space of bread, milk, and meat satisfy WARP, the truncated versions of the choices, when we look only at the quantities of bread and milk bought, can easily violate WARP. Thus, the issue of whether the violation of Condition α or WARP is to be regarded as an "inconsistent" or "irrational" choice on the part of the agent is inextricably intertwined with the issue of whether the space of options that the economist starts with in modeling the agent's behavior reflects the motives and concerns of the agent. Examples 3.1 and 3.2 illustrate this basic fact. In example 3.1, the violation of Condition α

does not seem to be unreasonable to us because we feel that the way the options have been specified does not capture all the concerns of the agent. Not only does the individual care about eating or not eating an apple, but he or she is also concerned with conforming to the accepted norms of politeness. When we realize this, we do not feel that the violation of Condition α, when the options are defined as having apple 1 or having apple 2 or not having an apple at all, does not, intuitively, constitute "odd" behavior on the part of the individual. In fact, when options are defined in this fashion, the insistence on Condition α would seem unreasonable. In the context of example 3.1, Condition α would seem far more reasonable if we start by specifying options as pairs of the following type: (having an apple, giving the impression of being a rude person), (not having an apple, not giving the impression of being rude), (having an apple, not giving the impression of being rude), and so on. However, one can specify the space of options in this fashion only when one has insight into the motives and concerns of the individual. Similarly, in example 3.2, once one realizes that the personality of the man with whom the woman may have tea is a relevant concern, one can reformulate the options as suitably defined lotteries (probability p of having tea with a "nice" person and probability $1 - p$ of having tea with an 'obnoxious' person, and so on) and the woman's choices with respect to such lotteries do not violate Condition α. The reasonableness of the specification of the options is closely linked with how we feel about the intuitive plausibility of Condition α, and the reasonableness of a particular specification of the options cannot be determined independently of the agent's objectives and motivations.

It is of interest to note that the basic argument, which Sen uses to challenge the interpretation of internal consistency conditions as intuitively plausible assumptions for choice without any reference to the agent's preferences and motives, can also be adapted to the case where the consistency conditions are treated simply as testable hypotheses. Before we take up this issue, however, consider first Sen's reason for not taking seriously the status of consistency requirements for choice as testable hypotheses.

In discussing the use of WARP in the theory of competitive consumers' behavior, Sen (1973) rightly points out that the class of budget sets that a consumer may face is an infinite class, and we cannot possibly observe the consumer's choices from an infinite number of budget sets. But, this only shows that, like all empirical hypotheses that take the form of universal statements about infinite classes, WARP is not verifiable. Nonverifiability can hardly be an objection to the introduction of a hypothesis (see Popper [1959] for a classic discussion of the role of verifiability and falsifiability in science). The second reason that Sen gives is that economists themselves have not collected much empirical evidence about WARP, and, therefore, economists could not be serious about WARP as an empirical hypothesis. It is true that the amount of empirical evidence regarding WARP that economists have collected is rather small, but the same is true also about many other empirical assumptions that economists make in their theories.

If we treat WARP as a testable empirical hypothesis, we face issues relating to the space of options, which are very similar to the questions raised by Sen about the intuitive plausibility of conditions such as WARP when they are completely divorced from considerations of the agent's objectives and motives. Before WARP can be introduced as an empirical hypothesis, one must specify the domain of the choice function of the agent. This, in turn, presupposes a specification of the alternatives before the agent. Thus, inevitably, WARP has to be combined with at least one other hypothesis, namely, a hypothesis about the type of alternatives that the agent chooses. A test of WARP as an empirical hypothesis is, therefore, a joint test of WARP and a hypothesis about the space of alternatives that the agent is faced with in his or her choice problem.[7] Suppose we observe the behaviour of the agent figuring in example 3.1. Then what is falsified is not WARP as such but the *conjunction* of WARP and the hypothesis that the alternatives that the agent is choosing are "having apple 1," "having no apple," "having apple 2," and so on. Given this falsification of the conjunction of the two hypotheses, the theorist has two options. If the theorist feels that his or her hypothesis about the nature of the alternatives is intuitively compelling, then the theorist can interpret his or her observations as casting doubts about the validity of WARP. Alternatively, he or she may feel that he or she has mis-specified the alternatives in posing the agent's choice problem. Then he or she can re-specify this space and proceed again to test the conjunction of WARP and the new hypothesis about the alternatives. We have already seen one such re-specification of the options in example 3.1, where one adds to the description of options another dimension, namely, whether one is appearing rude to others, but this is not the only way in which the options in example 3.1 can be re-specified so as to make the observations consistent with WARP. For example, Sen (1994) discusses an alternative re-specification where the "menu" as well as the option chosen from the menu in the original example figures in the description of the newly specified option. The main point, though, is this. Whether one would like to

---

[7] Cf. Boland (1981), Caldwell (1983), and Dasgupta et al. (2000).

change the description of options when faced with observations that falsify the conjunction of one's original hypothesis about the space of options and WARP defined with reference to those options, and how one would change the space of options if one wants to change it at all, would clearly depend on one's intuition about the options that the agent "really cares about," and that, in turn, would depend on one's intuition about the agent's objectives and motives. Thus, Sen's central point about the importance of knowing or guessing the agent's motives, objectives, and so forth turns out to be important even when one treats WARP as a testable empirical hypothesis.

4. THE PREFERENCE-BASED THEORIES OF CHOICE

In this section, we consider Sen's thoughts on preference-based models of choice, used extensively in economics.

4.1. Noncomparability, Indifference, and Choice

Before discussing the central features of Sen's assessment of the preference-based theory of choice, we first note what we consider to be a relatively less important part of his analysis.

Although Sen has serious reservations about choice-based theories that try to analyze choice without any reference to the agent's preference or motivations, he accepts that choices can serve as evidence for inferring the agent's preference ordering or utility ranking. However, he raises some issues regarding the role of choice as an indicator of preference. One of the problems that he raises has its origin in the possible nonconnectedness of the agent's preferences. Sen (1981: 205) writes,

> Buridan's ass with the same incomplete preference between the two haystacks, but more wisdom will choose one of the two haystacks rather than dying of hunger, but it will be wrong to conclude that the ass thought that the chosen haystack *must give more utility*.

The structure of the problem that Sen refers to is this. The agent has three alternatives: x, y, and z. The agent cannot compare x and y, but he considers both x and y to be superior to z. Then, faced with the problem of choosing from $\{x, y, z\}$, if the agent chooses x or y, anybody taking choice to be an indicator of preference will then wrongly conclude that the agent prefers x to y (when the agent chooses x) or that the agent prefers y to x (when the agent chooses y). The general implication is that, in the presence of noncomparability in preferences, choice may not serve as an indicator of preferences.

Sen interprets choice here in terms of a single act of picking exactly one alternative from a given set of feasible alternatives. Given this interpretation, even indifference can be problematic. Suppose the agent is indifferent between x and y, and prefers each of x and y to z. Then, no single act of choosing exactly one alternative can possibly serve as an indicator of preference. If he or she chooses x, then again the outside observer, trying to interpret the choice in terms of preference, will wrongly conclude that he or she prefers x to y. Thus, the problem that Sen has in mind can also arise in the case of indifference as distinct from noncomparability. Suppose, instead of interpreting choice in terms of a single act of actually picking up exactly one alternative from the feasible set of alternatives, we ask the agent to *say* what he or she would choose if confronted with the set $\{x, y, z\}$. Then, in the case where the agent is indifferent between x and y and strictly prefers x, as well as y, to z, the agent would tell us that he or she could choose either x or y and did not care which of them he or she chose. On the other hand, in the case where he or she cannot compare x and y, but strictly prefers x, as well as y, to z, the agent would tell us that he or she is unable to decide. We have here a broader interpretation of choice under which the agent is allowed to express verbally his or her inability to choose and also to tell us that he or she can choose either x or y and does not care whether he or she chooses x or y. In fact, Sen (1982: 9) has persuasively argued for this interpretation of choice. It seems to us that, insofar as economists often allow the set of chosen alternatives to have more than one option (see Arrow [1959] and Richter [1966] among others), and also insofar as they allow for the possibility that the agent's chosen options may not be defined for some feasible sets of alternatives, they have this broad interpretation of choice in mind.

4.2. Some Structural Assumptions: Self-Oriented Welfare, Self-Welfare Goal, and Self-Goal Choice

We now take up the core of Sen's critique of the preference-based theories of rational choice that economists typically use. The critique takes the form of an incisive analysis of some of the structural assumptions underlying the theory.

The abstract economic theory of preference and preference-based choice does not require any specific interpretation of the space over which the agent's preferences are defined; nor does it require any specific interpretation of the agent's preferences. However, in actual applications of this general theory, economists often commit themselves to specific views about the individual's preference. They typically assume that an individual's preferences are based exclusively on considerations of the individual's own welfare and that these self-interested preferences constitute the sole basis of the individual's behavior. In a series of contributions (see, for example, Sen [1973, 1977b, 1986b, 1987a, 1994]), Sen focuses on these explicit or implicit assumptions, on which so much of economic analysis is based.

Sen (1986b, 1987a) points out that economists generally use three distinct assumptions. The first is the assumption that the agent's welfare is determined exclusively by his or her own consumption. Sen (1986b: 7) calls this the assumption of self-centered welfare. Under this assumption, the agent's welfare depends only on his or her own consumption bundle; he or she does not care in any way about the consumption or production plan of any other agent and does not have either any sympathy or antipathy for others. The second assumption is that of a self-welfare goal, which says that the only goal of the agent is to maximize his or her own welfare; the agent's goals do not attach any weight, positive or negative, to other people's welfare. Finally, we have what Sen calls the assumption of self-goal choice, that is, the assumption that every action of the agent is guided exclusively by the motive of furthering his or her own goal. The assumptions of the self-welfare goal and self-goal choice together imply that an individual makes his or her choice exclusively to further his or her own welfare (the individual's own welfare may, however, incorporate either sympathy or antipathy towards others). In what follows, we shall sometimes treat this basic implication of the assumptions of a self-welfare goal and self-goal choice as an independent and primitive assumption; on such occasions, we shall call it the assumption of *self-welfare choice*.

The assumptions of a self-welfare goal and self-welfare choice are used widely in economics; economists also often use the assumption of self-centered choice, although perhaps less frequently. The two fundamental theorems of welfare economics, which show that, under suitable assumptions, every competitive equilibrium allocation must be Pareto optimal, and, conversely, every Pareto optimal allocation can be sustained by some competitive equilibrium, constitute a classic example of the use of these three assumptions. In the framework of these theorems, every individual chooses a consumption bundle to further his or her own goal, that goal being to maximize his or her own welfare. Every individual's welfare, in turn, depends only on his or her own consumption bundle. Another example of the use of the assumptions of self-oriented welfare, self-welfare goal, and self-goal choice is to be found in the game of prisoners' dilemma. The underlying

Table 1.1 Prisoner's Dilemma

		2	
		Not confess	*Confess*
1	Not confess	$(-3, -3)$	$(-25, 0)$
	Confess	$(0, -25)$	$(-10, -10)$

story of two prisoners, each of whom has two alternative strategies, confessing to having committed a crime together with the other prisoner or not making any such confession, is widely known (a reader unfamiliar with the story may like to consult Dixit and Skeath [2004: 90]). Table 1.1, where the numbers refer to the payoffs, gives only the formal structure of the game.

Each player's welfare, represented by his or her payoff in the table, depends only on his or her prison term. The goal of each player is to get the maximum payoff possible, and each player chooses a strategy to promote this goal. For each player, confessing is the strictly dominant strategy in the sense that, compared to the other strategy of not confessing, it yields a higher payoff regardless of the strategy adopted by the other player. When each player confesses to further his or her own welfare, each of them gets a payoff of –10, but both of them would be better off if both of them adopted the strategy of not confessing.

It may be worth noting that the assumption of self-oriented welfare is by no means universal in economics. A substantial body of economic theory investigates the implications of relaxing the assumption of self-oriented welfare and introducing what economists call "externalities." For example, although the two fundamental theorems make the assumption of self-oriented welfare, in the theory of general equilibrium itself, we also have a much more general analytical framework that allows a consumer's welfare to be affected by the consumption bundles of other consumers as well as the production plans of producers (for an incisive discussion of externalities, see Arrow [1969]). To some extent, it is also possible to accommodate antipathy and sympathy for others in this framework. Thus, in general, the economists' commitment to the assumption of self-centered welfare is far from complete, although the assumption does play a crucial role in the two fundamental theorems of welfare economics. However, even when economists relax the assumption of self-centered welfare, they typically retain the assumptions of a self-welfare goal and self-goal choice, which, together, imply self-welfare choice.

4.3. Self-Welfare Choice

Sen (1982: 6) distinguishes two aspects of self-welfare choice. First, it can be treated as an empirical hypothesis about how people act; the validity or invalidity of the hypothesis is then to be assessed by empirical evidence. Second, self-welfare choice can be treated as a requirement of rational action, so that to be rational a person must be always choosing his or her actions to maximize his or her own welfare.

Sen is skeptical about self-welfare choice both as an empirical hypothesis and as a condition for rationality (see, for example, Sen 1986a, 1986b, 1987a, 1994). Referring to its status as an empirical hypothesis, Sen (1986b:17) writes that

> as evidence has mounted against this assumption both in terms of empirical observations of actual economic behaviour and also in terms of observations of behaviour in experimental games, that traditional assumption seems neither secured nor securable.

Sen (1994) elaborates the allusion to empirical observations. Among other things, he cites authors who have drawn attention to "the special sense of collective responsibility that apparently prevails more abundantly in Japanese industrial relations than in the West" (Sen 1994: 387–8) and refers to suggestions by David Gordon (1994) that the wide variations in the monitoring of work efforts in different countries may be linked to social norms and institutions.

Two points may be noted here. First, when Sen questions the plausibility of self-welfare choice, he does not claim that people never act to maximize their own welfare; what he really questions is the assumption that people always act to maximize their own welfare (see Sen 1987a: 19). Secondly, it may be thought that, although in general people may not act exclusively to promote their own welfare, self-welfare choice is a plausible hypothesis in "economic contexts," that is, when making "economic" choices, people always act to maximize their own welfare. This, however, is not a serious objection to Sen's arguments, as many of the examples that he gives to demonstrate that the behavior of people often deviates from self-welfare choice are "economic" in nature (see, for example, his references to Japanese industrial relations and the monitoring of work efforts in different countries, cited earlier).

Sen is even more skeptical of the status of self-welfare choice as a condition of rational behavior (see, for instance, Sen 1987a: 15–22). He argues that, although rational people sometimes maximize their own welfare, to regard maximization of one's own welfare as a necessary condition for rational behavior will be to take too restrictive a view of rationality. Sen (1987a: 16) writes that

> it may not be quite as absurd to argue that people always *actually* do maximize their self-interest, as it is to argue that *rationality* must invariably demand maximization of self-interest. Universal selfishness as *actuality* may well be false, but universal selfishness as a requirement of *rationality* is patently absurd.

We consider this point again in section 4.4.

4.4. Self-Welfare Goal

If people's choices sometimes deviate from self-welfare choice, it must result from at least one of the following two reasons: (i) people do not always have the goal of maximizing their own welfare only (so that an agent's preference ordering R, which reflects his or her goals, is not exclusively based on considerations of his or her welfare); and (ii) they do not always act simply to pursue their own goals represented by their preference orderings.

Consider (i) first. There is nothing implausible about a person seeking to maximize some weighted combination of his or her own welfare and the welfare of other people. Nor is there anything implausible about an individual's objective function being based on his or her religious values, commitments, and so forth in addition to his or her own welfare and other people's welfare. If we retain for the moment the assumption of self-goal choice, it is clear that, in all such cases, although the agent's actions will be guided by the goal of maximizing some objective function, they will not be guided by the goal of maximizing his or her self-interest. Thus, the relaxation of the assumption of self-welfare goal, although retaining the assumption of self-goal choice, allows one to incorporate a richer and more realistic set of goals into the agent's ordering R that constitutes the basis of the agent's choice of actions.

In one important respect, this more relaxed interpretation of the agent objective function, represented by his or her ordering, is consistent with the notion of rational choice in economic theory. Recall that, at a more abstract level, positive economic theory conceives rational choice as choices generated by an ordering R over the universal set of alternatives, without postulating anything specific about the substantive content of the ordering R. At this level of abstraction, the positive economic theory of rational choice would not face any foundational problem if we permit R to be based on considerations other than the welfare of the agent himself or herself:

the central concept of maximization will remain intact, although maximization may not take the form of maximization of one's self-interest. In contrast, welfare economics would face difficulties. If an agent's choices are not guided by the sole objective of maximizing his or her self-interest, then choices, by themselves, would not allow us to infer anything directly about the agent's welfare. For example, if the preference ordering of an individual reflects considerations other than just the welfare of the individual, then it will not be possible to say much about the properties of a competitive equilibrium allocation in terms of the welfare of the individuals in the society. One possible way of escape from this problem may be to define the welfare of the agent to be whatever he or she seeks to maximize. If we adopt this suggestion, the problem of the gap between the agent's choice and his or her welfare that arises when we relax the assumption of self-welfare goal (while retaining the assumption of self-goal choice) would be solved, but it would be solved simply by an obtuse definition that would reduce the assumption of self-welfare goal to a tautology (see Sen 1986b: 8).

4.5. Self-Goal Choice

Sen questions the assumption of self-goal choice (see Sen 1977b; 1986b; 1987a: 88), as well as the assumption of self-welfare goal. This seems somewhat surprising, because the assumption that an agent will choose his or her actions to pursue exclusively his or her own goals seems intuitively plausible. Sen's objection to the assumption of self-goal choice is formulated in terms of the game of prisoners' dilemma. Suppose we continue to assume that the goal of each prisoner is to maximize his or her own welfare. If each of them pursues exclusively this goal, without taking into account the similar goal of the other person, each of them will end up by confessing, which will give each of them a lower level of welfare than what he or she would have if neither of them had confessed. Why would the two players not depart from the choice of strategies dictated by their individual goals once they realize that unrestrained pursuit of their individual goals leads to an outcome that is, for both of them, inferior to some other feasible outcome? Raising this question, Sen (1986b: 17) writes,

> When individual maximization is self-defeating for every one taken together, it is not at all clear why sophisticated social thinking must fail to take note of this important feature of social reality. And, if it does take note of this, there can surely be departures from self-goal choice. . . . This is, of course, where social norms about behaviour, constraining the pursuit of one's own goals play a part.

Sen (1974, 1977b) suggests an interesting framework for thinking about norm-based behaviour. The framework can be illustrated with reference to the prisoners' dilemma. The self-welfare goal of the prisoners, assumed to be reflected in the payoffs in Table 1.1, gives us the following orderings of the two prisoners, defined over the different pairs of strategies.

R_1 (1's ordering based on self-interest):

(confess, not confess), (not confess, not confess), (confess, confess), (not confess, confess)

R_2 (2's ordering based on self-interest):

(not confess, confess), (not confess, not confess), (confess, confess), (confess, not confess)

Now consider the following rankings that reflect the norm of not doing to others what you would not like others to do to you:

R_1^* (1's norm-based ordering):

(not confess, not confess), (not confess, confess), (confess, not confess), (confess, confess)

R_2^* (2's norm-based ordering):

(not confess, not confess), (confess, not confess), (not confess, confess), (confess, confess)

Suppose, after realizing the self-defeating nature of self-goal choice, the players consider choosing their strategies according to the norm-based orderings R_1^* and R_2^* above. Suppose the norm does not have any *intrinsic* value to them, and so conformity to these norms would not imply any change in their personal goal of maximizing self-interest. However, both the players realize that pursuing one's own goal in an unbridled fashion yields to everybody in the group achieving a lower level in terms of self-interest as compared to the situation where each of them conforms to the norm. If behaving according to the norm-based orderings serves their personal goals better, then why would they not behave in that fashion? And, further, would they not be rational to behave in that fashion? Thus, the players may have certain goals, but in deciding how to behave, they may prefer some other ordering as the basis of their choice rather than the ordering reflecting their personal goals simply because acting according to these other orderings would promote everybody's personal goals better. Each player can then be visualized as ordering the possible orderings over different pairs of strategies so as to choose an ordering that will constitute the basis of his or her choice. Note that here we have considered only two types of orderings for each player – an ordering based on self-interest and an ordering based on a particular norm – but the analysis can be easily made more general by permitting more than two orderings.

Do people behave in this way? Sen thinks so. Sen (1987a: 85) writes:

> Behaviour is ultimately a social matter as well, and thinking in terms of what 'we' should do or what should be our strategy, may reflect a sense of identity involving recognition of other people's goals and the mutual interdependencies involved.

Sen (1987a) argues that, when agents recognize such interdependence, they may adopt rules of behavior that serve to promote better the goals of all the members of the entire community.

4.6. Some Observations

We would like to conclude this section with a few observations. From the earlier discussion in this section, it is clear that Sen's critique of the preference-based theory of rational choice in economics consists of three distinct parts – his criticism of the assumption of the self-oriented welfare, his criticism of the assumption of the self-welfare goal, and, finally, his criticism of the assumption of self-goal choice. Very few economists would differ from him when he finds the assumption of self-oriented welfare a problematic empirical assumption. Although two central theorems in welfare economics dealing with competitive markets are based on this assumption, in general economists are keenly aware of the severe limitations of this assumption.

Economists are much more attached to the assumption of a self-welfare goal. Here, Sen's criticisms have been of immense importance in drawing attention to the restrictive nature of this assumption. His warning that the assumption of a self-welfare goal misses the considerable richness of the objective functions that individuals often have in real life is especially important when models based on the assumption of a self-welfare goal are becoming increasingly popular beyond the confines of economics. What, however, would be very valuable here is a wider range of specific analytical models and empirical research than we have now demonstrating that the use of more encompassing objective functions can yield insights likely to be missed when we use the assumption of a self-welfare goal.

Arguably, the most controversial part of Sen's critique of preference-based theories of choice is the part relating to self-goal choice, especially as it is very difficult to reconcile the negation of the assumption of self-goal choice with the fundamental assumption in economic theory that an agent always chooses his or her actions to maximize his or her personal objective function. Whereas we have some experimental and other evidence to show that people sometimes violate the assumption of self-welfare choice, there does not seem to be a large amount of evidence to show that such violation is because of the violation of the assumption of self-goal choice and not because of the violation of the assumption of self-welfare choice. Also, the argument that, after realizing that unrestrained pursuit of personal goals leads to a socially inoptimal outcome, the players in the game of prisoners' dilemma will contemplate adopting other rules of behavior without any intrinsic value for them does not seem intuitively any more compelling than the logic of adopting a strategy that strictly dominates every other strategy in terms of one's personal objective function. Sen himself recognizes this when, referring to these two very different types of behavior, one based on norms with only instrumental value and the other based on the notion of strict dominance, he writes (see Sen 1987a: 87), "The two alternative bases of behaviour are both quite deep, and both have excellent reasons for suggesting the respective course of action."

5. CONCLUDING REMARKS

In this chapter, we have outlined some of the salient aspects of Sen's thoughts on the theory of preference and choice. Given the enormous richness and volume of his contributions and given the constraints of space, we have chosen to focus on what we believe to be his most fundamental ideas. We believe that his deep and searching critique of the conventional economic theory of preference and choice in economics has reopened important foundational issues in a way that has far-reaching implications for economics. Therefore, we have devoted our entire chapter to this critique. There are, however, some aspects of his work on preference and choice that we have not covered in this chapter. We would like to note here two such omissions. First, we have not discussed the important contributions of Sen (1969, 1971, 1977a), where he has explored rationality conditions for preferences, which are weaker than the requirement of transitivity, introduced many internal consistency conditions for choice behavior, and clarified the interrelationship of such consistency conditions for choice. Second, Sen, perhaps more than any other economist, has explored various alternative notions of utility and clarified their limitations as articulations of the notion of an agent's well-being (see, for instance, Sen 1987b, 1987c). Given our emphasis in this chapter on the positive theory of choice and preference, we have not discussed this particular aspect of Sen's work although it is of much importance for normative economics.

References

Arrow, K. J. (1951). "An Extension of the Basic Theorems of Classical Welfare Economics," in Neyman (ed.), *Proceedings of the Second Berkeley Symposium on Mathematical Statistics and Probability* (Berkeley: University of California Press).

Arrow, K. J. (1958). "Utilities, Attitudes, Choices: A Review Note," *Operations Research*, 5, 765–74.

Arrow, K. J. (1959). "Rational Choice Functions and Orderings," *Economica*, 26, 121–7.

Arrow, K. J. (1969). "The Organization of Economic Activity: Issues Pertinent to the Choice of Market versus Non-market Allocation," in Joint Economic Committee, United States Congress, *The Analysis and Evaluation of Public Expenditures: The PPB System*, Vol. 1 (Washington, DC: Government Printing Office).

Arrow, K. J. (1971). "Exposition of the Theory of Choice under Uncertainty," in McGuire and Radner (eds.), *Decision and Organization* (Amsterdam: North-Holland).

Arrow, K. J., and L. Hurwicz (1972). "An Optimality Criterion for Decision-Making under Ignorance," in Carter and Ford (eds.), *Uncertainty and Expectations in Economics: Essays in Honour of G.L.S. Shackle* (Oxford: Basil Blackwell).

Boland, L. (1981). "On the Futility of Criticizing the Neo-classical Maximization Hypothesis," *American Economic Review*, 71, 1030–6.

Caldwell, B. J. (1983). "The Neoclassical Maximization Hypothesis: Comment," *American Economic Review*, 73, 824–30.

Chernoff, H. (1954). "Rational Selection of Decision Functions," *Economica*, new ser. 22, 422–43.

Dasgupta, I., S. Kumar, and P. K. Pattanaik (2000). "Consistent Choice and Falsifiability of the Maximization Hypothesis," in Pollin (ed.), *Capitalism, Socialism and Radical Political Economy: Essays in Honour of Howard J. Sherman* (Cheltenham, UK: Edward Elgar).

Dixit, A., and S. Skeath (2004). *Games of Strategy*, 2nd ed. (New York: Norton).

Debreu, G. (1959). *Theory of Value* (New York: Wiley).

Fishburn, P. (1970). *Utility Theory for Decision Making* (New York: Wiley).

Frank, R. H. (2003). *Microeconomics and Behavior*, 5th ed. (New York: McGraw-Hill/Irwin).

Gordon, D. M. (1994). "Bosses of Different Stripes: A Cross-National Perspective on Monitoring and Supervision," *American Economic Review* (Papers and Proceedings), 84, 375–9.

Herzberger, H. (1973). "Ordinal Choice Structures," *Econometrica*, 41, 187–237.

Houthakker, H. S. (1950). "Ordinal Preference and Rational Choice," *Economica*, 17, 159–74.

Hicks, J. R. (1939). *Value and Capital* (Oxford: Clarendon Press).

Hicks, J. R. (1956). *A Revision of Demand Theory* (Oxford: Clarendon Press).

Kannai, Y., and B. Peleg (1984). "A Note on the Extension of an Order on a Set to the Power Set," *Journal of Economic Theory*, 32, 172–5.

Koopmans, T. (1957). *Three Essays on the State of Economic Science* (New York: McGraw-Hill).

Kreps, D. M. (1988). *Notes on the Theory of Choice* (Boulder, CO: Westview Press).

Little, I. M. D. (1949). "A Reformulation of the Theory of Consumer's Behaviour," *Oxford Economic Papers*, 1, 90–9.

Little, I. M. D. (1957). *A Critique of Welfare Economics*, 2nd ed. (Oxford: Clarendon Press).

Luce, R. D., and H. Raiffa (1957). *Games and Decisions* (New York: Wiley).

Nash, J. F. (1950). "The Bargaining Problem," *Econometrica*, 18, 155–62.

Popper, K. (1959). *The Logic of Scientific Discovery* (London: Hutchinson).

Richter, M. K. (1966). "Revealed Preference Theory," *Econometrica*, 34, 987–91.

Samuelson, P. A. (1938). "A Note on the Pure Theory of Consumers' Behaviour," *Economica*, 5, 61–71.

Samuelson, P. A. (1947). *Foundations of Economic Analysis* (Cambridge, MA: Harvard University Press).

Savage, L. J. (1954). *The Foundations of Statistics* (New York: Wiley).

Sen, A. K. (1969). "Quasi-transitivity, Rational Choice and Collective Decisions," *Review of Economic Studies*, 36, 381–93.

Sen, A. K. (1970). *Collective Choice and Social Welfare* (San Francisco: Holden-Day).

Sen, A. K. (1971). "Choice Functions and Revealed Preference," *Review of Economic Studies*, 38, 307–17.

Sen, A. K. (1973). "Behaviour and the Concept of Preference," *Economica*, 40, 241–59.

Sen, A. K. (1974). "Choice, Ordering and Morality," in Körner (ed.), *Practical Reason* (Oxford: Blackwell).

Sen, A. K. (1977a). "Social Choice Theory: A Re-examination," *Econometrica*, 45, 53–89.

Sen, A. K. (1977b). "Rational Fools: A Critique of the Behavioral Foundations of Economic Theory," *Philosophy and Public Affairs*, 6, 317–44.

Sen, A. K. (1981). "Plural Utility," *Proceedings of the Aristotelian Society*, new ser., 81, 193–215.

Sen, A. K. (1982). *Choice, Welfare, and Measurement* (Oxford: Basil Blackwell).

Sen, A. K. (1986a). "Rationality, Interest and Identity," in Foxley, McPherson, and O'Donnell (eds.), *Development, Democracy, and the Art of Trespassing* (Notre Dame, IN: University of Notre Dame Press).

Sen, A. K. (1986b). "Prediction and Economic Theory," *Proceedings of the Royal Society of London, Series A, Mathematical and Physical Sciences*, 407, 1832, 3–22.

Sen, A. K. (1987a). *On Ethics and Economics* (Oxford: Basil Blackwell).

Sen, A. K. (1987b). *Commodities and Capabilities* (Oxford: Oxford University Press).

Sen, A. K. (1987c). *The Standard of Living* (Cambridge: Cambridge University Press).

Sen, A. K. (1989). "Economic Methodology, Heterogeneity and Relevance," *Social Research*, 56, 299–328.

Sen, A. K. (1991). "Utility," *Economics and Philosophy*, 7, 277–83.

Sen, A. K. (1993). "Internal Consistency of Choice," *Econometrica*, 61, 495–521.

Sen, A. K. (1994). "The Formulation of Rational Choice," *American Economic Review* (Papers and Proceedings), 84, 385–90.

Sen, A. K. (1995). "Rationality and Social Choice," *American Economic Review*, 85, 1, 1–24.

2 | Ethics and Economics
CHRISTOPHER W. MORRIS

Almost all of Amartya Sen's work has been, broadly speaking, about "ethics and economics." Sen's professional reputation rests in large part on work in normative areas of economics, welfare economics, and social choice theory, and on helping to restore "an ethical dimension to economics and related disciplines" (Nobel Committee 1998). His interests in poverty, justice, and development clearly are ethical. And, he has also made some substantial contributions to moral theory understood narrowly. In a way, virtually all of the chapters of this book take up topics in "ethics and economics."

My main concern in this chapter will be about the relation between the two, ethics *and* economics, and, in particular, the pressure that economics puts on ethics. Sen has long been concerned about the distance between the two fields of inquiry and has argued that "modern economics has been substantially impoverished by the distance that has grown between economics and ethics" (Sen 1987: 7). He thinks that the consequences to economics, both to the subfield of welfare economics and to the core predictive theory, have been serious (Sen 1987: 57).

1. SKEPTICISM ABOUT ETHICS

Economists in the twentieth century have often been skeptical about inquiries about value quite generally. They often have been concerned, first of all, to keep their field free of all normative elements, ethics included, so that it could be a "value-free" science. This concern was associated with views once widely held about the domain of the explanatory and the normative, articulated by many of the representatives of the logical positivist movement early in the last century. And economists have often been skeptical of ethics specifically.

I am grateful to Bruno Verbeek for comments on a draft of this chapter.

General skepticism about value and more particular skepticism about ethics are sometimes conflated. But, worries about value generally and about ethics in particular can be different. Ethical judgments are, of course, normative or evaluative. But, they do not exhaust the class. Skeptical concerns about the normative or the evaluative are much more general than those about ethics; the ethical or moral is merely a proper subset of the normative. The concern of economists that a genuine science needs to be value-free originally was linked to a more general form of skepticism. Lionel Robbins famously argued that economics and ethics had to be kept separate: "Economics deals with ascertainable facts; ethics with valuations and obligations" (Robbins 1935: 148–9). There has been considerable discussion of these questions since the early part of the last century. The most general point to be made is that it is very hard to conceive of science as an enterprise free of *all values*. Many of the activities of scientists are normative or evaluative. Graduate training, for instance, attempts to produce *good* scientists; the best journals have very high *standards* and reject submissions that are not very *good*; some questions are *interesting* and *worth pursuing*; some hypotheses or theories are rejected as *mistaken*.

There has also been considerable discussion in philosophy about the differences between normative and factual judgments. Some "naturalists" think that normative judgments are a species of factual ones (Lenman 2006). These controversies are not crucial for our concerns in this chapter and are mentioned merely to signal that matters are not as simple as they are often thought to be. Even if factual judgments are essentially different from normative or evaluative ones, it still may be that much can be said about the latter. Even if normative or evaluative judgments lack truth-values – that is, they cannot be true or false – many contemporary philosophers think that they nevertheless are assessable and criticizable.[1] Much like preferences, normative judgments at the very least are subject to consistency conditions.

In his early *Collective Choice and Social Welfare*, Sen (1970) presents an interesting argument against the project of a value-free welfare economics. He distinguishes between *basic* and *nonbasic* value judgments. A judgment is said to be basic to someone if it "is supposed to apply under all conceivable circumstances" (Sen 1970: 59). If someone, for instance, regards the judgment forbidding the killing of a person as one that applies in all circumstances, then it is basic for him or her. Now, someone might say that a basic value judgment cannot be disputed in the way that one might evaluate

---

[1] On the varieties of "noncognitivisms," see van Roojen (2008).

a factual or analytical claim (Sen 1970: 60). Sen goes on to argue that "no value judgment is demonstrably basic" (Sen 1970: 63). This means that even if one thinks that one cannot evaluate a basic value judgment, it is very hard to know when one is confronted with one. It seems, then, "impossible to rule out the possibility of fruitful scientific discussion on value judgments" (Sen 1970: 64).[2]

Moral skepticism, it is worth remarking, can take many forms. As we noted, economists in the twentieth century have been prone to believe that value judgments, or at least ethical ones, cannot be evaluated in the way in which factual judgments can be. As a consequence, many have concluded that economics must be value-free or ethics-free if it is to be a science. Sen's argument stated before is effective against this kind of skepticism. He has also been concerned with other ways in which economists are skeptical of ethics, and it is these that will concern us in this chapter.

Economics has long been associated with a view of human agents as self-interested maximizers. And, both self-interestedness and maximization can pose problems for ethics.[3] George Stigler, frequently cited by Sen, defends the general hypothesis that "we live in a world of reasonably well-informed people acting intelligently in pursuit of their self-interests" (Stigler 1981: 190). In his Tanner Lectures titled "Economics or Ethics?," Stigler raises the question, "Do people possess ethical beliefs which influence their behavior in ways not dictated by, and hence in conflict with, their own long-run utility-maximizing behavior?" (Stigler 1981: 175). Allowing that "altruism is strong within the family and toward close friends and diminishes with the social distance of the person" (Stigler 1981: 175) – a view he attributes to Smith – Stigler confidently makes a bold conjecture:

> Let me predict the outcome of the systematic and comprehensive testing of behavior in situations where self-interest and ethical values with wide verbal allegiance are in conflict. Much of the time, most of the time in fact, the self-interest theory (as I interpreted it on Smithian lines) will win. In a set of cases that is not negligible and perhaps not random with respect to social characteristics of the actors, the self-interest hypothesis will fail – at least without a subtle and unpredictable interpretation of self-interest.

---

[2] There are problems with Sen's characterization of a basic judgment, but they do not affect his conclusion and need not concern us here.

[3] Sen has rightly insisted that we distinguish between maximization and optimization. In contexts of choice, the latter requires choosing the best, whereas maximization, as he understands it, requires only choosing an alternative that is not judged worse than any other (Sen [1997] 2002: 158–205). Not all the theorists we discuss make this distinction.

I predict this result because it is the prevalent one found by economists not only within a wide variety of economic phenomena, but in their investigations of marital, child-bearing, criminal, religious, and other social behavior as well. We believe that man is a utility-maximizing animal. (Stigler 1981: 176)

"Ethical values," in Stigler's view, rarely beat self-interest when the two conflict.

Stigler's view is not uncommon in contemporary economics. Now moralists, ethical theorists, and ordinary people usually suppose that self-interest and morality will sometimes, perhaps often, conflict. So views like Stigler's represent a kind of skepticism about morality.

Many discussants, Stigler included, often are not very specific about the nature of the conflicts in question. Morality has different parts, and it does not seem that all will conflict with self-interest. Justice and benevolence are the two most important other-regarding virtues, and they may easily conflict with self-interest. But, most classical thinkers thought of temperance and courage as important virtues, even if largely self-regarding. Self-regarding virtues may be entirely consistent with *self-interest* or a person's *welfare*, however much they may conflict with a person's occurrent desires or preferences.[4] For instance, the virtue of courage would have one resist one's present inclination to flee, and temperance, one's present desire for more cake or another drink. On the other hand, justice, understood broadly as the part of morality that includes all of the obligations or duties owed to others, seems not infrequently to conflict with self-interest. Repaying one's debts, refraining from taking what belongs to another, and keeping one's word are all acts that often require a sacrifice and that seem to conflict with our interests. Now, some will argue that just acts are consistent with self-interest *in the long run*. Many, if not most, may well be. But, it is doubtful that *all* are (see Morris 2008). Few contemporary moral theorists think that self-interest and justice can be totally reconciled. If this virtual consensus is correct, then conjectures like Stigler's are a form of skepticism about justice or morality.

Sen is very critical of economists like Stigler on these matters. He remarks on the virtually complete absence of evidence in the latter's presentation: "The evidence for this belief presented by Stigler seems, however,

---

[4] It is commonplace for philosophers to distinguish between occurrent desires and self-interest. This distinction does not foreclose an account of the latter in terms of a person's coherent, informed, considered preferences. We need not linger on these matters here.

to be largely confined to predictions made by Stigler himself" (Sen 1987: 17).[5] Sen thinks this view distorts our understanding of humans:

> This narrow view of rationality as self-interest maximization is not only arbitrary; it can also lead to serious descriptive and predictive problems in economics (given the assumption of rational behavior). In many of our actions we evidently do pay attention to the demands of cooperation.... Indeed, within the narrow view, there are ongoing challenges in explaining why people often work together in interdependent productive activities, why public-spirited behavior is often observed (from not littering the streets to showing kindness and consideration to others), or why rule-based conduct standardly constrains narrowly self-seeking actions in a great many contexts. (Sen 2002: 23–4)

Sen notes some of the clever extensions of the traditional economic model in recent decades, for instance, by adding concerns for the usefulness of a good reputation.[6] He rightly doubts they can be extended to cover all of the phenomena in question. I shall return especially to the case of "rule-based conduct" later.

Sen notes the importance of the assumption of self-interested maximization for twentieth-century economics: "Not only is this assumption widely used in economics, but many of the central theorems of modern economics (e.g., the Arrow-Debreu theorems on the existence and efficiency of general equilibrium in a competitive economy without externality and without increasing returns) significantly depend on it."[7] The two Fundamental Theorems have significance in twentieth-century economics and social theory. They are often a centerpiece of presentations of welfare economics. One obvious interpretation of the significance of the two theorems is as a defense of competitive markets. When certain conditions are satisfied, competitive markets have some remarkable properties. The fact that these

---

[5] Sen is also very critical of the attribution of this view to Adam Smith, although I shall not consider these questions here. See the references he offers in Sen 2002: 22–3.

[6] See Sen 2002: 24–5. My criticisms of recent attempts to make use of the notion of reputation to save the hypothesis of self-interested maximization may be found in Morris 1999. I argue there that the notion of reputation used in much of the relevant literature has no explanatory value. One cannot have a reputation for, say, honesty, unless one can *be* honest, that is, have a stable disposition to act honestly even when it is not advantageous to so act.

Sen is also critical of the literature that introduces defects of rationality or knowledge to explain cooperative behavior. He notes the perversity of an account of *rational* choice that needs to depend in this way on ignorance (Sen 1987: 86).

[7] Sen 2002: 23; see note 30, where Sen briefly explains some of the ways in which the assumption can be relaxed without losing the results.

conditions are never fully satisfied is a difficulty for this defense, and the Theorem of the Second Best may be interpreted as telling us that approximating the conditions for perfect competition may not help us secure the benefits of perfect competition (Lipsey and Lancaster 1956). The debates here are controversial and beyond my competence. But, there is an interesting interpretation of the theorems of perfect competition that is relevant to our discussion of moral skepticism.

Suppose the world were a perfectly competitive market. This supposition may require radical suspension of belief for many, especially those who understand the conditions of perfect competition. But economists and philosophers alike are used to reasoning from idealized assumptions, and we shall proceed. In this perfectly competitive world, the outcome of production and trade will be both efficient in the Paretian sense and stable (a Nash equilibrium).[8] Any nonconsensual change to the conditions of this world will make some worse off (in terms of their preferences) than they otherwise would be. Consequently, it might be argued, there is no need for moral constraints on the interactions of agents. Such a world would be, in the words of the philosopher David Gauthier, a "morally free zone" (Gauthier 1986: 13).

In *Morals by Agreement*, Gauthier (1986), uses the theory of perfect competition to illustrate what he thinks is the rationale for moral constraints. In a perfectly competitive market, all agents are rational and self-interested, and all exchanges are mutually beneficial (or Pareto improving). In these markets, there is no way of rearranging things so as to improve the situation of some without making others worse off. In such a world there is no place, no need, for mutually beneficial principles of action; individual rational choice, through trade, exhausts mutually advantageous interaction.

Gauthier's purpose in focusing on perfectly competitive markets is first to give an example of a world, even if largely hypothetical, where there would be no need for a rational morality and secondly to have us think of moral principles as working to resolve a kind of externality. Markets typically presuppose the existence of a number of constraints on self-seeking behavior (for instance, norms governing contracts, a regime of property rights, and regulations to prevent fraud). And, in real markets, there are public goods and externalities (e.g., clean air, congestion) and many opportunities for mutually beneficial cooperative or collective action. Moral principles, especially principles of justice, presumably govern these matters.

---

[8] And in the *core*, an outcome where no coalition of agents can do better by cooperating among themselves.

Endorsing John Rawls's conception of a society as "a cooperative venture for mutual advantage,"[9] Gauthier expresses the view that morality promises mutual benefit. Sen would not entirely accept this, as he would think that justice may also call for some forms of redistribution that are not Pareto improvements.[10]

Neoclassical economics is an impressive edifice, and the theorems of welfare economics are instructive.[11] But, neither provides grounds for skepticism about ethics. Our world is not a "morally free zone." And even if mutual benefit were a condition of a rational morality, this would not be grounds for moral skepticism of the kind often found among economists.[12]

2. PREFERENCES, ETHICS, AND RATIONAL CHOICE

The formal framework of economics is not an obvious threat to ethics. It need not commit one to privileging self-interest in the way that economists like Stigler do. There are ways of addressing skeptical worries about ethics coming from economics. The most obvious route is to take a more expansive view of rationality and to be liberal about the values that utility functions can take. One can allow the preferences of rational agents to include not only their other-directed sentiments, but their moral values and principles as well. In his *Social Choice and Individual Values*, Kenneth Arrow includes a person's "entire system of values, including values about values" (Arrow 1951: 18). This is a very natural move to make. Economics might then cease to represent a skeptical alternative to ethics.

Sen thinks this move is insufficient to capture everything that is important to ethics, and I think that he is right. Starting in a famous article entitled "Rational Fools: A Critique of the Behavioral Foundations of Economic Theory," Sen distinguishes between *sympathy* and *commitment*.

---

[9] Rawls 1971: 4. Rawls came to regret this phrase.
[10] Some kinds of redistribution are, or can be, Pareto improvements. See the distinction between cooperative and noncooperative redistribution in Morris 1998: 277–80.
[11] "There is by now a long and fairly imposing line of economists from Adam Smith to the present who have sought to show that a decentralized economy motivated by self-interest and guided by price signal would be compatible with a coherent disposition of economic resources that could be regarded, in a well-defined sense, as superior to a large class of possible alternative dispositions.... It is important to understand how surprising this claim must be to anyone not exposed to this tradition" (Arrow and Hahn 1971: vi).
[12] See Hausman and McPherson 2006 for excellent discussions of the relevance of ethics to economics.

The former corresponds to the case in which the concern for others directly affects one's own welfare. If the knowledge of torture of others makes you sick, it is a case of sympathy; if it does not make you feel personally worse off, but you think it is wrong and you are ready to do something to stop it, it is a case of commitment. (Sen 1977: 326)

Sen notes that the choice of words may not be apt, but the distinction he thinks is important. He thinks that "behavior based on sympathy is in an important sense egoistic, for one is oneself pleased at others' pleasure and pained at other's pain" (Sen 1977: 326). Action based on commitment is not egoistic in this way. The contrast with commitment lies here. "One way of defining commitment is in terms of a person choosing an act that he believes will yield a lower level of personal welfare to him than an alternative that is also available to him" (Sen 1977: 327). I do not think this could be more than *part* of a definition, but the important point here is that commitment may require an agent knowingly to act in a way that will be costly to him or her.

Sympathy, Sen notes, is an externality, and it is thus excluded from models of perfect competition that are used to establish the important theorems about efficiency and stability discussed earlier. Sympathy nevertheless can be integrated into our economic models. Commitment, by contrast, is a more radical departure from orthodoxy. It "does involve, in a very real sense, counterpreferential choice, destroying the crucial assumption that a chosen alternative must be better than (or at least as good as) the others for the person choosing it" (Sen 1977: 328).

Commitment, as Sen understands it, is "concerned with breaking the tight link between individual welfare (with or without sympathy) and the choice of action (e.g., acting to help remove some misery even though one personally does not suffer from it)" (Sen 1982: 7–8; see also 1985: 214; 2002: 35). Like sympathy, commitment challenges the self-interestedness assumption of economic theory, but in different ways. Sen (2002: 33) distinguishes between different ways in which "the self may be central to one's self-interested preferences and choices":

> *Self-centered welfare:* A person's welfare depends only on her own consumption and other features of the richness of her life (without any sympathy or antipathy toward others, and without any procedural concern).

> *Self-welfare goal:* A person's only goal is to maximize her own welfare.

> *Self-goal choice:* A person's choices must be based entirely on the pursuit of her own goals. (Sen 2002: 33–4)

All three conditions are imposed by traditional economic models. The first, self-centered welfare, rules out sympathy (and antipathy). The second, self-welfare goal, "rules out incorporating within one's own objectives other considerations (such as welfare of others), except to the extent that it influences the person's own welfare." And the third, self-goal choice, "rules out the recognition of other people's goals, except to the extent that these goals shape the person's own goals" (Sen 2005: 6, italics omitted).[13]

Sympathy violates self-centered welfare, but not necessarily the other two. Commitment can, but need not, involve a violation of self-welfare goal (Sen 2002: 35; 1985: 214). What is interesting is the way in which commitment can challenge the third condition. It

> can take the form of modifying the person's *goals*, which can include effects on others beyond the extent to which these effects influence her own welfare (thereby violating self-welfare goal), or can alter the person's reasoned *choice* through a recognition of other people's goals beyond the extent to which other people's goals get incorporated within one's own goals (thereby violating self-goal choice). (Sen 2002: 35; see also Sen [1985] 2002: 214)

I shall apply Philip Pettit's apt labels of *goal-modifying commitment* to the first of these and *goal-displacing commitment* to the second (Pettit 2005: 18). Sen's notion of commitment is important for economics and rational choice theory. Commitment is

> not only important for characterizing the demands of rationality, but also for explaining behavioral variations between different societies and over time. The admission of committed behavior within a theory of rationality, not only enriches our conceptual understanding of rationality, but also helps us to understand actual behavior better, through taking note of the varying role of commitment in different social circumstances. (Sen 2005: 10)

He adds: "It is easy enough to see that ethics is somehow mixed up with the idea of commitment" (Sen 2005: 10). But, the importance of the notion does not mean that it is uncontroversial.

To the contrary, commitment, especially goal-displacing commitment, is an unorthodox proposal in economic theory and contemporary rational choice theory. It would have us abandon self-goal choice, and this is a radical departure from the dominant views. Philip Pettit finds goal-displacing

---

[13] See Chapter 1 of this volume for a parallel discussion of these conditions and associated questions about rationality.

commitment problematic, and his concerns will be widely shared. Commitment may be commonplace or perplexing, depending on how one conceives of it. Pettit notes that committing oneself to another in some of the ways that Sen describes

> is, on the face of it, a fairly common sort of exercise. Surely we often do take the goals of others into account in the manner proposed. We are bent on pursuit of our own ends, we discover that acting as they require will frustrate someone else's projects, and then we pause, take stock, and adjust what we were going to do so that the other will not suffer unduly at our hands. But though commitment is phenomenologically plausible in this way, it looks to be architecturally problematic. On Sen's conceptualization, it characteristically involves putting aside one's own goals and acting on those of another. But how can one ever fail to act on one's own goals? The idea offends against a picture of human psychology accepted on almost all sides, whether among professionals or among the folk. (Pettit 2005: 15)

Goal-modifying commitment, Pettit rightly argues, is less radical a departure from orthodoxy (Pettit 2005: 18). Goal-displacing commitment, by contrast, violates self-goal choice ("a person's choices must be based entirely on the pursuit of her own goals"). Pettit finds this possibility conceptually problematic. Rational choice theory, as well as common sense, he thinks, "picks up the assumption that when we act intentionally, then we try to advance certain goals in a way that is sensible in light of the apparent facts (Pettit 2002: Essay II.2). The claim that we can be executors of a goal-system that outruns our own goals is bound to raise a question" (Pettit 2005: 19). Pettit finds Sen's goal-displacing commitment unacceptable. Both rational choice theory and common-sense psychology understand intentional behavior as

> a form of behavior that is controlled by the agent's desire to realize a certain condition – the desired condition that will count as the agent's goal – and by the agent's beliefs about how best to do that. The goal represents the success condition of the action and will be discernible in how the agent is disposed to adjust the behavior as circumstances change and as different interventions are clearly needed for the realization of the condition. To imagine an action that is not controlled by a goal of the agent, by the lights of this approach, will be like trying to imagine the grin on the Cheshire cat in the absence of the cat itself. Let the agent have a goal and it becomes entirely obscure how the agent can be said to act; to act, or at least to act intentionally, is to act with a view of realizing a goal.

When Sen alleges that goal-displacing commitment takes the agent beyond
the control of his or her goals, then he is setting himself against our basic
common sense about action. What rational choice theory asserts on the minimal interpretation is that rational agents act out of a concern for maximizing
the expected realization of their goals. And that is precisely to argue, as in our
common-sense psychology, that rational agents aim at satisfying or fulfilling
their desires, according to their beliefs. It amounts to nothing more or less
than asserting the soundness of the belief-desire schema. (Pettit 2005: 21)

Goal-displacing commitment does not sit comfortably with economic
rationality and with some of our commonsensical notions. But, I think Sen
is right to urge us to consider it, especially as it seems necessary to make
sense of what I shall call *deontic constraint*.

3. RATIONALITY AND CONSTRAINT

I noted at the outset of this chapter that it can be important not to con-
fuse the ethical and the normative; the former is merely a proper subset of
the latter. Similarly, it will be important to distinguish between different
kinds of normativity, specifically between *values* generally and *constraints*.
A distinction of this kind will prove important both for understanding the
specific difficulties economic rationality poses for ethics and the potentially
radical nature of Sen's notion of commitment. There is no reason to think
that rationality as economists conceive of it need be hostile to values generally and moral values in particular. But, there are reasons to worry about
its compatibility with constraints understood in a certain way, and this may
be important for ethics and for rule-guided action in general.

It has long been noticed that maximizing conceptions of rationality or
of morality do not easily accommodate rules or principles. The worries the
early utilitarians had about moral rights were merely an instance of a more
general skepticism about norms or deontic constraints.[14] If rationality or
morality requires one to maximize the attainment of certain values, then
it is not clear what purpose norms can serve other than that of "rules of
thumb" or "summary rules" (e.g., "if it looks like rain, take an umbrella,"
"look both ways before crossing the street").

Suppose that we are to evaluate outcomes by certain optimizing standards (of rationality or morality). Suppose that there is a rule that instructs

---

[14] The term 'deontic constraint' I take from Heath (2008).

us how to act in certain situations. We find ourselves in such a situation, confronting a choice. Either the rule in question asks us to choose what is the best alternative (determined by the relevant optimizing standards of rationality or morality) or it does not. Suppose the rule asks us to choose the best alternative. Then it does not tell us anything more than we knew from applying the relevant standards. Suppose instead that the rule asks us to choose an alternative less good than the best one. Then it seems odd – indeed, irrational – to think that one should follow it.[15] It is hard to see what purpose norms have. Many social thinkers have concluded that taking norms as anything more than rules of thumb is irrational or immoral. Others, like Jon Elster, have "come to believe that social norms provide an important kind of motivation for action that is irreducible to rationality or indeed any other form of optimizing mechanism" (Elster 1989: 15).[16]

One can be skeptical of the rationality or morality of obeying norms without being skeptical of the standards that would have us evaluate and rank outcomes. The former kind of skepticism is directed against norms of all kinds. It is certainly directed against moral rules or principles, but it may also be directed against laws or other conventions of behavior. It should also not be confused with general skepticism about the moral or the normative. It is a very specific kind of skepticism. Given the kinds of conceptions of rationality that dominate economics, it is a kind of skepticism that is quite common in economics. I shall call it *constraint skepticism*.

Recall the inclusive view of the preferences of rational agents offered by Arrow, who suggests that for some purposes we can include in someone's preferences an "entire system of values, including values about values." Some think that such an inclusive view of preferences would avoid the skeptical implications of narrower views. I noted earlier that Sen is skeptical that this is the case. In a particularly helpful essay on Sen's views about preference and commitment, Daniel Hausman argues that the core notion

---

[15] The argument here is from Scott Shapiro; see Shapiro 2001, and McClennen and Shapiro 1998: 364. This argument is quite general, equally effective with norms generally or moral norms specifically. I have stated the argument using an optimizing conception of rationality or morality, but one can weaken this assumption and invoke only a maximizing conception (in Sen's sense) of either. One can also weaken the epistemic conditions.

[16] It might be noted that there is no special difficulty explaining how it is that the behavior of many agents *conforms* to norms (e.g., laws, coordination conventions). The problem is understanding *compliance* where this is conformity motivated by the norm itself. Hobbes's account of law, frequently thought to be a sanctions account, understands genuine laws to be reasons for action (laws are commands "where a man saith, *Doe this*, or *Doe not this*, without expecting other reason than the Will of him that sayeth it"; Hobbes [1651] 1991, chapters 25–6). On this view, political authority is not to be understood simply as justified force.

of preference that is central to economics and the theory of rational choice is that of *all-things-considered rankings*:

> An agent's preferences consist of his or her overall evaluation of the objects over which preferences are defined. This evaluation implies a ranking of these objects with respect to everything that matters to the agent: desirability, social norms, moral principles, habits – everything relevant to evaluation. Preferences thus imply all-things-considered rankings. In my view, all-things-considered rankings rather than choice ranking is "the underlying relation in terms of which individual choices can be explained" (Sen 1973: 67). It should be the single correct usage of the term "preference" in economics and decision theory. (Hausman 2005: 37)

The inclusive strategy and specifically Hausman's recommendation for economics and decision theory have much to recommend them, even if it turns out that some social theorists still need different notions of preference for their particular purposes. For our normative purposes, it may be useful sometimes to understand preferences as all-things-considered or rather, as I shall suggest, as *virtually*-all-things-considered. But, even if we do, this approach cannot address all the problems that we might want it to.

Some questions about justice or fairness, for instance, may not be answerable if preferences are all-things-considered. Consider this tale:

> Once upon a time two boys found a cake. One of them said, "Splendid! I will eat the cake." The other one said, "No, that is not fair! We found the cake together, and we should share and share alike, half for you and half for me." The first boy said, "No, I should have the whole cake!" Along came an adult who said, "Gentlemen, you shouldn't fight about this: you should compromise. Give him three quarters of the cake." (Smullyan 1980: 56)

We might be interested in what constitutes fair division of cakes. Including moral values and principles in utility functions cannot tell us how to divide the cake fairly or justly between the two boys, assuming, of course, that the adult's suggestion cannot be taken seriously.[17]

As the problem of fair division between the boys illustrates, some moral questions – especially problems of justice – remain unanswered even if preferences are allowed to include moral values and principles. The specific moral problems illustrated by the tale are *structural* ones. Questions of fairness or justice seem to arise even when the parties reason from the

---

[17] The proposed division is unfair. The first boy's interests are counted twice, and this double counting seems unfair as well as methodologically odd.

standpoint of (what seem to be) inclusive preferences. The inclusive strategy does not allow us to address certain kinds of moral questions.

Economists and game theorists have no difficulty understanding problems of interaction created by the *structure* of the situation in which agents find themselves. For instance, the familiar difficulties of securing efficient quantities of (many) public or collective goods result from structural features of the situations agents face. Whatever the others do, it often does not seem rational for one person to contribute to the production of a particular public good (e.g., clean air). The familiar prisoners' dilemma is a structural problem of interaction of this kind. I shall use it to discuss questions about the rationality of constraint that are central, it seems to me, to Sen's concerns about conceptions of rationality in economics.

Let us think of the familiar prisoners' dilemma (PD). Agents can find themselves in a PD defined by monetary payoffs. If their utility payoffs are different, then their real situation may not be a PD. But, of course, agents can be in a PD defined by their utility payoffs. For simplicity, let us focus on the single-play two-person PD. Even if it oversimplifies, the single-play PD is a useful model for an initial understanding of many collective action problems. There is an outcome that is mutually preferred to another, but, if agents act in ways that seem to be individually rational, the mutually preferred outcome will not be realized.

A number of solutions have been proposed for collective action problems, and we may think of these as "internal" or "external" to the underlying game. External solutions in this sense would include the "selective incentives" favored by Mancur Olson in his classical analysis, the introduction of sanctions, rewards, and the like (Olson 1965). External solutions alter the expected benefits of choice, effectively coordinating the different parties' actions so as to produce joint cooperation. They change people's preferences or beliefs (or expectations), whereas internal solutions take the structure of the game – the payoffs – to remain fixed. Internal solutions might include the introduction of norms that would have people cooperate in producing the desired goods.

We might then try to address troublesome PDs by introducing norms requiring agents to cooperate under certain conditions. The norms might simply require cooperation whenever one has adequate assurance that the other party will do the same.[18] On one understanding of norms, they are

---

[18] An agent "cooperates" here by choosing the act that, in conjunction with the similar act of others, will bring about the outcome that is jointly preferred to the Pareto-inferior equilibrium outcome.

practices that offer agents reasons to comply. It is not uncommon in the economic and game theoretical literatures to understand these reasons to comply as supported by coordination equilibria. I shall leave this view aside, as I wish to consider other ways in which norms might be reasons. The two main conceptions of norms I wish to discuss are different.

The first view is that norms in these contexts are essentially instructions backed up by sanctions: "Cooperate or suffer a penalty!" This view is still quite commonly found in economics and some other social sciences, although it ceases to have much influence in contemporary legal theory.[19] It may be the best account of rules governing, say, fouls in many competitive sports; these norms are often taken by players and their coaches to be nothing more than penalty schedules. For our purposes, such a view of norms, applied to PDs, functions to transform PDs into another game. They are external solutions.

Consider now a norm that instructs players of a PD to cooperate (when assured of the cooperation of others) that does not have penalties attached to it.[20] Suppose that this norm is an independent reason for action for the players. This assumption will immediately strike some as incoherent, but allow me to make it for the moment. Suppose then that a particular norm prescribing cooperation in a PD is a reason for action. How are we to understand the players' reasoning under this assumption? If the preferences that define the game are all-things-considered preferences as Hausman suggests, then these reasons are *already* included. If they are already included, and the game is a PD, then the agents will rationally defect, bringing about the familiar Pareto-inferior outcome. We are back where we started.[21]

Suppose that the agents' preferences are what I earlier called *virtually-*all-things-considered preferences. The reason introduced by the particular norm prescribing cooperation is not already included in their virtually-all-things-considered preferences. How are the agents to take this norm in their deliberations? Are they to reconsider their rankings of the outcomes and to reason with new preferences? Or are they to reason differently from familiar ways?

---

[19] Philosophers of law recognize, for instance, that many laws have no sanctions attached to them. See Hart 1961 for the seminal attacks on sanction accounts of law.

[20] Or where the sanctions are not needed to motivate most people's compliance, they merely provide law-abiding agents with assurance that others will comply (e.g., as in a game where some people have PD preferences and others Assurance Game preferences; for further explanation, see Sen [1974] 1982: 78).

[21] "It can be seen that even if the participants in a Prisoners' Dilemma were maximizers of *moral* (rather than selfish) orderings – different for different persons – the same 'dilemma' could result" (Sen 1984: 14).

The questions raised here are central to some important debates in the theory of rational choice today, and Sen's reflections about commitment have contributed to these discussions. For the most part, the familiar accounts of rational choice requiring optimization or some other form of consequential reasoning dominate the field. And these have difficulty explaining how rational agents might take the cooperative norm into account when they deliberate. It seems that they cannot rationally act on it. A number of revisionist accounts have been proposed to explain how rational agents might be guided by a cooperative norm like the one we are considering. I cited Sen's critical remarks about the "narrow view of rationality as self-interest maximization" earlier. This view, he argues, is misleading: "In many of our actions we evidently do pay attention to the demands of cooperation." We cannot explain a variety of characteristic human actions if we assume it to be true in all contexts, one of these being "why rule-based conduct standardly constrains narrowly self-seeking actions in a great many contexts" (Sen 2002: 23–4). The problem, as Sen has argued, is deeper than self-interestedness.

Sen's notion of goal-modifying commitment (Pettit's term) is the least radical way of integrating constraint into the theory of rational choice. Norms on this view can be understood as reasons to alter one's preferences. Rational choice will then require acting on the modified preferences.[22] In this view, preferences are "context-sensitive" and may change depending on the context of interaction. Rather than dwell on this view, I wish to mention two other kinds of revisionist views, neither of which makes use of goal-modifying commitment or anything similar. These views hold preferences constant. One, the *constraint model*, would understand norms as leading rational agents to revise their feasible set of alternatives. A norm requiring cooperation and forbidding noncooperative acts would lead a rational agent to remove the latter from the feasible set.[23] This view has some phenomenological support; most people find themselves "unable" to commit to or even to contemplate doing some wrongful acts.[24] A second revisionist approach, the *resolute choice model*, will have the norm function to alter the reasoning of rational agents. The latter will not change their views of what acts are feasible, much less their preferences; rather, they will

---

[22] In addition to the texts of Sen referred to in the text, see McClennen 1990. See also Schmidtz 1994.

[23] The label *constraint model* is adopted from McClennen and Shapiro 1998 and McClennen 2004. The two main contemporary proponents are Levi (1986, 1991) and Shapiro (1996).

[24] Humans characteristically find themselves unable to inflict certain harm on others in face-to-face situations and must often undergo training to overcome their reluctance.

come to think of the acts forbidden by the norm as unacceptable in certain contexts and will refrain from choosing them.[25]

Sen's goal-displacing commitment might be interpreted using these revisionist accounts, especially resolute choice. These views are not unproblematic and have their share of critics.[26] Rather than explore these questions in greater detail, let me merely frame the questions at issue here in a way that is both quite abstract and commonsensical. I wish to do this to explore the possibility, raised by Sen, of counterpreferential rational choice. We may think of economic rationality – that is, the optimizing views of rational choice that dominate economics and associated literatures – as a species of a more general, commonsensical "balance of reasons" conception of rationality. On a balance of reasons conception of rational choice, one chooses rationally whenever one selects an alternative that is favored by the balance of reasons. If one is faced with a choice between two options, one considers the reasons favoring each. One determines the weight of these reasons, and one then chooses the option favored by the "weightiest" reasons, that is, the reasons for an option that outweigh the reasons for the other. In this view, reasons may be compared for weight.[27]

Sen suggests that counterpreferential action may not always be irrational (Sen 1977: 328, quoted earlier in this chapter). How might that be? Might it ever be rational to act against the balance of reasons? Formulating the questions we have been raising about economic conceptions of rationality in terms of the broader balance of reasons account enables us to be able to introduce Joseph Raz's well-known revisionist account of the rationality of choosing against the balance of reasons (Raz [1975] 1990). Some norms, in his view, can be understood as reasons to act against the balance of reasons. They are to be understood as pairs of reasons. A norm requiring cooperation in certain contexts is (1) a first-order reason to choose a particular act and (2) a second-order "exclusionary" reason *not* to act on certain reasons

---

[25] I formulate the resolute choice model differently than do McClennen and Shapiro (1998) to emphasize the kind of goal-displacing account that David Gauthier developed. See Gauthier 1986, 1994, 1996, 1998a, and 1998b. The term *resolute choice* is originally McClennen's (1990); see McClennen 1988 for a comparison of his account with Gauthier's. The former's notion of "context-sensitive" preferences is similar to what Pettit calls goal-modifying commitments.

[26] And, there are other views, such as that of Michael Bratman, which are less revisionist and which may also offer support for Sen's criticisms of orthodox economic rationality. See Bratman 1987. For more references, see McClennen's excellent essay (2004).

[27] We can reformulate these views to allow for complications introduced by incomparable reasons.

favoring others. The suggestion is that goal-displacing commitment may be a kind of rational acting against the (first-order) balance of reasons.[28]

How best to understand rational deliberation and behavior in response to norms? Philip Pettit understands the accounts that dominate the theory of rational choice as developments of the dominant belief-desire schema for understanding and evaluating action (Pettit 2002). Thinking of these questions in terms of older belief-desire frameworks evokes an old criticism of this tradition that would have us add a third party to the pair, namely, will or intention or something like that. Belief and desire, the criticism was, do not explain action by themselves; for that they need the assistance of a third party, the will.[29] Our beliefs and desires may be reasons, for belief and action respectively. But, our decisions, commitments, and intentions, as well as our norms and principles, may also be a source of reasons for action. How to understand this possibility is a big question and central for the rationality of large parts of morality. Sen's reflections about rationality and moral motivation have helped both to raise the questions and to point in the direction of an answer.

References

Arrow, K. J. (1951). *Social Choice and Individual Values* (New York: Wiley).

Arrow, K., and F. Hahn (1971). *General Competitive Analysis* (San Francisco: Holden-Day).

Bratman, M. (1987). *Intention, Plans, and Practical Reason* (Cambridge, MA: Harvard University Press).

Elster, J. (1989). *The Cement of Society: A Study of Social Order* (Cambridge: Cambridge University Press).

Gauthier, D. (1986). *Morals by Agreement* (Oxford: Clarendon Press).

Gauthier, D. (1994). "Assure and Threaten," *Ethics*, 104, 690–721.

Gauthier, D. (1996). "Commitment and Choice: An Essay on the Rationality of Plans," in Farina, Hahn, and Vannucci (eds.), *Ethics, Rationality, and Economic Behaviour* (Oxford: Oxford University Press).

Gauthier, D. (1998a). "Intention and Deliberation," in Danielson (ed.), *Modeling Rationality, Morality, and Evolution* (Oxford: Oxford University Press).

---

[28] It may be necessary to have second-order relations (e.g., preferences, reasons) to understand constraints. The latter seem not to be first-order reasons with great weight. Sen introduces orderings of orderings in Sen 1974.

[29] Plato's may be the oldest version of this view (cf. his tripartite account of the soul in the *Republic*), but Kant's ethical writings will be more familiar to many readers.

Gauthier, D. (1998b). "Rethinking the Toxin Puzzle," in Coleman and Morris (eds.), *Rational Commitment and Social Justice: Essays for Gregory Kavka* (Cambridge: Cambridge University Press).

Hart, H. L. A. (1961). *The Concept of Law* (Oxford: Clarendon Press).

Hausman, D. M. (2005). "Sympathy, Commitment, and Preference," *Economics & Philosophy*, 21, 33–50.

Hausman, D. M., and M. S. McPherson (2006). *Economic Analysis, Moral Philosophy, and Public Policy*, 2nd ed. (Cambridge: Cambridge University Press).

Heath, J. (2008). *Following the Rules: Practical Reasoning and Deontic Constraint* (New York: Oxford University Press).

Hobbes, T. ([1651] 1991). *Leviathan*. R. Tuck, ed. (Cambridge: Cambridge University Press).

Lenman, J. (2006). "Moral Naturalism," in Zalta (ed.), *Stanford Encyclopedia of Philosophy*. http://plato.stanford.edu/entries/naturalism-moral/.

Levi, I. (1986). *Hard Choices* (Cambridge: Cambridge University Press).

Levi, I. (1991). "Consequentialism and Sequential Choice," in Bacharach and Hurley (eds.), *Foundations of Decision Theory: Issues and Advances* (Oxford: Blackwell).

Lipsey, R. G., and K. Lancaster (1956). "The General Theory of Second Best," *Review of Economic Studies*, 24, 11–32.

McClennen, E. F. (1988). "Constrained Maximization and Resolute Choice," *Social Philosophy & Policy*, 5, 95–118.

McClennen, E. F. (1990). *Rationality and Dynamic Choice* (Cambridge: Cambridge University Press).

McClennen, E. F. (2004). "The Rationality of Being Guided by Rules," in Mele and Rawlings (eds.), *The Oxford Handbook of Rationality* (New York: Oxford University Press).

McClennen, E. F., and S. Shapiro (1998). "Rule-Guided Behavior," in Newman (ed.), *The New Palgrave Dictionary of Economics and the Law* (New York: Palgrave Macmillan).

Morris, C. W. (1998). *An Essay on the Modern State* (Cambridge: Cambridge University Press).

Morris, C. W. (1999). "What Is This Thing Called 'Reputation'?" *Business Ethics Quarterly*, 9, 87–102.

Morris, C. W. (2008). "The Trouble with Justice," in Bloomfield (ed.), *Morality and Self-Interest* (New York: Oxford University Press).

Nobel Committee (1998). Statement of the award of the 1998 Nobel Memorial Prize in Economics, Press Release (Background Information). http://nobelprize.org/nobel_prizes/economics/laureates/1998/ecoback98.pdf.

Olson, M. (1965). *The Logic of Collective Action: Public Goods and the Theory of Groups* (Cambridge, MA: Harvard University Press).

Pettit, P. (1991). "Decision Theory and Folk Psychology," in Bacharach and Hurley (eds.), *Foundations of Decision Theory: Issues and Advances* (Oxford: Blackwell). Reprinted in Pettit 2002.

Pettit, P. (2002). *Rules, Reasons, and Norms* (Oxford: Clarendon Press).

Pettit, P. (2005). "Construing Sen on Commitment," *Economics & Philosophy*, 21, 15–32.

Rawls, J. (1971). *A Theory of Justice* (Cambridge, MA: Harvard University Press).

Raz, J. ([1975] 1990). *Practical Reason and Norms* (Princeton: Princeton University Press).

Robbins, L. (1935). *An Essay on the Nature and Significance of Economic Science*, 2nd ed. (London: Macmillan).

Schmidtz, D. (1994). "Choosing Ends," *Ethics*, 104, 226–51.

Sen, A. K. (1970). *Collective Choice and Social Welfare* (San Francisco: Holden-Day).

Sen, A. K. (1973). "Behavior and the Concept of Preference," *Economica*, 40, 241–59. Reprinted in Sen 1982.

Sen, A. K. (1974). "Choice, Orderings and Morality," in Körner (ed.), *Practical Reason* (Oxford: Blackwell). Reprinted in Sen 1982.

Sen, A. K. (1977). "Rational Fools: A Critique of the Behavioral Foundations of Economic Theory," *Philosophy & Public Affairs*, 6, 317–44. Reprinted in Sen 1982.

Sen, A. K. (1982). *Choice, Welfare, and Measurement* (Cambridge, MA: MIT Press).

Sen, A. K. (1984). *Resources, Values and Development* (Oxford: Blackwell).

Sen, A. K. (1985). "Goals, Commitment, and Identity," *Journal of Law, Economics and Organization*, 1, 341–55. Reprinted in Sen 2002.

Sen, A. K. (1987). *On Ethics and Economics* (Oxford: Blackwell).

Sen, A. K. (1997). "Maximization and the Act of Choice," *Econometrica*, 65, 745–79. Reprinted in Sen 2002.

Sen, A. K. (2002). *Rationality and Freedom* (Cambridge, MA: Harvard University Press).

Sen, A. K. (2005). "Why Exactly Is Commitment Important for Rationality?" *Economics & Philosophy*, 21, 5–13.

Shapiro, S. (1996). *Rules and Practical Rationality* (PhD dissertation, Columbia University).

Shapiro, S. (2001). "Judicial Can't," *Noûs*, 35, 530–57.

Smullyan, R. (1980). *This Book Needs No Title* (Englewood Cliffs, NJ: Prentice-Hall).

Stigler, G. J. (1981). "Economics or Ethics?" in McMurrin (ed.), *Tanner Lectures on Human Values*, Vol. 2 (Cambridge: Cambridge University Press).

Van Roojen, M. (2008). "Moral Cognitivism vs. Non-Cognitivism," in Zalta (ed.), *Stanford Encyclopedia of Philosophy*. http://plato.stanford.edu/entries/moral-cognitivism/.

3 | Capability and Agency

DAVID A. CROCKER AND INGRID ROBEYNS

INTRODUCTION

The capability approach is one of Amartya Sen's most significant contributions to philosophy and the social sciences. His writings on the capability approach are not only of theoretical interest on their own, but also provide concepts used in his work on social choice, freedoms, and development (see the chapters by Alkire, Pettit, and Roberts in this volume). Moreover, the capability approach has practical relevance for policy design and assessment, most famously through the work of the United Nations' *Human Development Reports* (United Nations Development Programme 1990–2007/8).

This chapter provides an overview of the conceptual and normative foundations of the capability approach and the role of agency within the approach. It puts aside the diverse ways in which the capability approach has been applied and implemented (Robeyns 2006). The chapter is divided into two parts. The first part, of which Ingrid Robeyns is the primary author, describes the main purpose of the capability approach, the concepts of functioning and capability, and the question of selecting and weighing capabilities. The second part, of which David A. Crocker is the primary author, focuses on the nature, value, and role of agency in the capability approach.

I. CAPABILITY

The Capability Approach

Scholars and policy makers use the capability approach in a wide range of fields, most prominently in development studies and policymaking, welfare economics, social policy, and social and political philosophy. It can be employed in both narrower and broader ways. In a narrower way, the capability approach tells us what information we should look at if we are to judge how well someone's life is going or has gone; this kind of information is needed in any account of well-being or human development. Because the capability approach contends that the relevant kind of information is that of human functionings and capabilities, the approach allows for interpersonal comparisons of well-being. This makes the approach attractive to a variety of theorists and scholars, as interpersonal comparisons are needed for a range of different exercises, such as comparing how well two persons (or societies) are doing at the same time or comparing one person (or society) at two different times. In the narrower use of the capability approach, the focus is often strictly on the evaluation of individual functioning levels or on both functionings and capabilities.

In its broader uses, the capability approach is more evaluative in nature and often pays attention to agency and other explicitly normative considerations. For example, the capability approach can be used as an alternative evaluative tool for social cost-benefit analysis. Or it can be used as a normative framework within which to evaluate and design policies, ranging from welfare-state design in affluent societies, to governmental and non-governmental development policies in poor countries, to policies that affluent countries and international institutions employ in their efforts to aid poor countries. The capability approach is not a theory to *explain* poverty, inequality, or well-being, although it does offer concepts that can be used in such explanations. Instead, it provides concepts and, in its broader forms, normative frameworks within which to conceptualize, measure, and evaluate these phenomena as well as the institutions and policies that affect them. Capability theorists differ as to whether the capability orientation can or should generate a cross-cultural or universal theory of justice: some argue against such a theory, whereas others aspire to a capability-based theory of justice. Although we can trace some aspects of the capability approach back to, among others, Aristotle, Adam Smith, and Karl Marx (see Nussbaum 1988; Sen 1993, 1999), it is economist-philosopher Amartya Sen who pioneered the approach and philosopher Martha Nussbaum and a growing number of other scholars across the humanities and the social sciences who have significantly developed it.

Well-Being and Agency

Sen conceives of *well-being* and *agency* as two distinguishable, but equally important and interdependent aspects of human life, each of which should be taken into account in our understanding of how individuals and groups are doing and each of which calls for respect (aid, protection) (Sen 1985b: 169–221; 1992: 39–42, 56–72; 1999: 189–91). The centrality of these two

	Well-Being	Agency
Achievements	Well-Being Achievements (Functionings)	Agency Achievements
Freedom	Well-Being Freedoms (Capabilities)	Agency Freedoms

Figure 3.1 Well-Being and Agency.

concepts in Sen's broader approach to evaluation in the field of well-being and development is suggested by the title of two essays: his 1984 Dewey Lectures, "Well-being, Agency and Freedom" (Sen 1985b), and his more recent essay "Agency and Well-Being: The Development Agenda" (Sen 1995a). To understand human beings, either individually or collectively, we should understand how well their lives are going and who or what controls them. Before explicating Sen's concepts of well-being and agency further, however, we must attend to a cross-cutting distinction, namely, achievement and freedom:

> A person's position in a social arrangement can be judged in two different perspectives, viz. (1) the actual achievement, and (2) the freedom to achieve. Achievement is concerned with what we *manage* to accomplish, and freedom with the *real opportunity* that we have to accomplish what we value. The two need not be congruent. (Sen 1992: 31)

Figure 3.1 shows Sen's two cross-cutting distinctions: (i) well-being and agency, and (ii) achievement and freedom. With the help of Figure 3.1, we explain the basic ideas.

As we shall see in more detail in the second part of this chapter, in his initial account of agency, set forth in articles and books through 1992, Sen describes agency achievement in the following way: "a person's agency achievement refers to the realization of goals and values she has reasons to pursue, whether or not they are connected with her own well-being" (1992: 56; see also 1985b: 203–4, 207; 1999: 19). A person's well-being achievements, in contrast, concern not "the totality of her considered goals and objectives" but rather only the person's "wellness" (Sen 1993: 37), "advantage" (Sen 1993: 30), or "personal welfare" (Sen 1993: 36). This state of a person, his or her beings and doings, may be the outcome of his or her own or other people's decisions and actions, or these achievements may be the result of causes internal or external to the person. Sen uses 'functionings' to designate well-being (and ill-being) achievements: they are "the state of a person – in particular the various things he or she manages to do or be in leading a life" (1993: 31).

> The well-being of a person can be seen in terms of the quality (the 'well-ness', as it were) of the person's being. Living may be seen as consisting of a set of interrelated 'functionings', consisting of beings and doings. A person's achievement in this respect can be seen as the vector of his or her functionings. The relevant functionings can vary from such elementary things as being adequately nourished, being in good health, avoiding escapable morbidity and premature mortality, etc., to more complex achievements such as being happy, having self-respect, taking part in the life of the community, and so on. The claim is that functionings are *constitutive* of a person's being, and an evaluation of well-being has to take the form of an assessment of these constituent elements. (Sen 1992: 39)

A person's well-being, for Sen, consists not only of his or her *current* states and activities (functionings), which may include the *activity* of choosing, but also of the person's freedom or real opportunities to function in ways alternative to his or her current functioning. Sen designates these real opportunities or freedoms for functioning as "capabilities." According to the capability approach, the ends of well-being, justice, and development should be conceptualized, *inter alia*, in terms of people's *capabilities to function*, that is, their effective opportunities to undertake the actions and activities they want to engage in, and to be whom they want to be. These "activities . . . or states of existence or being" (Sen 1985b: 197), and the freedom to engage in them, together constitute what makes a life valuable. The distinction between functionings and capabilities is between the realized and the effectively possible, in other words, between achievements, on the one hand, and freedoms or valuable options from which one can choose, on the other. Examples of functionings, as we have seen, are working, resting, being literate, being healthy, being part of a community, and so forth. What is ultimately important is that people have the freedoms or valuable opportunities (capabilities) for these functionings, hence the real freedom to lead the kinds of lives they want to lead, to do what they want to do, and to be the person they want to be. Once they effectively have these substantive opportunities, they can choose the options they value most. For example, every person should have the opportunity to be part of a community and to practice a religion, but if someone prefers to be a hermit or an atheist, he or she should also have these latter options.

A person's own well-being, whether functionings or capabilities or both, is often part and even all of a person's objectives. But one's own well-being may not be a person's exclusive goal, for a person may also pursue goals that reduce his or her well-being and even end his or her life. The concept of agency marks what a person does or can do to realize any of his or her goals and not only ones that advance or protect his or her well-being (see also the chapter by Morris in this volume).

Agency, like well-being, has two dimensions, namely, agency *achievements* and the *freedom* for those achievements. As agents, persons individually and collectively decide and achieve their goals – whether altruistic or not – in the world, and as agents they have more or less freedom and power to exercise their agency: "Agency freedom is freedom to achieve whatever the person, as a responsible agent, decides he or she should achieve" (Sen 1985b: 204). Although agency "is inescapably qualified and constrained by the social, political, and economic opportunities available to us" (Sen 1999: xi–xii), not only do people have more or less freedom to decide, act, and make a difference in the world, but social arrangements can also extend the reach of agency achievements and agency freedom. In the second part of this chapter, we analyze Sen's concept of agency in more detail and argue that it has evolved to have at least two uses. Given this introductory distinction between well-being and agency, we turn now to a further clarification of Sen's distinction between capability and functioning.

Well-Being: Functionings and Capabilities

A key analytical distinction in the capability approach is between the means and the ends of, for example, well-being, agency, and development. The capability approach evaluates policies according to their impact on people's capabilities as well as their actual functionings. It asks whether people are *able* to be healthy, and whether the means or resources necessary for this capability, such as clean water, adequate sanitation, access to doctors, protection from infections and diseases, and basic knowledge on health issues, are present. It asks whether people are well-nourished, and whether the conditions for the realization of this capability, such as having sufficient food supplies and food entitlements, are being met. It asks whether people have access to a high-quality educational system, to real political participation, and to community activities that support them, that enable them to cope with struggles in daily life, and that foster real friendships. For some of these capabilities, the main input will be financial resources and economic production, but for others it may be political practices and institutions, such as effective guarantees and protections of freedom of thought, political participation, social or cultural practices, social structures, social institutions, public goods, social norms, and traditions and habits. The capability approach thus proposes a broad, rich, and multidimensional view of human well-being and pays much attention to the links between material, mental, and social well-being, or to the economic, social, political, and cultural dimensions of life. The following sections describe the capability approach in more detail.

An Alternative Framework for Evaluation of Well-Being

In its broader form, we have said, the capability approach is a perspective that can be used for a wide range of evaluative purposes. The approach focuses on the information that we need to make judgments about individual well-being (and agency), social policies, and so forth, and consequently rejects alternative approaches that it considers normatively inadequate, for example when an evaluation is done exclusively in monetary terms. In its broader use, the capability approach also identifies social constraints that influence and restrict well-being (and agency) and those institutions and policies that promote or protect well-being (and agency). The approach can also be applied to efficiency evaluations. For example, Alkire (2002) used the capability approach to evaluate three Oxfam projects in Pakistan, comparing a conventional cost-benefit analysis with an evaluation based on a range of valuable functionings. Wolff and de-Shalit (2007) have developed a capabilities-based theory to develop policies to support the disadvantaged in affluent societies.

The capability approach can serve as an important constituent for a theory of justice, but, as Sen argues, the capability approach specifies an evaluative space, and this does not amount by itself to a theory of justice (Sen 2004: 337). He stresses that a theory of justice must include not just a choice for a specific "currency of justice" (that is, the information on well-being that will be taken into account when making the judgments of justice), but also aggregative considerations and distributive principles that the capability approach itself does not specify. Moreover, as we shall see, given his commitment to the agency of individuals and communities, and to democratic decision making, Sen contends that "foundational ideas of justice can separate out some basic issues as being inescapably relevant, but they cannot plausibly end up . . . with an exclusive choice of some highly delineated formula of relative weights as being the unique blueprint for 'the just society'" (1999: 286–7).

The capability approach entails a critique of other evaluative approaches, mainly of the welfarist approaches in welfare economics and of

utilitarian and income- or resource-based theories. Sen characterizes welfarist theories as those consequentialist theories that restrict "the judgments
of state of affairs to the utilities in the respective states (paying no direct
attention to such things as the fulfillment or violation of rights, duties,
and so on)" (Sen 1999: 59). He rejects such theories because, whatever
their further specifications, they rely *exclusively* on utility and thus exclude
nonutility information from our moral judgments (Sen 1999: 62). Sen is
concerned not only with the information that is included in a normative
evaluation, but also with the information that is excluded. The nonutility
information that is excluded by utilitarianism includes a person's additional
physical needs, resulting from being physically disabled for example, but
also social or moral principles, such as human rights or the specific principle that men and women should be paid the same wage for the same work.
For a utilitarian, these features of life and principles have no intrinsic value.
Men and women, for example, should not be paid the same wage as long as
women are satisfied with lower wages or total utility is maximized. But, Sen
believes it a mistake to think that such egalitarian and other moral principles
would not be taken directly into account in our moral judgments. Thus,
the normative theories that Sen attacks include those that rely exclusively
on mental states. This does not mean that Sen thinks that mental states,
such as happiness, are unimportant and have no role to play, for they too
are functionings that we sometimes have reason to value. Rather, it is the
exclusive reliance on mental states that he rejects.

Although Sen has often acknowledged his debt to John Rawls (1971),
he also criticizes Rawls's use of primary goods for interpersonal comparisons, because primary goods are mere means, not intrinsically worthwhile
ends, and as a consequence would not be able to account for the full range
of the diversity of human beings (Sen 1980; 1992: 81–7; 2004: 332). If all
persons were identical, then an index of primary goods would yield similar freedoms for all; but, given human diversity, the comparisons in the
space of social primary goods will fail to note that different people need
different amounts and different kinds of goods to reach the same levels
of well-being or advantage. The right amount of food to enable one person to labor effectively may be insufficient for a second person and too
much for a third.[1] However, Thomas Pogge (2002) has argued against the

---

[1] More recently, Martha Nussbaum has significantly extended the capability critique of Rawls
by not only focusing on the difference between primary goods and capabilities, but also by
examining the implications of the fact that Rawls's theory of justice belongs to the social
contract tradition, whereas the capability approach does not (Nussbaum 2006).

capability approach to justice and in favor of a Rawlsian approach. The debate between Rawlsians and capability theorists is certainly not settled (Brighouse and Robeyns, forthcoming). In a similar vein, Sen has criticized other resource-based normative theories, such as Ronald Dworkin's (1981) account of equality of resources, which has also generated a highly abstract philosophical debate on the precise differences between these two theories (Dworkin 2000: 299–303; Kaufman 2006b: 125–8; Pierik and Robeyns 2007; Sen 1984; Williams 2002).

In its narrower understanding, as we adumbrated earlier in this chapter, the capability approach serves as a metric for interpersonal comparisons of well-being freedom and well-being achievement. Yet, some economists have taken this to imply that the capability approach must provide a *formula* for interpersonal comparisons of well-being, in the sense that the capability approach would provide a neat recipe or even an algorithm to carry out empirical exercises in welfare comparisons. They have tried in vain to find in Sen's writings such a formula or algorithm and then criticized it based on this restrictive assumption of what the capability approach should deliver (Roemer 1996: 191–3; Sugden 1993: 1953–4). Similarly, some political philosophers criticize the capability approach for not providing for a complete outline of a theory of equality or social justice (Dworkin 2000: 299–303). In both cases, it should be stressed that the capability approach delineates a class or family of possible criteria for or measures of interpersonal well-being, but that within this family there are still many different options, depending on the selection of capabilities and their relative weights. As we shall see, the ideal of individual and group agency plays an important role in Sen's (but not Nussbaum's) way of addressing capability selection, weighting, and sequencing.

Conversion Factors and Human Diversity

Recall that a crucial distinction in the capability approach is the distinction between the means (such as goods and services) and the ends of well-being and development, which are conceptualized, *inter alia*, as functionings (the realized dimensions of well-being) and capabilities (those dimensions of well-being that are potentially available to a person). Goods and services (which may include nonmarket goods and services), have certain characteristics that make them of interest to people. For example, we may not be interested in a bike because it is an object made from certain materials with a specific shape and color, but because it can take us to places where we want to go, and in a faster way than if we were walking. These characteristics of a good or commodity, we might say, enable or contribute to a functioning. A bike enables the functioning of mobility, to be able to move oneself freely and more rapidly than walking.

The relation between a good and the achievement of certain beings and doings is influenced by *conversion factors*. There are several different types of conversion factors, and the conversion factors discussed in Sen's writings can be categorized into three groups. All conversion factors influence how a person can be or is free to convert the characteristics of the good or service into a functioning, yet the sources of these factors may differ. *Personal conversion factors* are internal to the person, such as metabolism, physical condition, sex, reading skills, or intelligence. If a person is disabled, is in bad physical condition, or has never learned to cycle, then the bike will be of limited help in enabling the functioning of mobility. *Social conversion factors* are factors from the society in which one lives, such as public policies, social norms, practices that unfairly discriminate, societal hierarchies, or power relations related to class, gender, race, or caste. *Environmental conversion factors* emerge from the physical or built environment in which a person lives. Among aspects of one's geographical location are climate, pollution, the proneness to earthquakes, and the presence or absence of seas and oceans. Among aspects of the built environment are the stability of buildings, roads, bridges, and means of transportation and communication. The three types of conversion factors all stress that it is not sufficient to know the goods a person owns or can use to be able to assess the well-being that he or she has achieved or could achieve; rather, we need to know much more about the person and the circumstances in which he or she is living. Sen uses 'capability,' not to refer exclusively to a person's abilities or other internal powers, but to refer to an opportunity made feasible, and constrained by, both internal and external conversion factors (Crocker 2008: 171–2; Robeyns 2005: 99).

The capability approach thus takes account of human diversity in at least two ways: (i) by its focus on the plurality of functionings and capabilities as an important evaluative space, and (ii) by the explicit focus on personal and socio-environmental factors that make possible the conversion of commodities into functionings, and on the whole social, institutional, and environmental contexts that affect the conversion factors and the capability set directly.

Moreover, goods and services are not the only means to people's capabilities. There are other means that function as "inputs" in the creation or expansion of capabilities, such as social institutions broadly defined. The material and nonmaterial circumstances that shape people's opportunity sets, and the circumstances that influence the choices that people make from the capability set, should receive a central place in capability evaluations. For example, both Sen and Nussbaum have paid much attention to the social norms and traditions that form women's preferences and that influence their aspirations and their effective choices (Nussbaum 2000; Sen 1990a, 1995b). The capability approach does not only advocate an evaluation of people's capability sets, but also insists on scrutinizing the context in which economic production and social interactions take place, and whether the circumstances in which people choose from their opportunity sets are enabling and just.

A focus on functionings and capabilities does not imply that a capability analysis would pay no attention to resources, such as food availability, or the evaluation of social institutions, economic growth, technical advancement, social cohesion, and so forth. Although functionings and capabilities are of ultimate normative concern, other values may be important as well. For example, in their evaluation of development in India, Jean Drèze and Amartya Sen (2002: 3) have stressed that working within the capability approach in no way excludes the integration of an analysis of resources, such as food, or other means. In sum, all the means of well-being, like the availability of commodities, legal entitlements to them, other social institutions, and so forth, *are* important, but the capability approach presses the point that they are not the ends of well-being, only their means. Food may be abundant in the village, but a starving person may have nothing to exchange for it, no legal claim on it, or no way of preventing intestinal parasites from consuming it before he or she does.

Capabilities as Real Opportunities

A terminological note concerns the meaning of the term "basic capabilities." In Sen's work, basic capabilities are a subset of all capabilities. A basic capability, says Sen, is "the ability to satisfy certain elementary and crucially important functionings up to certain levels" (1992: 45 n. 19). Basic capabilities refer to the freedom to do some basic things considered necessary for survival and to avoid or escape poverty or other serious deprivations. The relevance of basic capabilities is "not so much in ranking living standards, but in deciding on a cut-off point for the purpose of assessing poverty and deprivation" (Sen 1987: 109). Hence, although the notion of capabilities refers to a very broad range of opportunities, basic capabilities refer to the real opportunity to avoid poverty or to meet or exceed a threshold of well-being. Basic capabilities will thus be crucial for poverty analysis and in general for studying the well-being of the majority of the people in poor countries. In affluent countries, by contrast, well-being analysis would often focus on capabilities that are less necessary for survival. It is important to acknowledge that the capability approach is not restricted to poverty and deprivation analysis, but can also serve as a framework for, say, project or policy evaluations or inequality measurement in affluent communities.

A second misunderstanding concerns the use of the term "freedom." Especially in his more recent work, Sen often equates capabilities with freedoms, without always specifying in more detail what kind of freedoms he is referring to. Yet, this equation can easily be misunderstood, because Sen insists both that there are many kinds of freedom (some valuable, some negative, and some trivial) and that "freedom" means very different things to different people. One misunderstanding to get out of the way is that capabilities as freedoms refer exclusively to the "free market." Functionings and capabilities are conceptualizations of well-being achievement and well-being freedoms. Sen does argue that people have reason to value the freedom or liberty to produce, buy, and sell in markets. This point, however, is a very different matter than the highly disputed question in economics and politics regarding the benefits and limits of the market as a system of economic production and distribution.

What kind of freedoms are capabilities? A careful reading of Sen's work clarifies that capabilities are freedoms conceived as real opportunities (Sen 1985a: 3–4; 1985b: 201; 2002: chapter 20). For Sen, capabilities as freedoms refer to the *presence* of valuable freedoms or alternatives, in the sense of opportunities that do not exist only formally or legally, but are also effectively available to the agent. Understanding capability as an opportunity concept of freedom, rather than some other kind of freedom, may undermine mistaken critiques of Sen's work (Kaufman 2006a).

Functionings or Capabilities?

In addition to these terminological remarks, capability proponents have addressed the question of whether the appropriate well-being metric should be capabilities or functionings. What considerations are relevant for this choice? The first consideration is normative, and this is the argument Sen and Nussbaum most often offer: by focusing on capabilities rather than functionings, we do not privilege a particular account of good lives, but instead aim at a range of possible ways of life from which each person can choose. Thus, it is the liberal nature of the capability approach, or an antipaternalist consideration, that motivates a principled choice for capabilities rather than functionings. A second normative consideration stems from the importance given to personal responsibility in contemporary political philosophy: each person should have the same real opportunity (capability), but once that is in place, each individual should be held responsible for his or her own choices. This responsibility-sensitivity principle is widely endorsed, not only in political philosophy, but also in the mathematical models being developed in normative welfare economics. If one wants to endorse and implement this principle of responsibility-sensitivity, then specifications and applications of the capability approach should focus on capabilities, rather than functionings. Yet, even at a highly abstract theoretical level, philosophers disagree on whether we should endorse responsibility-sensitivity in developing the capability approach (e.g., Fleurbaey 2002; Vallentyne 2005; Wolff and de-Shalit 2007). Third, there are cases in which a capability is available to a person, but only if other people do not also want to realize that capability (Basu 1987: 74; Basu and López-Calva, forthcoming). For example, two spouses may each have the capability of holding demanding jobs incompatible with large caring responsibilities. However, if these spouses also have children or relatives with extensive needs for care, then at best only one of the spouses may effectively realize that capability. As capability sets may therefore include freedoms that are conditional (because they depend on the choices of other people), it might be better to focus both on the individual's capability set and also on what people have been able to realize from their own capability sets, that is, their functionings or well-being achievements. The question of who decides or *should* decide this sort of spousal question highlights the importance of agency.

It should also be mentioned that the concept of functioning has particular relevance for our relations to those human beings who are not yet able to choose (infants), who will never be able to choose (severely mentally disabled individuals), or who have lost this ability through advanced dementia or serious brain damage. Whether or not these persons can decide to be well nourished and healthy, we (through families, governments, or other institutions) have the obligation to promote or protect their nutritional and healthy functioning.

Finally, the choice between functionings and capabilities can also be bridged by a conceptual move. Sen (1987: 36–7) has proposed the concept of "refined functioning" to designate functioning that takes note of the available alternatives. Sen (1992: 52) notes: "'fasting' as a functioning is not just starving; it is *choosing to starve when one does have other options.*" That is, one could focus on achieved functionings levels but – where appropriate – include the exercise of choice as one of the relevant functionings (Fleurbaey 2002; Stewart 1995).

In addition to these normative and conceptual arguments, there are also concerns related to the application and measurability that influence the choice of capabilities, functionings, or a combination of the two (Robeyns 2006). It is, for example, often easier to observe and measure functionings than capabilities (Sen 1992: 52–3).

Selecting and Weighing Capabilities

Other major points of debate in the capability literature are the questions of which capabilities should be selected as relevant and who should decide. At the level of ideal theories of justice, some have argued that each and every capability is relevant and should count in our moral calculus (Vallentyne 2005). Others have argued that considerations of justice require that we demarcate morally relevant from morally irrelevant and morally bad capabilities (Nussbaum 2003; Pogge 2002). This demarcation could be done in various ways. Anderson (1999) argues that, for purposes of political justice, the only relevant capabilities are those needed for a person to participate as a citizen. Nussbaum endorses a well-defined list of capabilities, which, she argues, should be enshrined in every country's constitution (Nussbaum 2000, 2003, 2006; see the appendix to this chapter). Sen, we shall argue, draws on his ideal of agency to argue that each group should itself select, weigh, trade off, and sequence capabilities as well as prioritize them in relation to other normative considerations, such as agency, efficiency, and stability.

Moving from ideal theory to nonideal theory and empirical applications makes the selection of relevant capabilities even more complicated, for other concerns such as feasibility, data availability, practical relevance, and even parsimony may play significant roles. Several proposals are offered ranging from substantive proposals with elaborate theoretical underpinnings, through several procedural methods, to the *a*theoretical practice that an investigator should simply conduct a survey to collect rich data (or use an existing survey) and let a statistical technique, such as factor analysis, "decide." At one end of this spectrum is Martha Nussbaum's well-known list, which contains prescribed capabilities that are grouped together under ten "central human capabilities" (see the appendix to this chapter). Nussbaum defends these capabilities as being the moral entitlements of every human being on earth. She formulates the list at an abstract level, and the translation to implementation and policies should be done at a local level, taking into account local differences. Nussbaum claims that this list can be derived from a Rawlsian overlapping consensus and stresses that her list remains "open-ended and humble" (Nussbaum 2000: 77) and always open for revision, yet this avowal has not convinced critics who have argued that there is insufficient scope for democratic deliberation and respect for agency in her capabilities approach (e.g., Crocker 2008; Robeyns 2003; Sen 2004). Amartya Sen consistently and explicitly refuses to defend "one pre-determined canonical list of capabilities, chosen by theorists without any general social discussion or public reasoning" (Sen 2005: 158). Of course, groups and theorists might construct lists for various purposes, and lists need not be "pre-determined" or "canonical," however we might under-stand these terms. And, Sen's refusal to endorse Nussbaum's list has not prevented him from using – for various purposes – particular selections of capabilities in his empirical as well as his normative work. However, beyond stating in general terms that some democratic process and public reasoning should be involved, Sen has never explained in detail how such a selection could and should be done. Several capability scholars, including Anderson, Alkire, Robeyns, and Crocker, have sought in various ways to fill this lacuna. Anderson (1999: 316) argues that people should be enti-tled "to whatever capabilities are necessary to enable them to avoid or escape entanglement in oppressive social relationships" and "to the capa-bilities necessary for functioning as an equal citizen in a democratic state." Alkire (2002: chapter 2) proposes to select capabilities based on John Fin-nis's practical reasoning approach. By iteratively asking "Why do I do what I do?," one comes to the most basic reasons for acting: life, knowledge, play, aesthetic experience, sociability (friendship), practical reasonableness, and religion. Robeyns (2003) has proposed some pragmatic criteria, mainly relevant for empirical research, for the selection of capabilities for the con-text of inequality and well-being assessments. Crocker (2006; 2007; 2008: chapters 9–10) explores the theory and practice of deliberative democ-racy to bring more specificity to democratic procedures and participative institutions.

Suppose that, by whatever method, we (whoever the "we" is) unany-mously agreed on a selection of capabilities. We still would be left with the question of whether the capabilities should be aggregated and, if so, what their relative weights will or should be. How should different capa-bilities be traded off against each other when they cannot all be realized fully? Some have argued against trade-offs on the basis that the differ-ent capabilities are incommensurable or that each capability is an absolute entitlement that never should be overridden by another entitlement or other normative consideration. For example, Nussbaum argues that the ten capabilities on her list, being incommensurable, cannot be traded off against each other (and, hence, have no relative weight), and also that the state should provide each citizen with a minimum threshold of each capability.

In existing empirical applications, investigators employ the most prevalent weighing systems and simply adopt certain weights (with or without attempting to justify them) or to use a conventional statistical procedure. The United Nations Development Programme uses the first approach in its construction of the Human Development Index in which the three functionings (educational achievement, life expectancy, and an economic standard of living) each receive an equal weighting. Many economists find this procedure entirely arbitrary and disapprove of the explicit value judgments involved, but others appreciate the clarity that such an explicit weighting procedure brings. Obviously, one can always change the relative weights and test the robustness of the empirical results for a change in weights. The second approach, one that derives weights in a statistical way, also has proponents and opponents. The proponents believe that their deployment of statistical information enables them to determine the weights without appealing to "simplistic" or unscientific methods such as explicit choices. But, there is very little discussion about the validity and plausibility of either the normative assumptions underlying these statistical methods or the related conceptions of good science.

Another possible weighting system is to use a democratic or some other social choice procedure (Chakraborty 1996). The basic idea would be to encourage or prescribe that the relevant group of people decide on the weights. In some contexts, such as small-scale projects or evaluations, such capability weighting (and selection) could be done by participatory techniques. For larger-scale policy contexts, researchers (Gastil and Levine 2005) are exploring ways in which representative citizen panels or deliberative polling may generate a deliberated majority opinion on relative weights such that policy makers may be guided and even mandated to choose whether to invest public funds in education, health care, mobility infrastructure, or other public goods that they deem contextually urgent. For large-scale measurement applications, information on the weights could in theory be collected in the same way that data on functionings are collected (i.e., with household surveys or other types of questionnaires) or through other exercises, such as deliberative polling. Finally, it has also been suggested that we may determine the weights of capabilities as a function of how much they contribute to overall life satisfaction (Graham and Pettinato 2002; Schokkaert 2007).

II. AGENCY

Sen's concept of agency – although often misunderstood or neglected by followers and critics alike – has come to be crucial in his solution to the problem of the selection and weighting of capabilities and, more generally, in his social-scientific and normative outlook. It is important to ask not only what it means for an individual's life to go well or for a group to be doing well, and which capabilities and functionings are most important, but also who should decide these questions, how they should do so, and who should act to effect change. If well-being freedoms and functionings were the only items with normative importance, it would not matter who decided what was important or the process by which these decisions were made or enacted. With the concept of agency, however, Sen (1999: 11, 53, 281) signals an "agent-oriented view" in which individuals and groups should decide these matters for themselves, "effectively shape their own destiny and help each other" (Sen 1999: 11), and be "active participant[s] in change, rather than . . . passive and docile recipient[s] of instructions or of dispensed assistance" (Sen 1999: 281).

Sen's Descriptive Concept of Agency

What does Sen mean by agency? How does he come to this focus on agency, and how does he support it? What role does individual and collective agency play in what we may call the "agency-oriented" capability approach?

Initially, Sen's concept of agency was descriptive or explanatory (with normative implications): it described human motivation as often going beyond self-interest, even enlightened self-interest. Recall that, for Sen, a person's well-being concerns his or her own wellness, his or her own "advantage," whether from the person's own efforts, those of others, or the force of circumstances. Yet, with the concept of agency, Sen makes the point that one's own well-being – whether functionings or capabilities – need not exhaust one's motivations or objectives. We may also pursue goals that reduce our well-being and even end our lives. To achieve either well-being or non-well-being goals and to have the freedom of will and action to do so is to realize agency freedom in agency achievements. A person's agency achievement is his or her deciding and acting on the basis of what he or she values and has reason to value, whether or not that action is personally advantageous. A person's agency freedom is the freedom to so decide and the power to act and be effective.

What is the point of Sen's initial distinction between well-being and agency? It provides space for a conception of freedom and responsibility that breaks decisively with any egoism that claims that humans are no more than – and are bound to be – "strict maximizers of a narrowly defined self-interest" (Sen 1990b: 54). Some people most of the time and many people some of the time *do* strive to increase their own well-being. However, insofar as humans can and do devote themselves to causes beyond and even against their own welfare, with his descriptive concept of agency, Sen (1990b: 54) can answer a skeptical realist's concern about any normative theory that proposes a just treatment of conflicting interests or freedoms: "If . . . individuals as social persons have broader values and objectives, including sympathy for others and commitment to ethical norms, then the promotion of social justice need not face unremitting opposition at every move" (Sen 1990b: 54).

Moreover, Sen might have added, as he did in a 2006 address (Sen 2006), that effective implementation of development policies can and should build on people's sense of fairness and concern that they and others be treated fairly. Sen (1987, 1999, 2002) himself provides empirical content for this sort of altruistic conceptual space by referring to his own social-scientific work and that of many other social scientists, such as Albert Hirschman (1977). Also relevant are experiments that show that participants in controlled games often choose not to maximize their own self interest (Frolich and Oppenheimer 1992). In sum, employing the distinction between well-being and agency, Sen provides conceptual space for the commonplace that agents pursue not only their own self-interest, but also altruistic goals for the sake of which they may sacrifice their health, friends, and even life itself. Although an agent may exercise agency only in seeking his or her well-being, he or she also may exercise it in seeking other ends.

Sen's Normative Ideal of Agency

After 1992, Sen increasingly supplements this *descriptive* account of agency, one that makes room for both self-regarding and other-regarding human motivation, with an explicitly *normative* account that proposes human agency as something we have reason to value, realize in our lives, and exercise jointly in our groups and institutions. The ideal of agency now plays such an important role that there is good reason to call this perspective the "agency-oriented" capability approach. Not only should individuals exercise their agency by shaping or determining their own lives, but it is by exercising joint agency that communities can and should select, weigh, and trade off capabilities, functionings, and other normative considerations.

Already in 1992, Sen edged toward a normative account of agency when he ramified his initial distinction between well-being and agency and distinguished two kinds of agency achievement or success: (i) "*realized* agency success," a generic concept of agency, and (ii) "*instrumental* agency success," a more specific and "participatory" concept of agency (Sen 1992: 58).

In "realized agency success," one's objectives – whether self-regarding or other-regarding – are realized, but someone or something else may be the cause or the "lever" of the achievement. Only in "instrumental agency success" – the specific and "more *participatory*" variety of agency – does agency require that the person *himself or herself* either bring things about by his or her *own* efforts or play an "active part" in some collective action. Sen's generic concept of agency permits an individual or group – other than the person or group whose aims are realized – to exercise or "control" the "levers" of change. A person's agency freedom, in this account, is enhanced not only when he or she actually does something but when something he or she values occurs – such as the elimination of famines – even when the person had nothing to do with its occurrence, but would have chosen it *had he or she had* the chance and the means (Sen 1992: 57–8).

This generic concept of agency freedom and achievement does, we concede, point to something important. It permits us to say that institutions and *other* people can bring about or contribute to the realization of our own goals: a person's ability to achieve various valuable functionings may be greatly enhanced by public action and policy (Sen 1999: xi–xii). Moreover, infants, severely mentally disabled individuals, and very old people are capable of healthy functioning even though they make few if any decisions and are dependent on others for care. Many good (and bad) things happen to people because of what other agents do for (or to) them. It is not the case that an individual's evening meal is drained of worth unless he or she personally freely cooked it. Nor is it the case that Sen is claiming that the best life is a life of self-help or strenuous action rather than quiet reflection or equanimity, for one may exercise agency in the latter cases as well as the former.

It does not follow, however, that we should accept Sen's conclusion and say that the actions of others that realize a person's goals, which the person would have realized by himself or herself if he or she could have, are cases of *that person's* agency. Here we must distinguish a variety of cases, only some of which qualify as agency achievement. Then, within agency achievement, we may distinguish between two kinds of agency but draw the distinction in a different way and for a different purpose than does Sen. Let us distinguish not between the generic "realized agency" and the more specific "instrumental" agency but rather between (i) the agency of others (and force of circumstances), (ii) a person's *indirect* agency, and (iii) a person's *direct* agency.

Using one of Sen's examples, suppose governmental officials intend to eliminate and succeed in eliminating famine from their country and that such an achievement was also the goal of citizen Soumya. Soumya, however, did not exercise his own agency in this case, even though his goal was achieved, because he did nothing to bring it about. (He did not even decide not to block the government's efforts.) Even if he intended to bring an end to famine, he would not be an agent in this feat, unless his intention was causally efficacious in some way in producing the desired event. Agency was exercised, but the agency was that of others and not Soumya's. Soumya could be an agent in famine elimination in two ways. He would be a *direct agent* if he planned the extermination or played an important (and intentional) role in executing the plan. He would be an *indirect or remote agent* if he played a minor role in the causal chain between the formation and the execution of the plan. Such action might range from doing some minor paperwork connected with the project to protesting to or communicating with appropriate officials. And, as a democratic citizen, Soumya exercises his *indirect agency* insofar as he makes known his desire that famine end and this view contributes to government officials' – fearing the loss of the next election or anticipating destabilizing protest in the streets – taking action. But, if Soumya's desire or intention to exterminate famine in fact had no causal efficacy, even though he would have done his part if he had had a chance, he exercised no agency – direct or indirect – in the realization of his goal. Hypothetical or nonefficacious conditional agency is not actual agency.

Rather than extending, as does the notion of "realized agency success," the notion of agency to include whatever event happens to realize an individual's preferences (and would be chosen by him or her if he or she had had the chance), the notion of indirect agency enables us to make Pettit's (1997, 2001) important point that tyrants are restrained not only by their so-called subjects' direct doing (for example, mass agitation), but also by the tyrant's knowledge that the subjects intend to blockade the city should the tyrant fail to accede to certain popular demands. A person's indirect agency, with both backward and anticipatory reference, also occurs when a citizen's senator casts a vote to disconfirm the president's nomination for attorney general. The senator casts the vote, and the citizen does not. But, the citizen has exercised indirect agency if he or she purposefully influenced the senator's decision, perhaps because the senator expects that this constituent will hold him or her accountable if he or she votes against the expressed will of this and other constituents. If the senator knows what the constituents have elected him or her to do and stand for, and if he or she expects to lose their support if he or she votes for the nominee, then our citizen's agency has been indirectly exercised through the representative.

This last example leads us to see the merit, but also a limitation, in what we have called indirect agency. In modern society's complex organizations, such as representative democracy, Sen correctly recognizes that "it is often very hard, if not impossible, to have a system that gives each person all the levers of control over her own life" (Sen 1992: 65; cf. Sen 1985b: 210). It does not follow, however, that even in complex societies no further issue exists as to who makes decisions, who is in charge, or "how the controls are, in fact, exercised" (Sen 1992: 65). One challenge of movements to deepen and broaden democracy is, as Iris Marion Young (2000: chapter 4) argues, to find ways to strengthen and extend direct agency, make indirect agency less indirect, and link direct and indirect agency, for instance, by establishing venues for representatives and constituents to deliberate together between elections for or votes in representative bodies.

Even in 1992, Sen did recognize that what he called "active" or "participatory" agency is "closely related to the nature of our values" (Sen 1992: 58; cf. 1985b: 212) in the sense that we place a high value on bringing about our goals through our *own* efforts or jointly *with* others. After 1992, Sen drops or at least downplays the generic meaning of agency, refrains from discussing nonparticipatory agency, and emphasizes agency only in the sense of what in 1992 he called "instrumental agency success." Again, we agree with Sen that it is important to recognize that others can realize our goals on our behalf even though we have had no role – direct or indirect – in the process. But, rather than including this sort of case under the category of one's "realized agency," it is more perspicuous to classify these cases not as sorts of agency, but rather as one class of "realized goals."

The abandonment of the generic category "realized agency" is, we believe, no great loss. What is important is that people individually and collectively conduct their own lives, sometimes realizing their own self-regarding goals, sometimes realizing (or helping realize) others' goals, and sometimes by forming joint intentions and exercising collective agency. We exercise agency or control not when our goals are merely realized (as important as that may be) but when, in addition, we decide on and *intentionally* realize or contribute directly or indirectly to the realization of our goals.

The Dimensions of Agency

How does Sen understand agency? The term "agency," like the term "capability," confuses many people. Not only does one think of travel agencies and real estate agents rather than individual or collective actors (in Spanish, *protagonistas*), but the word does not occur in some languages, such as Dutch. Moreover, agency, as Sen uses the term, has little to do with the principal-agent distinction used by institutional economists and some lawyers. Rather than denoting "a person who is acting on someone else's behalf (perhaps being led on by a 'principal'), and whose achievements are to be assessed in the light of someone else's (the principal's) goals," Sen explains that he uses the term "in its older – and 'grander' – sense as someone who acts and brings about change, and whose achievements can be judged in terms of her own values and objectives, whether or not we assess them in terms of some external criteria as well" (Sen 1999: 18–19).

Especially in *Development as Freedom* (1999), but also in other writings after 1992, Sen employs a complex *ideal* of agency (and a related ideal of empowerment as, among other things, the acquisition of this kind of agency). Although he has not yet subjected the ideal to the careful analysis that we have come to expect of him, we draw on his scattered remarks to offer the following interpretation or "rational construction" of his current view. A person (or group) is an agent with respect to action X, to the extent that the following four conditions hold (the labels are ours and not Sen's): (i) *self-determination*: the person decides for himself or herself rather than someone or something else making the decision to do X; (ii) *reason orientation and deliberation*: the person bases his or her decisions on reasons, such as the pursuit of goals; (iii) *action*: the person performs or has a role in performing X; and (iv) *impact on the world*: the person thereby brings about (or contributes to bringing about) change in the world.[2] Rather than make each one of these four conditions necessary and together sufficient for agency, let us say that the more fully an agent's action fulfills each condition, the more fully is that act one of agency. As Rob Reich (2002: 93) argues in relation to what he calls "minimalist autonomy," agency is a matter of

---

[2] Although we put the point in a way that suggests that exercises of agency are positive doings, we also mean to include (as agency achievements) decisions to omit or refrain from positive action when such decisions are intentional and make a difference in the world (cf. Alvarez 2005: 49–52). When a handshake is customary, (the decision) not to shake an offered hand is, at least in Western culture, an act that rebuffs.

degree rather than "an 'on/off' capacity or condition." We comment briefly on each of these four components:

Self-determination

Even though an agent gets what he or she wants, the agent has not exercised agency unless he or she personally decides to perform the act in question. When external circumstances or internal compulsions or addictions *cause* the agent's behavior or when other agents force or manipulate him or her, the person does not exercise agency even though he or she gets what he or she wants: "There is clearly a violation of freedom [i.e., agency freedom]" when an agent "is being forced to do exactly what she would have chosen to do anyway" (Sen 2004: 331). When the agent is coerced ("Your money or your life") in contrast to being forced (being carried to the paddy wagon), there is some – but minimal – agency freedom.

Reason Orientation and Deliberation

Not just any behavior that an agent "emits" is an agency achievement, for acting on whim (let alone impulse) is behavior not under the agent's control. Sometimes Sen says "free" or "active" agency to characterize internally caused behavior that is freely self-determined. Agency takes place when a person acts on purpose and for a purpose, goal, or reason. Such activity Sen and coauthor Jean Drèze sometimes call "reasoned agency" (Drèze and Sen 2002: 19) or "critical agency" (Drèze and Sen 2002: 258) because it involves more or less scrutiny of and deliberation about reasons and values: "What is needed is not merely freedom and power to act, but also freedom and power to question and reassess the prevailing norms and values" (Drèze and Sen 2002: 258). The agent's decision is not for *no* reason, based on a whim or impulse, but is for *some* reason or to achieve some goal, regardless of whether that goal is self-regarding or other-regarding. The more that the agent values the options, the more he or she is able to exercise agency: choosing to surrender money at gunpoint rather than die is an exercise of agency, but a minimal one.

Action

Agency achievement involves more than the freedom to act, more than deciding, and more than scrutiny of reasons and norms for action. For people lack full agency if they decide (on the basis of reasons) to act and either take no action or utterly fail to realize their goals. And, as we have seen, even though an agent gets what he or she intends – for instance, the elimination of famine – if he or she did not get it, at least partially, because of his or her own (direct or indirect) action (individually or with others), he or she is not an agent in that regard.

Impact on the World

The more an agent's actions make a difference in the world, the more fully does the agent exercise agency. Not only does one's exercise of agency include a doing and not merely an intention, the doing must have a larger or smaller impact. Because of this act, the agent alters the world – sometimes in ways intended, sometimes in ways not intended but foreseen, and sometimes in unintended or unexpected ways. When, by his or her action, the agent intentionally achieves a goal, he or she is in this instance an agent, the author of his or her own life. What is true of individuals is also true of groups who engage in joint actions: "The basic approach [of Drèze and Sen 2002] involves an overarching interest in the role of human beings – on their own and in cooperation with each other – in running their lives and in using and expanding their freedoms" (Drèze and Sen 2002: 33). To realize an individual's or a group's goals and to change the world, to have an ability to do the things we value (Drèze and Sen 2002: 17–20), requires that the individual or collective agent have agency freedom and effective power: "Greater freedom enhances the ability of people to help themselves and also to influence the world, and these matters ["the 'agency aspect' of the individual"] are central to the process of development" (Sen 1999: 18).[3]

---

[3] Sen's concept of agency differs not only from the notion of agent in institutional economics, but also from the concept that the World Bank employs in its *World Development Report 2006: Equity and Development* (World Bank 2005: 5, 48–50, 205). The report defines agency as "the socioeconomically, culturally, and politically determined ability to shape the world around oneself" (2005: 5). Not only does this definition, with its notion of a "determined" ability, undermine the agent's self-determination or "free agency," but it also unacceptably includes under the concept of full agency any impact that people have on the world, no matter how unthinking or unconscious: "Some [agency] is unconscious – for example when people engage in land transactions without questioning them, they reproduce the institutions of land tenure and the markets in land" (2005: 48–9). At best, such agency is pretty thin. We leave open the question of whether unintended, but foreseen, or reasonably foreseeable consequences are themselves expressions of agency – either because there is some higher-order intention or for some other reason.

The Value of Agency

Why is agency valuable, and how valuable is it? Sen believes that agency is valuable in three ways. It is *intrinsically* valuable: we have reason to value agency for its own sake (although the exercise of agency may be used for trivial or nefarious actions). In defending the intrinsic value of agency, we may only be able to appeal to what Rawls (1971: section 9) calls a "considered judgment" that, all things considered, it is better to act than be acted upon either as someone else's tool or a pawn of circumstance. Isaiah Berlin captures this judgment:

> I wish to be the instrument of my own, not other men's, acts of will. I wish to be a subject, not an object.... I wish to be a somebody, not nobody; a doer – deciding, not being decided for, self-directed and not acted on by external nature or by other men as if I were a thing, or an animal, or a slave incapable of playing a human role, that is, of conceiving goals and policies of my own and realizing them. (Berlin 1969: 131; quoted in Reich 2002: 100)

Some agency theorists seek additional justification by explaining agency's intrinsic value in relation to our conception of persons as morally responsible (Sen 1999: 288), worthy of respect (Berlin: "a somebody, not nobody"), or having the capacity to "have or strive for a meaningful life" (Nozick 1974: 50).

Agency is also *instrumentally* valuable as a means to good consequences. If people are involved in making their own decisions and running their own lives, their actions are more likely to result, when they so aim and act, in achievement of their well-being freedoms, such as being able to be healthy and well-nourished. Moreover, when individuals are agents in a joint enterprise, rather than mere "patients" or pawns, they are more likely to contribute sustainably and loyally to the joint action.

Finally, agency is what Sen calls "constructively" valuable,[4] for in agency freedom the agent freely scrutinizes, decides on, and shapes its values. Included in the constructive value of agency is the agent's selecting, weighing, and trading off of capabilities and other values that we discussed in the last section of this chapter's first part (see also Crocker 2006; 2008: chapter 9).

---

[4] We leave open the question of whether Sen's notion of "constructive" value straddles the "intrinsic-instrumental" value distinction instead of falling on one side or the other.

Agency and Democracy

It is clear that Sen considers the "agency role" of individuals, acting alone or in concert, to be of fundamental importance in his vision of good institutional arrangements and change. Rather than stressing, as he did in 1992, the difficulty of citizens purposefully operating the "levers" of change, Sen now emphasizes the importance of direct as well as indirect citizen involvement in democratic governance, and he seeks ways to close the gap between the two (Drèze and Sen 2002: chapters 1, 10).

In other writings one of us considers the implications of this ideal of agency for a deepening of democracy and citizen participation from the local to the global (Crocker 2008: chapters 9, 10). One reason that development, conceived as good social change, is important for Sen is that it provides a variety of social arrangements in which human beings express their agency or become free to do so. The responsibility-sensitive analyst evaluates policies and practices – in both rich and poor countries – in light of, among other things, the extent to which these policies and processes enhance, guarantee, and restore the agency of individuals and various groups (Sen 1999: xii–xiii).

> Societal arrangements, involving many institutions (the state, the market, the legal system, political parties, the media, public interest groups, and public discussion forums, among others) are investigated in terms of their contribution to enhancing and guaranteeing the substantive freedoms of individuals, seen as active agents of change, rather than passive recipients of dispensed benefits. (Sen 1999: xii–xiii)

One challenge for Sen and others is to give an account of how democracy, including public discussion, provides procedures for *collective* agency, procedures in which many agents can reason together to arrive at policy that is wise and action with which most can agree. For Sen, groups as well as individual persons can and should be authors of their own futures. Public deliberation and democratic decision making are arguably defensible ways in which citizens and their representatives both exercise their agency and forge good policy.

FURTHER CHALLENGES

Much work remains for those in agreement or sympathy with an agency-oriented capability approach. On the practical side, researchers should consider the ways in which individual and group agency might be measured (see Alkire: 2009). On the conceptual side, scholars should evaluate Sen's concepts of agency in relation to different conceptions of autonomy (see Alvarez 2005; Buss and Overtone 2002; Taylor 2005) as well as recent work on collective agency and action and its similarities to and differences from individual agency and action (Bratman 1999; Tuomela 1995). More normative work is called for to answer the questions of why and how much we should care about agency, and what should be done when agency is at odds with well-being freedoms and achievements or with other values such as stability or efficiency. Political philosophers should also take up the question of conflict resolution, when the agency (freedoms and achievements) of different individuals or of different groups conflict, and also the question of what would count as a fair distribution of agency freedom and achievement within and between groups. Policy analysts should consider what agents are most likely to bring about progressive change and which strategies and institutions are most likely to protect, promote, and restore agency. If we adopt an "essentially 'people-centered' approach, which puts human agency (rather than organizations such as markets or governments) at the centre of the stage" (Sen 2002: 6), what are the implications for what ought to be done and who ought to do it?

CONCLUDING REMARKS

In this chapter, we have provided an overview of Sen's notions of capability and agency. We also have sought to dispel misunderstandings of these concepts and have called attention to their neglected or underappreciated nuances. We have discussed the evolution of Sen's formulations of these notions, and his employment of them in both his social scientific and normative inquiries. We have identified ongoing work of scholars developing these concepts and taking up new challenges in their clarification and defense. We conclude by underscoring that well-being (capabilities and functionings) and agency, although conceptually and normatively distinct, are also linked in various ways.

Both agency and those capabilities (and functionings) that we have reason to value are intrinsically good as well as instrumentally good in relation to each other. If people exercise their own agency in deciding on and realizing their well-being freedoms (capabilities), they are more likely to realize well-being achievements (functionings), such as a reduction of deprivation, than if they depend on luck or on the development programs that others provide. Moreover, when people make their own decisions, run their own lives, and make a mark on the world, this exercise of agency is often accompanied by a sense of satisfaction – a component of well-being achievement (Alkire 2009; Sen 1985b: 187).

If people have and realize capabilities they have reason to value, such as health, nutritional well-being, education, and valuable employment, they are more likely to have the ability to decide on and the power to achieve what they want. It is difficult if not impossible for people suffering from severe deprivation to be able to run their own lives and help decide the direction of their communities. The more people are responsible for their own lives, the more they can and should "be in charge of their own well-being; it is for them to decide how to use their capabilities" (Sen 1999: 288).

Without agency freedom, without "the liberty of acting as citizens who matter and whose voices counts," people run the risk of "living as well-fed, well-clothed, and well-entertained vassals" (Drèze and Sen 2002: 288). Without an adequate level of well-being, freedom, and achievement, people are unable to realize their potential as agents. Because of the important linkages between well-being and agency, there is good reason to advocate an "agency-focused capability approach."

APPENDIX: MARTHA NUSSBAUM'S LIST OF CENTRAL HUMAN CAPABILITIES

From: Martha Nussbaum (2006), *Frontiers of Justice*, Harvard University Press, pp. 76–8.

The Central Human Capabilities

1. *Life*. Being able to live to the end of a human life of normal length: not dying prematurely, or before one's life is so reduced as to be not worth living.

2. *Bodily Health*. Being able to have good health, including reproductive health; to be adequately nourished; to have adequate shelter.

3. *Bodily Integrity*. Being able to move freely from place to place; to be secure against violent assault, including sexual assault and domestic violence; having opportunities for sexual satisfaction and for choice in matters of reproduction.

4. *Senses, Imagination, and Thought*. Being able to use the senses, to imagine, think, and reason – and to do these things in a "truly human" way, a way informed and cultivated by an adequate education, including, but by no means limited to, literacy and basic mathematical and scientific

training. Being able to use imagination and thought in connection with experiencing and producing works and events of one's own choice, religious, literary, musical, and so forth. Being able to use one's mind in ways protected by guarantees of freedom of expression with respect to both political and artistic speech, and freedom of religious exercise. Being able to have pleasurable experiences and to avoid nonbeneficial pain.

5. *Emotions.* Being able to have attachments to things and people outside ourselves; to love those who love and care for us, to grieve at their absence; in general, to love, to grieve, to experience longing, gratitude, and justified anger. Not having one's emotional development blighted by fear and anxiety. (Supporting this capability means supporting forms of human association that can be shown to be crucial for their development.)

6. *Practical Reason.* Being able to form a conception of the good and to engage in critical reflection about the planning of one's life. (This entails protection for the liberty of conscience and religious observance.)

7. *Affiliation.*
   A. Being able to live with and toward others, to recognize and show concern for other human beings, to engage in various forms of social interaction; to be able to imagine the situation of another. (Protecting this capability means protecting institutions that constitute and nourish such forms of affiliation, and also protecting the freedom of assembly and political speech.)
   B. Having the social bases of self-respect and nonhumiliation; being able to be treated as a dignified being whose worth is equal to that of others. This entails provisions of nondiscrimination on the basis of race, sex, sexual orientation, ethnicity, caste, religion, and national origin.

8. *Other Species.* Being able to live with concern for and in relation to animals, plants, and the world of nature.

9. *Play.* Being able to laugh, to play, and to enjoy recreational activities.

10. *Control over One's Environment*
    A. *Political.* Being able to participate effectively in political choices that govern one's life; having the right of political participation, protections of free speech and association.
    B. *Material.* Being able to hold property (both land and movable goods), and having property rights on an equal basis with others; having the right to seek employment on an equal basis with others; having the freedom from unwarranted search and seizure. In work, being able to work as a human being, exercising practical reason and entering into meaningful relationships of mutual recognition with other workers.

References

Alkire, S. (2002). *Valuing Freedoms: Sen's Capability Approach and Poverty Reduction* (New York: Oxford University Press).

Alkire, S. (2009). "Concepts and Measures of Agency" in Basu and Kanbur (eds.), *Arguments for a Better World* (Oxford: Oxford University Press).

Alvarez, M. (2005). "Agents, Actions, and Reasons," *Philosophical Books*, 46, 1, 45–58.

Anderson, E. (1999). "What is the Point of Equality?" *Ethics*, 109, 2, 287–337.

Basu, K. (1987). "Achievements, Capabilities, and the Concept of Well-being," *Social Choice and Welfare*, 4, 69–76.

Basu, K., and L. López-Calva (forthcoming). "Functionings and Capabilities," in Arrow, Sen, and Suzumura (eds.), *Handbook of Social Choice and Welfare*, Vol. 3 (North Holland: Elsevier Science).

Berlin, I. (1969). *Four Essays on Liberty* (Oxford: Oxford University Press).

Bratman, M. (1999). *Faces of Intention: Selected Essays on Intention and Agency* (Cambridge: Cambridge University Press).

Brighouse, H., and I. Robeyns (eds.) (forthcoming). *Measuring Justice: Primary Goods and Capabilities* (Cambridge: Cambridge University Press).

Buss, S., and L. Overtone (eds.) (2002). *Contours of Agency: Essays on Themes from Harry Frankfurt* (Cambridge, MA: MIT Press).

Chakraborty, A. (1996). "On the Possibility of a Weighting System for Function-ings," *Indian Economic Review*, 31, 241–50.

Crocker, D. A. (2006). "Sen and Deliberative Democracy," in Kaufman (ed.), *Capabilities Equality: Basic Issues and Problems* (New York: Routledge).

Crocker, D. A. (2007). "Deliberative Participation in Local Development," *Journal of Human Development*, 8, 3, 431–55.

Crocker, D. A. (2008). *Ethics of Global Development: Agency, Capability, and Deliberative Democracy* (Cambridge: Cambridge University Press).

Drèze, J., and A. Sen (2002). *India: Development and Participation*, 2nd ed. (Oxford: Oxford University Press).

Dworkin, R. (1981). "What is Equality? Part 2: Equality of Resources," *Philosophy and Public Affairs*, 10, 283–345.

Dworkin, R. (2000). *Sovereign Virtue: The Theory and Practice of Equality* (Cambridge, MA: Harvard University Press).

Fleurbaey, M. (2002). "Development, Capabilities and Freedom," *Studies in Comparative International Development*, 37, 71–7.

Frolich, N., and J. Oppenheimer (1992). *Choosing Justice: An Experimental Approach to Ethical Theory* (Berkeley: University of California Press).

Gastil, J., and P. Levine (eds.) (2005). *The Deliberative Democracy Handbook: Strategies for Effective Civic Engagement in the 21st Century* (San Francisco: Jossey-Bass).

Graham, C., and S. Pettinato (2002). *Happiness and Hardship* (Washington, DC: Brookings Institution Press).

Hirschman, A. (1977). *The Passions and the Interests: Political Arguments for Capitalism before Its Triumph* (Princeton: Princeton University Press).

Kaufman, A. (2006a). "Capabilities and Freedom," *Journal of Political Philosophy*, 14, 3, 289–300.

Kaufman, A. (2006b). "What Goods Do to (and for) People: Duality and Ambiguity in Sen's Capabilities Approach?" in Kaufman (ed.), *Capabilities Equality: Basic Issues and Problems* (New York: Routledge).

Nozick, R. (1974). *Anarchy, State, and Utopia* (New York: Basic Books).

Nussbaum, M. (1988). "Nature, Functioning and Capability: Aristotle on Political Distribution," *Oxford Studies in Ancient Philosophy*, 6, suppl. vol., 145–84.

Nussbaum, M. (2000). *Women and Human Development: The Capabilities Approach* (Cambridge: Cambridge University Press).

Nussbaum, M. (2003). "Capabilities as Fundamental Entitlements: Sen and Social Justice," *Feminist Economics*, 9, 2/3, 33–59.

Nussbaum, M. (2006). *Frontiers of Justice: Disability, Nationality, Species Membership* (Cambridge, MA: Harvard University Press).

Pettit, P. (1997). *Republicanism: A Theory of Freedom and Government* (Oxford: Clarendon Press).

Pettit, P. (2001). "Capability and Freedom: A Defense of Sen," *Economics and Philosophy*, 17, 1–20.

Pierik, R., and I. Robeyns (2007). "Resources Versus Capabilities: Social Endowments in Egalitarian Theory," *Political Studies*, 55, 1, 133–52.

Pogge, T. (2002). "Can the Capability Approach be Justified?" *Philosophical Topics*, 30, 2, 167–228.

Rawls, J. (1971). *A Theory of Justice* (Cambridge, MA: Harvard University Press).

Reich, R. (2002). *Bridging Liberalism and Multiculturalism in American Education* (Chicago: University of Chicago Press).

Robeyns, I. (2003). "Sen's Capability Approach and Gender Inequality: Selecting Relevant Capabilities," *Feminist Economics*, 9, 2/3, 61–92.

Robeyns, I. (2005). "The Capability Approach: A Theoretical Survey," *Journal of Human Development*, 6, 1, 93–114.

Robeyns, I. (2006). "The Capability Approach in Practice," *Journal of Political Philosophy*, 14, 3, 351–76.

Roemer, J. (1996). *Theories of Distributive Justice* (Cambridge, MA: Harvard University Press).

Schokkaert, E. (2007). "Capabilities and Satisfaction with Life," *Journal of Human Development*, 8, 3, 415–30.

Sen, A. K. (1980). "Equality of What?' in McMurrin (ed.), *Tanner Lectures on Human Values* (Cambridge: Cambridge University Press).

Sen, A. K. (1984). "Rights and Capabilities," in *Resources, Values and Development* (Cambridge, MA: Harvard University Press).

Sen, A. K. (1985a). *Commodities and Capabilities* (Amsterdam: North-Holland).

Sen, A. K. (1985b). "Well-being, Agency and Freedom: The Dewey Lectures 1984," *Journal of Philosophy*, 82, 4, 169–221.

Sen, A. K. (1987). "The Standard of Living," in Sen, Muellbauer, Kanbur, Hart, and Williams, *The Standard of Living: The Tanner Lectures on Human Values* (Cambridge: Cambridge University Press).

Sen, A. K. (1990a). "Gender and Cooperative Conflicts," in Tinker (ed.), *Persistent Inequalities* (New York: Oxford University Press).

Sen, A. K. (1990b). "Individual Freedom as a Social Commitment," *New York Review of Books*, 37, 10 (14 June).

Sen, A. K. (1992). *Inequality Re-examined* (Oxford: Clarendon Press).

Sen, A. K. (1993). "Capability and Well-being," in Nussbaum and Sen (eds.), *The Quality of Life* (Oxford: Clarendon Press).

Sen, A. K. (1995a). "Agency and Well-Being: The Development Agenda," in Heyzer, Kapoor, and Sandler (eds.), *A Commitment to the World's Women* (New York: UNIFEM).

Sen, A. K. (1995b). "Gender Inequality and Theories of Justice," in Nussbaum and Glover (eds.), *Women, Culture and Development: A Study of Human Capabilities* (Oxford: Clarendon Press).

Sen, A. K. (1999). *Development as Freedom* (New York: Knopf).

Sen, A. K. (2002). *Rationality and Freedom* (Cambridge, MA: Harvard University Press).

Sen, A. K. (2004). "Elements of a Theory of Human Rights," *Philosophy & Public Affairs*, 32, 4, 315–56.

Sen, A. K. (2005). "Human Rights and Capabilities," *Journal of Human Development*, 6, 2, 151–66.

Sen, A. K. (2006). "The Importance of Ethics for the Efficient Design and Implementation of Development Policies and Projects," International Social Capital, Ethics and Development Day, Inter-American Development Bank, 24 February.

Stewart, F. (1995). "Basic Needs, Capabilities and Human Development," *Greek Economic Review*, 17, 2, 83–96.

Sugden, R. (1993). "Welfare, Resources, and Capabilities: A Review of Inequality Reexamined by Amartya Sen," *Journal of Economic Literature*, 31, 1947–62.

Taylor, J. S. (ed.) (2005). *Personal Autonomy: New Essays on Personal Autonomy and Its Role in Contemporary Moral Philosophy* (Cambridge: Cambridge University Press).

Tuomela, R. (1995). *The Importance of Us* (Stanford: Stanford University Press).

United Nations Development Programme (1990–2007/8). *Human Development Report* (Oxford: Oxford University Press).

Vallentyne, P. (2005). "Debate: Capabilities versus Opportunities for Wellbeing," *Journal of Political Philosophy*, 13, 359–71.

Williams, A. (2002). "Dworkin on Capability," *Ethics*, 113, 23–39.

Wolff, J., and A. de-Shalit (2007). *Disadvantage* (Oxford: Oxford University Press).

World Bank (2005). *World Development Report 2006: Equity and Development* (Washington, DC: World Bank / Oxford University Press).

Young, I. (2000). *Inclusion and Democracy* (Oxford: Oxford University Press).

4 | Freedom in the Spirit of Sen
PHILIP PETTIT

From his earliest research on social choice theory through to his more recent development of the idea of capability, Amartya Sen has given the idea of freedom pride of place in his thoughts. I think that his conception of freedom is of the greatest interest, and I try to bring out its distinctive character in this chapter. I shall not be discussing the notion of capability directly – nor, more generally, the place of freedom in Sen's theory of justice – although my comments have implications for how his normative position should be understood (Pettit 2001a). My analysis will focus entirely on how freedom is to be interpreted within the approach taken by Sen. I have titled this chapter "Freedom in the Spirit of Sen," because I suggest some ways in which his approach can be developed that are not discussed explicitly in his work.

This chapter is divided into five main sections. In the first, I present Sen's conception of freedom as having two forms, direct and indirect, and in the second I show how he associates freedom, direct and indirect, with the idea of agent control. In the third section, I introduce a further distinction, between active and virtual control, which is independent of that between direct and indirect control but ought to appeal to Sen, being of a kind with it. In the fourth section, I show where Sen's conception of freedom, articulated in line with these distinctions, leads in thinking about the nature of democratic institutions. And, then, in the final section, I explore the significance of his new departures in the theory of freedom generally.

I am grateful to the participants at a 2003 colloquium on philosophy at MIT for a useful set of comments; they led me to make a number of changes to the paper on which this chapter is based.

1. DIRECT AND INDIRECT FREEDOM

Sen's Distinction[1]

Sen's (1970a, 1970b) "Liberal Paradox" purports to show that no satisfactory rule for aggregating individual preferences into a social preference – no satisfactory social decision function – can simultaneously satisfy certain attractive conditions. Specifically, a social decision function cannot guarantee a consistent, complete ordering of relevant social states and meet these three constraints: first, work for any profile of preferences among individuals; second, ensure that if everyone prefers a social state, x, to a social state, y, then x will be chosen over y; and third, guarantee that liberalism, even liberalism in a minimal sense, will prevail. The minimal liberal condition is that there are at least two persons in the society – not necessarily all – who are decisive in relation to issues in their "recognised personal sphere" (Sen 1983a).

One question raised in the discussion of Sen's impossibility result was how the notion of decisiveness should be understood in the statement of the liberal condition (Nozick 1974; Gaerdenfors 1981; Sen 1983a; Sugden 1981). Two readings are possible, as that literature made clear. One would say that a person is decisive in relation to either A or B just in case they can choose between A and B. The other would say that the person is decisive just in case a weaker condition is fulfilled: so, they can actually choose either A or B or the fact of what they would counterfactually have chosen, should they have a choice, determines whether they decide on A or B. In the first reading, decisiveness requires direct control or direct freedom; the exercise of choice determines what happens. In the second, it requires only indirect control or indirect freedom; if the exercise of choice does not determine what happens, how the person would have chosen does.

When Sen speaks of things turning out as the agent would have chosen in a counterfactual case, I assume that how the agent would have chosen in the counterfactual case is a function of how he or she is now configured in the actual world: that is, that it expresses an actual disposition to choose in that imagined case after a certain pattern (a pattern that may differ from how the agent is actually disposed to choose in the actual case). This assumption is entirely plausible. Measures that make an agent's counterfactual choices

---

[1] The discussion in this subsection draws heavily on (Pettit 2001b), as does the discussion in section 2.

decisive will give a degree of power to that agent, as he or she actually is, only if those counterfactual choices express something about the agent's actual nature.

This means that whereas it is the exercise of choice that has to be determinative of results under the narrower conception of freedom, it is the agent's disposition to choose – for short, his or her preference[2] – that must be determinative under the broader; this disposition determines whether A or B is chosen, either on a direct or on an indirect basis. Under the narrower reading, then, freedom consists in the enjoyment of decisive choice; under the broader it consists in the enjoyment of decisive preference.

Sen points out that his impossibility theorem holds under either of the two readings of freedom, but acknowledges that social choice theory represents freedom as requiring only indirect power. "The social-choice characterization of liberty compares what emerges with what a person *would have chosen*, whether or not he actually does the choosing" (Sen 1983a: 20). More than that, however, Sen defends the broader conception under which freedom on a given issue consists in enjoying decisive preference, and not necessarily decisive choice, in relation to that issue. He acknowledges, particularly in more recent work, that the "process" aspect of freedom – say, the fact that one has a decisive choice, not just a decisive preference – may be important in many cases (Sen 2002: chapters 20–21). But, he remains faithful to the thought that the enjoyment of "opportunity" – in effect, decisive preference – retains its claim to constitute a way of enjoying freedom, regardless of the "process" involved.

There is one point of contrast between decisive choice and decisive preference that should be mentioned, although Sen does not himself advert to it. When I exercise decisive choice, I am bound to be aware of the fact, and presumably to acquiesce to it: to consent to the choice having the effects

---

[2] Notice that a person's preference in relation to an issue between A and B will be made decisive, not when his or her preference in the actual case on hand is made decisive for all possible cases where the issue arises, but when his or her actual preference for any possible case where that issue arises dictates what happens in that case. The fact that the agent prefers A to B in the actual case on hand, for example – say, a case where others are not involved – does not mean that in all possible cases, including those involving others as well, A will prevail; for some such cases, in particular for cases where others want the agent to ensure B, the agent's actual preference may be that B should prevail there. This observation is important because it explains why there is no inconsistency between saying that a person's preference is decisive under Sen's conception of liberty and agreeing with him that choice may sometimes be dictated by the preferences of others and sometimes not; what this means is that the agent's meta-preference to respect such preferences may be relevant in some cases – some choices between A and B – and not in others (Sen 1982).

that make it decisive.[3] But this need not strictly be the case, for all that has been said, with decisive preference. I think that Sen takes it for granted, however, that when someone's preference is made indirectly decisive, then the person is aware of that fact or its likelihood – although perhaps not at the very moment when it is made decisive – and acquiesces in its being so. On this assumption, he would be unwilling to say that someone's freedom was increased without his or her being aware of the control exercised by his or her preference or without his or her agreeing to that exercise of control.

Sen illustrates his view with reference to the example of a person whose preference in regard to medical treatment is respected, even when the person is unconscious. The person's preference for avoiding a certain treatment guides the doctors, although they think that this will reduce the chances of his or her recovery. Believing that the person's liberty – indirect liberty – is well served in such a case, Sen draws a conclusion in favor of the broader conception. "To see liberty exclusively in terms of who is exercising control is inadequate," he says, where by "control" he means direct choice-mediated control (Sen 1983a: 19).

Sen's Distinction Extended

This particular example may not serve Sen well, however, because it misses out on a further distinction between two different ways in which I may enjoy decisive preference (Pettit 2007b). One is the case where I depend on the services of a deputy, as we might say: someone, as in the surgery case, who is disposed to act on whatever my preference is. The other is the case where I depend on the services of a proxy: someone who is disposed to act on what my preference actually is and whom I recruit or co-opt, for that very reason, to serve my purposes.

There are many ways in which I may commission or co-opt others, actively or virtually, in the role of proxies. I may come across some individuals who think as I do or whose ends are such that if they are satisfied, then my ends are satisfied; this may be in the neighborhood or workplace, in politics or in the market. And having found such duplicates of my attitudes, or complements to my projects, I may make use of them by choosing to operate in the same environment as they or by providing reasons for them to remain there or to continue to act as they do. Think of how I might always

---

[3] I abstract here from the sort of issue raised in Frankfurt 1988 as to whether I am in control if I do not actually want the preference on the basis of which I choose to be effective, as in the case of the unwilling alcoholic or drug addict. For further discussion, see Pettit 2001b.

try to walk through a rough neighborhood in the company of a muscular colleague, or of how I might inveigle that colleague to accompany me by being a reliable source of a drink. I will have endorsed the process whereby a proxy generates a certain result – in this case a safe space – and I will have established myself as the controller, if not of the fact that that space exists, at least of the fact that I am within it.

A similar pattern prevails if I go one better and help to create or appoint the proxies on whom I rely, not just exploit proxies already available. I will do this, for example, if I construct a robot that pursues certain goals that support my own. And I will do it, more realistically, if I provide incentives for some individual or body to play a proxy role, or impose constraints on some individual or body that makes him, her, or it likely to play that role; the body may be one that I find in existence or organize myself. The exploitation of any such proxy, of course, is likely to be a hazardous enterprise. Like Hal, the computer in *2001: A Space Odyssey*, the individual or body may form a will that fails to serve the creator and may even prove downright hostile.

What I can affect by my own efforts may fall well short of what can be achieved on my behalf, if deputies can be recruited to act on my manifest preferences or if things can be arranged so that proxies reliably satisfy those wishes, manifest or not. Deputies and proxies can give me a presence in the world, which extends well beyond my own physical body. If they are sufficiently reliable, indeed, then they may be seen as prosthetic extensions through which I gather information on matters beyond my personal access and act upon things beyond my personal reach. They may relate to me as my eyes and ears, my hands and legs. They may count as organs and members of an extended body that provides me with enhanced information and gives me an enhanced impact. Thus, they may extend my control and my freedom so long as I am aware of the role they play and acquiesce to their playing it.

In what follows, I shall take it that proxies may serve as well as deputies to enhance my indirect freedom, although I shall not comment very often on the differences between how they would do so.[4] The surgery example that Sen gives suggests that he thinks of indirect freedom as having to be mediated by deputies, but other examples, as we shall notice later, suggest that he may be equally open to the idea that proxies might play this role. Both mediators can make my preference decisive over certain domains.

---

[4] To remain faithful to Sen's terminology, I take both deputies and proxies to exemplify indirect control and freedom. In Pettit 2007b, I speak of indirect control in the case of deputies, oblique in the case of proxies.

2. THE CONTROL REQUIRED BY FREEDOM

Perhaps Sen's most striking innovation in the theory of freedom is the idea that it requires decisive preference, not necessarily decisive choice. But, it is important to recognize that decisive preference requires more than just the satisfaction of preference. I do not enjoy decisive preference in regard to certain alternatives just so far as my preference happens to be satisfied, even routinely satisfied. It must be that my preference is satisfied because it is my preference, and not for any other reason. It must be that my preference is in control, so that what I get is robustly connected, not just connected by chance, with what I prefer.

This is worth noting, in particular, because Sen has been accused of describing situations in which my preference just happens to be satisfied as ones where I enjoy decisive preference and indirect freedom (Cohen 1994). If he does this, then that is a slip from the intent of his theory. Quite clearly, what that theory requires for freedom in a certain domain is that my preference be in control of what happens there. It will be in direct control, so far as I get whatever I choose; we may assume that choice generally tracks preference. And, it will be in indirect control so far as things are arranged so that what happens depends on what I would prefer to happen.

But, the requirement that my preference be satisfied just because it is my preference, and not for any other reason, is more demanding than this may make it seem. Not only does it mean that the satisfaction of the preference should not come about just by chance or coincidence or whatever. It also means that the satisfaction of the preference should not be contingent on the satisfaction of certain conditions over and beyond the fact that I have the preference.

There are two particularly salient conditions such that if my preference's being satisfied requires that either is fulfilled, then the control I have is intuitively too circumscribed to count as freedom. The first condition would stipulate that the content of the preference falls within a certain range; the other, that certain powerful parties bestow goodwill or favor on me, giving me a permit to behave as I would. Neither content-dependent control nor permit-dependent control is sufficient, I would say, for the sort of control required intuitively under Sen's account of freedom.

For a person to have content-independent control in an issue between A and B, it is required that his or her preference be decisive regardless of its content, regardless of whether the preference is for A or for B. I am free in relation to A or B only if, depending on how my preference may go, I get A or I get B. Thus, it will not be enough for freedom that I get A if my preference is for A, when it is not the case that I get B if my preference is for B. Freedom requires that my preference be empowered in a content-independent way; it is decisive, regardless of which of the relevant options is preferred.

The best argument for this first claim is that if we reject it, we must say that a person can make himself or herself free just by adapting his or her preferences appropriately (Berlin 1969: xxxviii). Suppose that I prefer B in a choice between A and B, but that I will get what I prefer only if I prefer A. Well, then, if freedom does not require content-independent control, it appears that I can make myself free just by adapting my preferences so that I do indeed prefer A (Sen 1985: 191). Having A may mean being in prison, having B being at large. I can come to be freely in prison, it seems, just by adapting my preferences so that I desire to be inside rather than outside the jail walls.

It may be that under common usage I can be properly said to get A freely, when my preference for A is content-dependently decisive. But, this should not tempt us to say, as theorists, that such content-dependent control is sufficient for freedom. The problem is that the decisiveness of my preference is too circumscribed and contingent to deserve the name of freedom.

Sen explicitly endorses the claim, as I am putting it, that freedom on a given issue requires the agent's preference between options to be decisive in a content-independent way. He notes that in standard consumer theory, "the contribution of a set of feasible choices is judged exclusively by the value of the best element available" and that "the removal of all the elements of a feasible set (e.g. of a 'budget set') other than the chosen best element is seen, in that theory, as no real loss" (Sen 1993: 39). He argues that if we see freedom in his sense as important, then we must reject any such approach. We must recognize that it is important, not just that a person get what he or she is disposed to choose from among a given set of alternatives – say, option A – but also that this does not depend on his or her being lucky enough to want that particular alternative (see also Sen 1999: 76). The person must be assured of getting whatever he or she is or might be disposed to choose; his or her choice-disposition – or preference – must be content-independently decisive.[5]

But for someone's preference to be in control in the manner required intuitively for the enjoyment of freedom it is also necessary, I would say,

---

[5] The points made here are consistent with the claim made by Sen (1993: 34–5) that how good it is to be free in respect of a choice between A and B depends on how one values A and B. Sen (1996) argues this point forcibly in response to a criticism by Ian Carter (1996).

that the control not be conditioned on a second front. Not only must the control be independent of what it is that the agent prefers – independent of content – it should also be independent of whether the agent happens to enjoy the goodwill of those with power over their affairs. The agent should not have to depend on others' being willing not to exercise any power of interference that they may happen to have; the agent, as it is sometimes said, should not be dominated by others: his or her freedom should not be hostage to the fortune of their favor.[6]

The need for this further dimension of independence is not explicitly endorsed in any of Sen's earlier work, although Christian List (2004) shows that it is implied in his social-theoretic treatment of the liberal paradox. In commenting on my introduction of the dimension, Sen (2001: 56) agrees that permit-independence represents "an important aspect of freedom." He rightly notes that evaluative assessment should take account of how far each form of independence is realized, not go for an all-for-nothing analysis in terms of freedom; such an analysis might deprive us of important information. But, such qualifications in place, he appears to be willing to go along with the idea that freedom – freedom but not perhaps capability – requires permit-independence as well as content-independence. For purposes of this chapter, I shall take him to follow that line.

Imagine that you have a disposition to choose between A and B that is content-independently decisive, but that your enjoyment of such decisive preference depends on the goodwill of those around you. You are not powerful enough in relation to them to be sure of your preference's being decisive regardless of how they feel about blocking you. You have a decisive preference only so far as you enjoy the grace and favor of those others. You can get A or you can get B, depending on your preference, but this results from their allowing it to be so. Whatever you obtain as a result of your preferences, then, you obtain by virtue of your good fortune in being subject to dominating powers who look kindly on you; by virtue of your success in securing their complacence; or by virtue of your cunning in managing to avoid their notice. You may be said to have decisive preferences, but this decisiveness is permit-dependent.

The main argument against associating content-dependently decisive preference with freedom was that it would enable a person to attain freedom

---

[6] It is important that the favor in question here is the favor exercised by someone with a power of interference, when he or she chooses not to interfere. I did not make this sufficiently clear in Pettit 2001a, and this occasioned the misunderstanding present in Sen's (2001: 56) remark: "We live in a world in which being completely independent of the goodwill and help of others may be particularly difficult to achieve."

just by adapting his or her preferences appropriately. A similar argument suggests that permit-dependently decisive preference, in the sense just illustrated, is not sufficient for freedom either. Imagine those individuals whose preferences mean that they stay on the wrong side of their masters or betters, so that their preferences are systematically nondecisive; they suffer serious interference in their lives and affairs. If permit-dependence does not matter, then such individuals can make their preferences decisive, and secure freedom, just by adapting their preferences so that their relations to their superiors improve. Suppose that they learn to like those masters, and secure reciprocal favor; or that they come to tolerate having to humor or flatter or appease them; or that they reduce their distaste for having to hide their true intentions and their actual doings from them. By developing an acceptance of such self-abasement, ingratiation, and duplicity they would be able, it appears, to make themselves free. And, that flies in the face of our intuitions as to when it is appropriate to say that a person enjoys freedom.

We noted earlier, in the spirit of Sen's argument, that a person who gets A in the presence of a content-dependently decisive preference for A may be said to get A freely, but that the decisiveness of the preference is too circumscribed and contingent to constitute anything we would happily describe as freedom. I suggest now that we should say the same about preference that is, in the sense just illustrated, only permit-dependently decisive. We may be able to say in this case, by parallel with the other, that the person who gets A in the presence of a permit-dependently decisive preference for A gets A freely; no block or difficulty hinders him or her, and indeed no block or difficulty would be put in his or her way if he or she happened to prefer B instead. But still, the decisiveness of the preference is too circumscribed and contingent to deserve the name of freedom. The enjoyment of permit-dependently decisive preference is quite consistent with the person's living in a position of total subjugation to another, being available just so far as the other happens to be a kindly or gullible or evadable master. Let the master withdraw favor on a capricious basis, or let the agent become more careless or less competent in retaining that favor, and the decisiveness of the preference is immediately undermined. This sort of fragility is too great, I suggest, to allow us to think of permit-dependently decisive preference as sufficient for freedom. We would not be happy to speak of freedom from hunger or disease or ignorance, as Sen regularly does, if the freedom amounted only to the sort of fragile good fortune envisaged.

I make this point without explicitly taking into account the fact that permit-independence may come in degrees, depending on how difficult it is for others to impose their will on a person. That is not a serious disanalogy with content-dependence, for this may also come in degrees, depending on the relative ease of the agent's access to different options. It will be a matter of judgment or stipulation as to the degree of dependency on content or favor at which we are to say, not that the agent enjoys freedom in such and such a measure, but that he or she cannot be said to be free at all. The problem is a familiar one. It is akin to the problem of stipulating the degree of confidence – less than 0.5 perhaps – at which we say, not that someone believes with that degree of confidence that something is the case, but that they do not believe it to be the case, period.

3. CONTROL, ACTIVE AND VIRTUAL

We have been speaking about how my preference between certain options, say A and B, might control whether A or B happens, and have seen that Sen distinguishes between two cases. In one, the preference assumes hands-on control, leading the agent to choose appropriately. In the other, it assumes only arm's-length control, operating via the interventions of others. This arm's-length control may materialize in either of two ways, as we have seen. Deputies will be disposed to act on whatever I prefer, and will have a more or less permanent commission to serve me. Proxies will be disposed to act for the ends that I happen actually to prefer, and will have a commission to serve me that is conditional on this remaining the case.

This picture of two forms of control, direct and indirect – this picture of direct and indirect freedom – can be extended in a way that Sen should find congenial. In both the case where preference exercises control through leading the agent to choose appropriately, and, in the case where it does so via the actions of others, the control normally takes an active form. The preference is at the origin of a causal sequence that fixes the alternative to be realized, and it leads to that result in the usual cause-effect way. In the first case, the causal chain materializes entirely within the agent, going via the deliberative process connecting preference and choice. In the other case, it materializes via inputs to the larger domain constituted by the agent's deputies and proxies. That preference, once manifest, will affect what deputies decide to do in the agent's name. And that preference, or at least the likelihood of that sort of preference, will be the explanation as to why suitable, preference-satisfying proxies are commissioned, wittingly or unwittingly, to act in the agent's interest.

There are many varieties of active preferential control, in particular of indirect active control. But, there is also a nonactive way in which preferential control may be exercised. I speak of this mode of control as virtual rather than active.

Imagine that someone has preferences over what happens in a certain domain, but that the causal process whereby results are determined does not normally involve that person's preferences in any way. And, now, suppose that three further conditions are fulfilled. First, the causal process normally produces results that satisfy the person's preferences. Second, should the process fail to produce such results, this fact will tend to activate the person, or a deputy or proxy, and lead him or her to reverse the result or amend the process. And third, active control will be returned to the independent process, however amended, once the intervention has done its work. Where such conditions are fulfilled, we may say that the person's preferences are in virtual control of what happens. They may not be at the causal origin of what occurs, but they are positioned so that whatever occurs is required to conform to them (Pettit 1995; Pettit 2007b; Pettit 2007c).[7]

There are many sorts of situations where someone's preferences can exercise this sort of virtual control. The causal process that actually produces virtually controlled effects may be an impersonal one, in which the agent may let it operate as it will and only intervene on a need-for-action basis. This, in the tradition of the Western movie, is how the cowboy ensures that the cattle go in the right direction. He rides herd, letting the cattle follow their instinct and only taking action when one of them strays in the wrong direction. This exemplifies direct but virtual control of an effect.

But, virtual control may be indirect too, as when a person exercises virtual control over a deputy or a proxy. Consider the case of the wealthy person who gives control of his or her affairs to a deputy, relying on that agent to work out what he or she is likely to want in any situation – he or she does not actively manifest his or her preferences – and relying on his or her own power to check or replace that deputy should performance fail to satisfy. Or consider the case of someone with the potential to intervene effectively in some area who is quite content to select a proxy to exercise power there and only check or override where necessary. The proxy may have similar interests and be disposed for that reason to act congenially, or the proxy may be constrained by surrounding institutions to act in a congenial way.[8]

In any case of this kind, we have to say that the person's preferences are in control of what happens, although they are not causally active. They are standby factors that ensure that what happens will normally assume a

---

[7] In this discussion, I assume that causal factors are positive factors, so that the absence of a preference cannot be designated as a cause in the same way as the presence of a preference.

[8] A further complexity that may be put in the picture is that the control of the deputy or proxy may itself be active or virtual, as indeed it may be direct or indirect.

satisfactory shape, but they do this from the position of a manager, as it were, not a worker. They let the causal work be done by other factors and assume an active role only if this is absolutely required to keep the work on track: only if it is necessary to ensure that the results generated are the results desired.

Where Sen distinguishes between direct and indirect control and liberty, then, this observation suggests that, in the same spirit of tolerating indirection, he should allow a distinction between the case where either sort of control is active and the case where it is virtual. Direct control is hands-on, whereas indirect control is exercised at arm's length. And, either sort of influence may operate in an active, productive manner or in the virtual manner of the manager or monitor. The possibilities are represented by the four boxes in this matrix.

	Direct control	*Indirect control*
Active	1.	2.
Virtual	3.	4.

Before leaving this topic, I should mention that with the category of virtual control in place, we can provide another argument for why the control associated with freedom has to be permit-independent as well as content-independent. Suppose that I am able to make certain choices, but only to the extent that certain dominating agents are happy with the choices I happen to make, or are happy for the moment to let me choose whatever appeals to me. That means that those others have virtual control over what I choose; it is this that makes them dominators. I may be the active source of the actions chosen, but I will be allowed to operate in the generation of such actions only when the powerful figures in my life are happy with this. They are in virtual control of what I do, standing by in a position to interfere with me, should their tastes lead them that way; explicitly or implicitly, they invigilate my performance (Pettit 2007c). If permit-dependence means that I am controlled in this way by others, then, intuitively, it means that I do not myself control what I do, and it implies that I am not free.

4. FREEDOM AND DEMOCRATIC INSTITUTIONS

One of the recurring themes in Amartya Sen's work is that well-designed institutions, in particular the institutions associated with democratic society, can serve the cause of freedom. They enable people to control public practices indirectly and, although Sen does not note the distinction, by proxies as well as by deputies. "The relevance of *indirect* liberty seems quite substantial in modern society. Police action in preventing crime in the streets may serve my liberty well – since I don't want to be mugged or roughed up – but the control here is exercised not by me, but by the police" (Sen 1983a: 19). Or, as he says elsewhere: "Being free to live the way one would like may be enormously helped by the choice of others, and it would be a mistake to think of achievements only in terms of active *choice by oneself*" (Sen 1993: 44). It is this connection between freedom and institutional arrangements that leads Sen to link development – development that involves political institutions as much as economic prosperity – to freedom (Sen 1999).

We are now in a position to see why freedom in Sen's sense is liable to be enhanced in this way by social institutions. Once we allow that people's freedom may be enhanced through the empowerment of their preferences rather than their choices, and when we recognize that this may occur in virtual, not in active mode, then the way is open to recognizing that various social institutions can increase people's freedom, as Sen conceives of freedom.

Consider the example of the police that Sen gives. I have a preference for crime-free streets, and the police operate, let us suppose, to see that this is satisfied. Does that increase my freedom? Well, not for all we have been told so far. It might be just an accident that what the police ensure is something that I want them to ensure. I might not exercise any degree of control over their ensuring this, and such control is essential if we are to think of my freedom as being increased by police action. My preferences may be satisfied without my preferences ruling. And, my preferences must rule if my freedom is to be involved (Cohen 1994).

There is more that should be said about this sort of example, however, and I think that it is probably taken for granted by Sen. What needs to be said is that the three following assumptions are also in place:

- my preference for crime-free streets is a preference that I share in common with law-abiding, fellow citizens;
- were the streets not to be generally free of crime, then we law-abiding citizens would protest to government; and
- should we protest in this way, then government would increase expenditure on the police and improve the situation.

These assumptions mean that although the police control crime levels directly and actively, my fellow citizens and I control them indirectly and virtually: should the police fail to do the job properly, then we would step in and ensure via government that things were changed. This is to say that my law-abiding fellows and I share in the enjoyment of preferential control and of the associated freedom. And that means, in turn, that each one of us has a partial degree of control in this domain and a partial measure of freedom. The preference that each one of us has is in partial control, although of course only very partial control, of what happens.[9]

But, however partial in character, it is worth noting that the control is independent of content and indeed independent of the goodwill of any powerful party, at least in the ideal democratic society. If the preferences that we, the majority of citizens, have argued for supported a different arrangement – if they supported gated communities, in indifference to the streets in general, for example – then they also would be likely to prevail. And, this power of shared, popular preference is not contingent on the goodwill of any independent authority, such as a colonial government or a background dictator. It operates more or less unconditionally. We shall see in the next section why such partial but robust control can be very important, surprisingly, in the ledger books of liberty.

The line of thought that Sen suggests in relation to the police can be readily extended to cover other cases. There are three broad categories of situation where my fellow citizens and I, or at least certain groups among us, can share in the control of those in government and can have our freedom therefore enhanced. The control exercised in these cases is indirect, and it is often virtual rather than active. I think of the three categories, alliteratively, as cases where government is controlled by fear of our *reaction*, by the role of *regulation* in forcing the authorities to act after a certain pattern, and by the presence of those who claim to speak for us as (elected or unelected) *representatives*.

The rule of reaction is easily illustrated. In an expressive, democratic society, the people will have influence over government – it will become the indirect executor of their preferences – not just by virtue of electing government officials, but by the fact that those whom they elect to government are going to be fearful of prompting a negative reaction in the populace. If the people understand what government is doing in any instance, and if this is manifest to all – an idealized but not impossible condition – then they are going to be a power that those in government are generally going to have to placate, for fear of losing out in elections; those in government will have to behave as deputies. Even if they do nothing to influence government

---

[9] For further fairly speculative thoughts on this topic, see Pettit 2007b.

actively, they will enjoy a measure of virtual control over governmental actions, so far as they are there in the position of an informed and effective invigilator.

People will enjoy regulative control of government so far as there are institutional devices in position that they can change should they find them unsatisfactory and that serve, as things stand, to pressure government into conforming with their wishes; they mean that those in government act as their proxies, if not their deputies. Regulative control can be mediated via any of the standard, democratic devices, ranging from separation of powers to the requirement to support decisions with reasons, to the constraints associated with the rule of law. A good example is the fundamental democratic arrangement whereby those who make the laws have to live under them. Thus the seventeenth-century republican Algernon Sidney (1990: 571), could write of legislators: "They may make prejudicial wars, ignominious treaties, and unjust laws. Yet when the session is ended, they must bear the burden as much as others."

The dual place of regulative and reactive power was marked by many traditional political writers. Adam Ferguson illustrates the approach in the answer he gives to the question as to what ensures the sort of law and order that that he saw eighteenth-century Britons enjoying and savoring. He argues that the existence of that sort of order "requires a fabric no less than the whole political constitution of Great Britain, a spirit no less than the refractory and turbulent zeal of this fortunate people, to secure it" (Ferguson 1767: 167). In our terms, the unwritten political constitution represents regulative control and the zeal of the people represents reactive control; and both are rightly said to be essential to the good working of the polity.

A last mode of control in which Sen can claim to see the promotion of people's freedom is that which is exercised on their behalf when elected and unelected representatives (Pettit, 2009) – say, the members of environmental and consumer movements – direct government into behaving in a manner that conforms to people's general wishes. This direction may itself take an active or virtual form: the representatives may actively influence the authorities or may just stand by, ready to respond to what government does. And, in either case, the direction may derive from the preferences of the people represented in an active or virtual way: the representatives may actively track those preferences, for example, or they may be in a position where they will be challenged by ordinary people should they fail to reflect some widely held preferences.

Why say that such representatives, particularly those of an unelected kind, act on behalf of the people? Because the fact that they are not challenged about the role that they play – they may of course be challenged, as we just saw, about particular matters – means that they have the virtual support of those on whose behalf they claim to speak. They may not be actively elected or recruited to that role, but they could be ejected from it and they are not.

Unelected representatives are of growing importance in the world of contemporary democracy. Given that government now acts on many fronts, and on issues of great complexity, people's only hope of forcing the authorities to track their widely held preferences – indirectly extending their freedom, as Sen conceives of it – is to introduce specialization and a division of political labor. This is precisely what can be achieved, at least in principle, with the appearance of ever more fine-tuned social movements (Pettit, 2009).

5. THE THEORY OF FREEDOM

Sen is clearly concerned with social freedom rather than with freedom in the sense in which it may be affected by psychological malaise or malfunction: if you like, psychological freedom. But what impact do his observations make on the theory of social freedom, considered as a whole?

There are really two quite different topics addressed in the theory of social freedom. These might be described as "option-freedom," which is the main area of concern in contemporary thinking, and what I describe as "status-freedom" (Pettit 2007a). Sen is explicitly concerned with option-freedom, suggesting some radical innovations in charting and measuring what it involves. But, as we shall see, his theory also has important implications for how we ought to think of status-freedom.

Option-Freedom

Option-freedom is often described as freedom of choice or freedom of opportunity. It is freedom of choice in the sense in which the standard assumptions are, first, that individuals and societies may vary in how much freedom they enjoy; second, that more freedom of choice is better than less; and, third, that how much freedom is available is something worth measuring for purposes of assessing how well individuals and societies fare (Carter 1999).

Freedom in this sense is often invoked by economists in support of the free market; by increasing the commodities and services at people's disposal, the market is assumed thereby to increase their option-freedom. One issue that has dominated the discussion of option-freedom is whether this is so and, more generally, whether every increase in the number of options that are available to a person or a society should be taken as a way of increasing freedom (for an overview, see Sugden 1998).

On this issue Sen (2002) argues that it is not just the number of options that matter in computing how far people enjoy option-freedom. What is also of importance is the extent to which the options are diverse and valuable – by whatever criteria of value – for the agents involved. It would be methodologically simpler if the level of option-freedom were a function of the number of options alone, but it runs against common observations to the effect that my freedom is more substantially improved by the addition of a valued as distinct from an unvalued option, or by a novel option as distinct from an option of a familiar sort. Sen is not willing to discount those powerful intuitions and is willing to sacrifice theoretical simplicity to accommodate them.

But, if Sen makes things more complex and difficult in this respect for the measurement of option-freedom, the new departures we have charted make them more complex in two other respects too. His approach implies, on the one hand, that an option is added to an agent's repertoire of choice only if it is brought under the agent's content-independent and permit-independent control; and on the other, that the range of options relevant for option-freedom extends beyond those that are directly and actively controlled by the agent. The first implication is that the quality of control required for option-freedom is higher than is generally assumed; the second is that the quantity or extent of options in which option-freedom may be enjoyed is larger than standard approaches suggest.

The first implication means that it is not enough for control in a choice, and for the achievement of option-freedom there, that it be physically possible for me to make the choice (Carter 1999; Kramer 2003; Steiner 1994). I must have the ability to make the choice in the sense that the choice is not just possible, but relatively accessible. With each option in the choice I must be so positioned, by ordinary criteria – here we return to the issue of degree – that I can take it or not take it, as I will. I must not be exposed to the virtual control of other persons, I must not be inhibited by their power or threat or opposition, and I must not have to run a gauntlet of physical danger or difficulty. If any option requires me to do this or be that, then, in Sen's words, I must be "actually able to do this or be that" (Sen 1987: 57).[10]

---

[10] In a usage that differs from Berlin (1969), he describes such freedom as "positive" in nature. For Berlin, positive freedom means, roughly, either psychological autonomy or democratic enfranchisement.

The second implication of Sen's ideas for the theory of option-freedom derives from the observation that although control may have to be content-independent and permit-independent to count toward the agent's option-freedom, it can be indirect as well as direct, virtual as well as active. The first implication is negative in suggesting that people may have fewer options within their control than are ordinarily allowed. The second is positive in suggesting that in another respect they may have more options – those they control virtually and/or indirectly – than are routinely recognized.

This implication is particularly striking when we add, as charted in the last section, that much of the control that any one of us enjoys is enjoyed in company with others, as in the democratic control of how our lives go. Not only do we benefit from how we can rely on individual deputies and proxies to make our preferences decisive, we benefit from the way in which we can rely on collective deputies and proxies – for example, the politicians and the police – to make our shared preferences decisive.

Status-Freedom

The nuanced contributions that Sen makes to the theory of option-freedom have the paradoxical consequence that option-freedom no longer looks like a useful yardstick by which to measure how well individuals or societies of individuals fare. The reason is that option-freedom becomes just too complex a target. It may be for this reason that Sen turns in his later work to the idea of capabilities for functioning as a yardstick by which to make social assessments.

But, there is an alternative approach to social freedom that Sen ignores and that I would like, finally, to put in the frame. This prioritizes status-freedom, as I shall call it, rather than option-freedom.

The status-centered approach to social freedom builds on the tradition in which it is people or agents that are primarily assessed for how free they are, not choices or options. In this tradition the focus is on how far an individual is a "freeman" rather than a "bondsman," and how far the members of a society are established in general as freemen. The tradition used to be associated with the narrow assumption that only propertied, mainstream males are to count in the ledger of liberty. But, this feature is dispensable. We may focus, more broadly, on how far able and adult individuals count as fully free citizens and the extent to which a society is one in which membership or citizenship entails freedom.

The status-centered way of thinking is best presented as a set of interconnected claims.

- The state should promote the free choice of its members.
- The state should promote the free choice of members equally.
- Specifically, it should provide equal, effective protection against unfreedom.
- In particular, it should protect against unfreedom in choices that are equally accessible to each.
- Citizens are free to the extent that they are given that protection in those choices.

The first two points are likely to be endorsed in almost any contemporary theory of the state and its duties: the first makes free choice important; the second, equality. The third and fourth points provide an interpretation of what it is for the state to promote the free choice of members equally. That interpretation focuses on protection against forces that would undermine free choice, and it construes equality as requiring equal protection in a domain of choices that is equally accessible to each. The account leaves room for different construals of what protection requires and of what choices should figure in the favored domain, but it suffices to identify a rival ideal to that of option-freedom.

What is freedom, then, on this approach? It is the status that goes with being incorporated equally – and, as protection itself requires, being recognized as being incorporated equally – into the matrix of protection that state and society provide.

Does the quantity of free choice matter on this approach? Yes, for the approach naturally suggests that all equally accessible choices, not just a proper subset, are to be protected. But, there is no abstract target that is hailed as a quantity to be maximized; there is nothing that corresponds in that way to option-freedom (O'Neill 1979–80). The assumption is that certain choices can be identified as equally accessible to all and that the set of such choices that is protected should not be unnecessarily restricted. And that is all. Suppose, then, that there are two candidate sets of choices that might be equally accessed by everyone. Consistently with the status-centered approach, there need be no abstract basis for determining that one produces more abstract liberty than the other. The choice about which set to protect may have to be made on the basis of values that are distinct from the value of liberty: say, the value of protecting a set of

choices that fits well with existing mores and that promises to be relatively
stable.

The status-centered way of thinking about liberty is closely associated
with the long republican tradition in which, as one Roman commentator
puts it, liberty becomes more or less synonymous with citizenship: "full
libertas is coterminous with *civitas*" (Wirszubski 1968: 3). In this tradition,
the cause of freedom is the cause of establishing people equally in the
enjoyment of a standing in which they can walk tall, conscious of being
equally protected against others – including the state itself – in a common
domain of choice. Freedom does not wax and wane with marginal shifts
in the commodities or services over which choice can be exercised. It is a
more stable quality of persons, albeit one that is defined by reference to the
notion of freedom in choice.

I think that Sen should find the status-centered conception of freedom
more attractive and important as a normative ideal than the option-centered
conception. The complexities he unearths in the notion of option-freedom,
as I mentioned, make it very difficult to think of it as a workable basis for
assessing individual or social fortunes. And, in addition to that negative
consideration, there are three positive reasons why he should find the ideal
of status-freedom attractive.

The first is that insisting on the importance of permit-independence as
well as content-independence goes very naturally with focusing on status-
freedom. If I have to depend on the permit or leave of another to be
able to make a certain choice, then I am not a free agent; I am not my
own person. I may be said with some plausibility to be able to make
that choice freely, if my masters give me free rein and let me choose as
I will. But, I cannot possibly be ascribed status-freedom. Sen's assumption
that freedom requires rich, permit-independent control sits very nicely,
then, with the status-centered rather than the option-centered approach to
freedom.

That assumption, as it happens, has been traditionally associated with
the status-centered way of thinking (Pettit 2007a). Perhaps the most central thesis in the long republican tradition is that the protection that is
needed for someone to enjoy freedom has to ensure permit-independent
as well as content-independent choice (Pettit 1997; Skinner 1998; Viroli
2002). The protection provided has to ensure that in making his or her
choices, the agent does not have to rely on the leave or permission of
others; the agent does not have to act *cum permissu*. The protection
must establish the person as *sui juris*, under their own jurisdiction. It has

to guard the person against living *in potestate domini*, in the power of a master.[11]

But, there is also a second positive reason why Sen should find the status-centered way of thinking about freedom more attractive and important than the option-centered alternative. This is that it fits very well with his more recent emphasis on capabilities for functioning and their importance in assessing the quality of life. There are two central questions to resolve in developing a status-centered theory of freedom. The first, just touched upon, is to say what sort of protection has to be provided for citizens that they should count as free. The second is to determine the types of choices in which people should have that protection; I describe these, in a common phrase, as the basic liberties. It is on this second question that status-freedom connects with the idea of functioning capabilities.

The usual way to identify the basic liberties is by means of a list or inventory: they include the freedom to speak your mind, associate with others, adopt a religious affiliation, live in one or another part of the country, and so on (Hart 1973; Rawls 1958). But, the basic liberties can be characterized, more perspicuously, as liberties that satisfy three constraints (Pettit 2008). They are personally significant for people in general, involving choices that anyone is more or less bound to care about. They are choices that everyone can exercise at once, and do so without the exercise of the choice losing its motivating point; they are not essentially competitive or collectively counterproductive. And, they are all the choices of those kinds that a society can protect, not just a proper subset of them; they are not unnecessarily restricted. The choices identified as basic liberties may often presuppose rules that can vary between societies, say because of the differing demands of local mores; the liberty to own property, for example, will vary with different rules of ownership. But, regardless of how they vary in that way, they will have to be personally significant, equally accessible to all, and not unnecessarily restricted.

---

[11] The equal protection stipulation might be taken to require protection against natural misfortune in the same way that it requires protection against interpersonal domination (Van Parijs 1995). I reject that approach on two grounds. First, the impact of natural misfortune on status-freedom, unlike that of interpersonal domination, gives cause for regret, but no cause for complaint and does not have the same significance for us. And, second, protecting against interpersonal domination will require a degree of protection against natural misfortune and a degree of redistribution in favor of the less well-off; absolute or relative poverty makes people prone to being dominated.

Let basic liberties be understood in this fashion, and providing for the protection of basic liberties – in particular, their protection against domination – will come very close to what Sen (1982) and Nussbaum (2006) think of as enabling people to enjoy basic functioning capabilities. To have such capabilities is, as Sen (1983b) suggests, to be able to live without shame in one's society. And, that is quite close to the idea of having such a protected space for the exercise of basic liberties that one is not subject to the dominating control of others. One does not live *in potestate domini*, in the power of a master.

The third positive reason why Sen should be attracted to the status-centered way of thinking about freedom is that it would make good sense of his commitment to connecting issues of freedom with issues of democracy. The good polity, by the criterion of status-freedom, will have to provide each of us with suitable protection in suitable choices. But, a polity might do that and yet figure in our lives as itself a source of domination: an agency with a power of interfering in our lives that effectively gives it virtual control over what we do. If the polity is subject to control in the democratic manner envisaged by Sen, however, then this danger may be avoided. Hence democracy may be said to serve the cause of freedom well.

Suppose that the public officials who control the state – a state that identifies and protects our basic liberties – operate under our indirect, democratic control, as Sen imagines: ideally, under our equally shared, collective control. The fact that there is such a coercive state may be regarded as a historical necessity, akin to the fact of living under natural limitations, so that its mere existence will not dominate us (Pettit 2007b). And, the fact that we share equally in democratic control of that state means that the exercise of state authority in shaping and guarding our basic liberties will not be dominating either. Thanks to its democratic structure, the agency that protects us against domination by others will not perpetrate domination in the act of doing so. The control it exercises over us individually will be subject to our own control in the maximal measure possible for each of us in a democratically egalitarian society. Such controlled control – such nonarbitrary control, in the old republican phrase – is no danger to freedom, once freedom is understood in the republican, status-centered way.

The considerations just rehearsed are set out rather briefly. Without expanding on them in any more detail, however, I hope that they give some ground for thinking that the rich and varied considerations generated in Sen's work on freedom support an approach that has a long ancestry in political theory, but not much currency in contemporary thought. His personal trajectory has led from recognizing ever more complexities in the notion of control and choice, and in the received, option-centered notion of freedom, to the development of an approach that starts from the idea of functioning in one's society and looks for a state that would provide for the equal functioning capability of every citizen. That trajectory, as I see it, describes a path whereby he moves from a focus on option-freedom to a perspective in which something close to the old ideal of status-freedom assumes center stage.

References

Berlin, I. (1969). *Four Essays on Liberty* (Oxford: Oxford University Press).

Carter, I. (1996). "The Concept of Freedom in the Work of Amartya Sen," *Politeia*, 12, 43–4, 7–29.

Carter, I. (1999). *A Measure of Freedom* (Oxford: Oxford University Press).

Cohen, G. A. (1994). "Amartya Sen's Unequal World," *New Left Review*, 203, 117–29.

Ferguson, A. (1767). *An Essay on the History of Civil Society* (Edinburgh: Millar and Caddel; reprinted, New York: Garland, 1971).

Frankfurt, H. G. (1988). *The Importance of What We Care About* (Cambridge: Cambridge University Press).

Gaerdenfors, P. (1981). "Rights, Games and Social Choice," *Noûs*, 15, 341–56.

Hart, H. L. A. (1973). "Rawls on Liberty and its Priority," *University of Chicago Law Review*, 40, 534–55.

Kramer, M. H. (2003). *The Quality of Freedom* (Oxford: Oxford University Press).

List, C. (2004). "The Impossibility of a Paretian Republican? Some Comments on Pettit and Sen," *Economics and Philosophy*, 20, 1–23.

Nozick, R. (1974). *Anarchy, State, and Utopia* (Oxford: Blackwell).

Nussbaum, M. C. (2006). *Frontiers of Justice: Disability, Nationality, Species Membership* (Cambridge, MA: Harvard University Press).

O'Neill, O. (1979–80). "The Most Extensive Liberty," *Proceedings of the Aristotelian Society*, 80, 45–59.

Pettit, P. (1995). "The Virtual Reality of Homo Economicus," *Monist*, 78, 308–29. Expanded version in Maki (ed.), *The World of Economics* (Cambridge: Cambridge University Press, 2000); reprinted in P. Pettit, *Rules, Reasons, and Norms* (Oxford: Oxford University Press, 2002).

Pettit, P. (1997). *Republicanism: A Theory of Freedom and Government* (Oxford: Oxford University Press).

Pettit, P. (2001a). "Capability and Freedom: A Defence of Sen," *Economics and Philosophy*, 17, 1–20.

Pettit, P. (2001b). *A Theory of Freedom: From the Psychology to the Politics of Agency* (Cambridge: Polity; New York: Oxford University Press).

Pettit, P. (2007a). "Free Persons and Free Choices," *History of Political Thought*, 28, 709–18.

Pettit, P. (2007b). "Joining the Dots," in Smith, Brennan, Goodin, and Jackson (eds.), *Common Minds: Themes from the Philosophy of Philip Pettit* (Oxford: Oxford University Press).

Pettit, P. (2007c). "Republican Liberty: Three Axioms, Four Theorems," in Laborde and Manor (eds.), *Republicanism and Political Theory* (Oxford: Blackwell).

Pettit, P. (2008). "The Basic Liberties," in Kramer (ed.), *Essays on H.L.A. Hart* (Oxford: Oxford University Press).

Pettit, P. (2009). "Varieties of Public Representation," in Shapiro, Stokes, Wood, and Kirshner (eds.), *Political Representation* (Cambridge: Cambridge University Press).

Rawls, J. (1958). "Justice as Fairness," *Philosophical Review*, 67, 164–94.

Sen, A. (1970a). *Collective Choice and Social Welfare* (Edinburgh: Oliver and Boyd).

Sen, A. (1970b). "The Impossibility of a Paretian Liberal," *Journal of Political Economy*, 78, 152–7.

Sen, A. (1982). *Choice, Welfare, and Measurement* (Oxford: Blackwell).

Sen, A. (1983a). "Liberty and Social Choice," *Journal of Philosophy*, 80, 18–20.

Sen, A. (1983b). "Poor, Relatively Speaking," *Oxford Economic Papers*, 35, 153–68.

Sen, A. (1985). "Well-being, Agency and Freedom," *Journal of Philosophy*, 82, 169–221.

Sen, A. (1987). *On Ethics and Economics* (Oxford: Blackwell).

Sen, A. (1993). "Capability and Well-Being," in Nussbaum and Sen (eds.), *The Quality of Life* (Oxford: Oxford University Press).

Sen, A. (1996). "Freedom, Capabilities and Public Action: A Response," *Politeia*, 12, 43–4, 107–25.

Sen, A. (1999). *Development as Freedom* (New York: Anchor Books).

Sen, A. (2001). "Reply to Pettit, Anderson and Scanlon," *Economics and Philosophy*, 17, 51–66.

Sen, A. (2002). *Rationality and Freedom* (Cambridge, MA: Harvard University Press).

Sidney, A. (1990). *Discourses Concerning Government* (Indianapolis: Liberty Classics).

Skinner, Q. (1998). *Liberty Before Liberalism* (Cambridge: Cambridge University Press).

Steiner, H. (1994). *An Essay on Rights* (Oxford: Blackwell).

Sugden, R. (1981). *The Political Economy of Public Choice* (Oxford: Martin Robertson).

Sugden, R. (1998). "The Metric of Opportunity," *Economics and Philosophy*, 14, 307–37.

Van Parijs, P. (1995). *Real Freedom for All* (Oxford: Oxford University Press).

Viroli, M. (2002). *Republicanism* (New York: Hill and Wang).

Wirszubski, C. (1968). *Libertas as a Political Ideal at Rome* (Oxford: Oxford University Press).

5 | Social Choice Theory and the Informational Basis Approach

KEVIN ROBERTS

1. INTRODUCTION

Social choice theory is concerned with the principles underlying choice and preference when a group of individuals have different preferences over the options available. In the sense that it is thought desirable to reflect individual preferences in a group preference, social choice theory deals with the principles of aggregation of preference. At this general level, social choice theory is applicable to decision making by committees, the political voting process, and most aspects of welfare economics.

In narrower terms, social choice theory is concerned with the formal analysis of the aggregation of information to generate a social choice or preference. The basic building block for this theory is the work of Kenneth Arrow (1951); the generalization to permit an understanding of how the aggregation of information is sensitive to the nature of information available is because of Amartya Sen, most notably in his book *Collective Choice and Social Welfare* (Sen 1970a). This book remains a tour de force in terms of being both a map to guide researchers and an inspiration to them in their endeavors. Indeed, the flowering of the subject in the 1970s and later is directly from the clarity of the issues that Sen laid out in that book.

The purpose of this chapter is to critically examine the informational basis approach to social choice as developed by Sen.[1] The major finding of Arrow – his famous General (Im)possibility Theorem – is that aggregation in the social choice is impossible if the aggregation process is to satisfy a set of "reasonable" conditions. Sen's work points to the informational

---

[1] In the field of social choice, broadly conceived, Sen has made many contributions across a wide range of fields. Within the field more narrowly conceived, one can separate out at least three subfields where his contribution has been fundamental – the conditions under which majority rule gives rise to an ordering of social states (Sen 1966; see also Sen and Pattanaik 1969), the conflict between rights and Paretianism (Sen 1970a), and the generalization of the Arrow paradigm to social welfare functionals, which is the subject of this chapter.
The author is grateful to Marc Fleurbaey for his comments.

restrictions inherent in the Arrow setup and shows that aggregation with richer information permits social choices to be made with more "appealing" mechanisms. In particular, this richer information may include utility or individual welfare information that is interpersonally comparable. The nature and extent of this comparability is a major focus of the subject and of this chapter.

I start with a presentation of Arrow's approach to the analysis of social choice, based upon the use of a social welfare function, and of Sen's extension to this, based upon the use of a social welfare functional. I then consider alternative informational bases for interpersonal comparisons and the use of invariance transforms as pioneered in the social choice context by Sen.[2]

Given the nature of the original Arrow result, it is not surprising that Sen's approach has been viewed as a solution to its negativeness. However, part of the purpose of this chapter is to demonstrate that conventional notions of comparability of utilities imply, through their informational parsimony, a restrictiveness in terms of mechanisms for social choice. This is particularly the case if comparability information is restricted because more detailed information is considered meaningless, rather than being considered meaningful but not available. Within a welfarist context, feasible mechanisms to generate social welfare from the aggregation of individual welfares remain restrictive. In a more general nonwelfarist context, it will be shown that mild restrictions on utility information become very important when welfare information must be compared with nonwelfare information.[3] This will be demonstrated by exposing the difficulties of moving beyond welfarism, even when welfarist conditions like the Pareto criterion are not invoked.

2. SOCIAL CHOICE THEORY

Social choice has a long history, dating back at least to ancient Greece. A recurring theme has been the difficulty of aggregating individual

---

[2] Following Sen, the term 'informational basis' is assumed to relate to the structure of individual utility or welfare information. A wider interpretation can also be adopted (Fleurbaey 2003).

[3] It is not the purpose of this chapter to examine Sen's work on the role of nonutility information and the conflict of rights and the Pareto principles (Sen 1970a). Here, the conflict is less stark, but it does not require the sledgehammer of the Pareto principle (Sen 1979) to expose the difficulties of adopting a pluralist approach, encompassing welfarist and nonwelfarist principles.

preferences into a social preference. This has been demonstrated by considering examples of situations where difficulties occur, the most well-known being the paradox of majority voting associated with Condorcet (1785): consider three individuals, where individual 1 prefers social state or outcome x to y to z, 2 prefers y to z to x, and 3 prefers z to x to y. A majority (1 and 3) prefer x to y, a majority (1 and 2) prefer y to z, and a majority (2 and 3) prefer z to x. Thus, for any state, there is another state preferred by a majority, and a ranking of states based upon majority rule is intransitive. Other voting methods would give more satisfactory results in this situation, but possess other problems, again demonstrated by invoking examples. The problem with analyses of this sort is that they do not move beyond a collection of examples, and we owe to Arrow (1951) the debt for creating a more general approach to the subject. In essence, he sought to move away from an investigation of how particular aggregation mechanisms work in particular cases to how classes of mechanisms work in all "feasible" scenarios.

We lay out some formalities. Assume that we wish to construct a social ordering of social states. An ordering is complete (two states can be compared), reflexive (a state is as good as itself), and transitive (if x is at least as good as y and y is at least as good as z, then x is at least as good as z). The set of social states is X, and xRy, where $x, y \in X$, denotes the fact that x is socially weakly preferred to y ($x\ I\ y$ denotes indifference and $x\ P\ y$ denotes strict preference). Arrow considers the aggregation of individual preferences that, themselves, are orderings over X. Thus, assume that there is a set of individuals N and, for $i \in N$, R_i denotes i's ordering of the social states. A *social welfare function* (SWF) f is an aggregation mechanism, which determines a social ordering as a function of individual orderings: $R = f(\langle R_i \rangle_{i \in N})$. The most obvious examples of social welfare functions are voting mechanisms like majority rule. It is inherent in the Arrow structure that individual utility information consists of individual orderings – there is no intensity of preference or ranking of utility levels across individuals.

In a particular situation or example, the individual preferences are specified and f determines some social ordering. Arrow lays down four conditions that should be satisfied by an SWF:

(U)   Unrestricted domain: f is defined for all possible individual orderings.

(I)   Independence: If $\langle R_i \rangle_{i \in N}$ and $\langle R'_i \rangle_{i \in N}$ coincide over some pair of states x and y, then $R = f(\langle R_i \rangle_{i \in N})$ is the same as $R' = f(\langle R'_i \rangle_{i \in N})$ over the pair $\{x, y\}$.

(P)   Pareto: If xP_iy for all $i \in N$ then xPy (where P is derived from $R = f(\langle R_i \rangle_{i \in N})$ and R_i is each individual's ordering giving rise to the strict preference over $\{x, y\}$.

(ND)   Nondictatorship: For each individual d, there exists a set of preferences $\langle R_i \rangle$ and a pair $\{x, y\}$ such that xP_dy and yRx $(R = f(\langle R_i \rangle_{i \in N}))$.

Arrow's impossibility theorem shows that there exists no SWF satisfying these four conditions; for example, majority voting fails condition (U) because in some situations the ranking it creates is not an ordering.

Condition (U) demands that an ordering can be created for all individual preferences – it forces a consideration of counterfactuals so that a social ordering needs to be created not only for individual orderings that actually occur but also for hypothetical possibilities.[4] Condition (I) relies upon the use of counterfactuals to ensure that the social choice between a pair $\{x, y\}$ is independent of the individual rankings of any other pairs of states – it is by intention consequentialist. Condition (P) is a welfarist condition pointing to both a desire to respect individual preference and a willingness to be guided only by individual preference when there is unanimity. Condition (ND) requires that social preference does not reflect one person's individual preference *regardless* of the preferences of other individuals.

In the Arrow framework, what is the information on which the social ordering is based? Utility information enters directly through the individual orderings of states. Other information enters through the description of each state, which, for instance, serves to differentiate state x from y. This information can be rich in terms of a description of society in each state, but condition (U) can only be reasonable if states x and y are described sufficiently loosely for individuals to have any preference between x and y. It could be possible to say that individual i has an adequate well-being in state x as a description of state x, but it would not then be possible to say that i's well-being in state y is inadequate, given that it is possible that yR_ix and condition (U) demands that it is reasonable to construct a social ordering in this situation. Thus, if condition (U) is to be reasonable, nonutility information can enter into the primitive description of states in limited ways.

---

[4] One can avoid the use of hypothetical possibilities if the set of social states is sufficiently large and the set of individual orderings is sufficiently rich, this richness extending to triples of states that are viewed as similar apart from individual preference over the triples. See Parks (1976). For aggregation based upon social welfare functionals as developed later in this chapter, see Roberts (1980c).

3. SEN'S SOCIAL WELFARE FUNCTIONAL

It is now commonplace to view the Arrow problem as an attempt to determine a reasonable social ordering with too little information, particularly utility information. We owe this interpretation to Sen (1970a). He proposes a generalization of the Arrow approach to make possible the incorporation of richer utility information. Utility information is captured by a numerical representation of utility so that $u(x, i)$ denotes utility in state x of individual i. Instead of an SWF, we have a *social welfare functional* (SWFL) f mapping utility representations into a social ordering: $R = f(\langle u(x, i) \rangle_{x \in X, i \in N})$. The Arrow conditions can be straightforwardly amended to apply to SWFLs, and condition (I), for instance, can be reformulated as follows:

(I^*) Independence:[5] If $\langle u \rangle$ and $\langle u' \rangle$ are two numerical representations that coincide over a pair of states x, y, that is, $u(x, i) = u'(x, i)$ and $u(y, i) = u'(y, i)$ for all $i \in N$, then $R = f(\langle u \rangle)$ and $R' = f(\langle u' \rangle)$ coincide over $\{x, y\}$.

Conditions (U), (P), and (ND) can be similarly reformulated as (U^*), (P^*), and (ND^*).

The usefulness of using SWFLs is that utility information can incorporate more information than is contained in a simple individual ordering. The information content of utility information can be fine-tuned by imposing conditions that ensure that an SWFL treats different numerical representations as equivalent. Let $\mathcal{U}$ be the set of all real valued functions defined over $X x N$. Consider partitioning $\mathcal{U}$ into a collection of subsets $P_1, \ldots, P_K$ where $\mathcal{U} = \cup_{k=1, K} P_k$ and $P_k \cap P_l = \phi$ for all k, l. We call $P = \{P_1, \ldots, P_K\}$ a partition and let $\mathcal{P}$ be the set of all partitions of $\mathcal{U}$. A partition captures the informational context of utilities and this suggests the following definition:

$(P\text{-}I^*)$ P-invariance: An SWFL f is P-invariant with respect to partitioning $P = \{P_1, \ldots, P_k\}$ if for all $u, u' \in P_k$, for some k, $f(\langle u \rangle) = f(\langle u' \rangle)$.

If the partitioning of $\mathcal{U}$, call it $\tilde{P}$, is such that u and u' are in the same partition if they induce the same ordering of states for each individual, that is, for all $i \in N, x, y \in X$: $u(x, i) \geq u(y, i) \Leftrightarrow u'(x, i) \geq u'(y, i)$, then an SWFL that is P-invariant with respect to $\tilde{P}$ ignores all utility information other than individual orderings. By Arrow's theorem, there is no such SWFL satisfying $(U^*), (I^*), (P^*)$, and (ND^*) that is P-invariant with respect to $\tilde{P}$.

---

[5] We use an asterisk to denote that the condition applies to SWFLs.

The idea of capturing utility information as a partition of $\mathcal{U}$ is that utility functions in the same partition are informationally equivalent. The coarser the partition, the more demanding is P-invariance.

4. INFORMATION BASES OF INTERPERSONAL COMPARABILITY AND INVARIANCE TRANSFORMS

In this section, we show how different types of interpersonal comparability can be captured using partitions generated through the use of invariance transforms. We go on to examine the extent to which richer informational structures as captured by finer partitions overcome the pessimism generated by Arrow's impossibility theorem.

In terms of utility information, it is usual to view utilities as being ordinal or cardinal. Looking first at just one individual's utility function, ordinality captures the idea that utility information defines an ordering of states – the levels of utility can be ordered – but no more.

Thus, the primitive notion is an individual ordering. This ordering can be given a numerical utility representation by assigning higher utility to more preferred outcomes, and the arbitrariness of the particular representation is captured by P-invariance with the partitioning $\tilde{P}$.[6] An alternative method of defining equivalence of utility functions is to use the idea of an *invariance transform* $<\phi_i>$ that has the property that $\phi_i(u(.,i))$ is equivalent to $u(.,i)$ – under ordinalism, ϕ_i can be any strictly monotonic transformation.[7]

Ordinality allows levels of utility to be compared. Cardinality allows utility differences to be compared: the ordering of $u(x,i) - u(y,i)$ over the set XxX is the same for all utility functions with the same information partition. In terms of an invariance transform, ϕ_i is a strictly increasing affine transformation: $\phi_i(u_i) = \alpha_i + \beta_i u_i$ where $\beta_i > 0$.

The informational content of utility functions becomes interesting when there is comparability across individuals (Sen 1970a, 1977). Levels of utility are comparable, for example, the statement can be made that individual i in state x is better off than j in state y, if the partitioning of the utility space distinguishes between two utility functions $u(.,.)$ and $u'(.,.)$

---

[6] If the number of states is a continuum, then some continuity assumption is required to ensure the existence of a numerical representation. With cardinal utility representations, there are extra technical demands (Basu 1983; Roberts 1997).

[7] For a set of invariance transforms Φ_i to define a partitioning of the utility space, it is required that (i) Φ_i contains the identity transform; (ii) if $\phi_i \in \Phi_i$, then $\phi_i^{-1} \in \Phi_i$; and (iii) $\phi_i' \in \Phi_i$ and $\phi_i'' \in \Phi_i \Rightarrow \phi_i'(\phi_i'') \in \Phi_i$.

with a different ordering in XxN space. Thus, level comparability is an ordinal notion, and an example of an SWFL satisfying (U^*), (I^*), (P^*), (ND^*), and $(P\text{-}I^*)$ with this information partition is a Rawlsian maximin rule that ranks states according to the well-being of the worst off in each state.

If differences in utility are comparable, then $u(x, i) - u(y, i)$ can be ordered in $XxXxN$ space, for example, statements of the form that i gains more from the move from x to y than j gains from the move from w to z can be made. This is a cardinal notion and, in terms of invariance transforms, it is necessary that if $\phi_i(u_i) = \alpha_i + \beta_i u_i$ and $\phi_j(u_j) = \alpha_j + \beta_j u_j$ then $\beta_i = \beta_j$. Comparability of differences – often termed unit comparability – underlies what is necessary for the implementation of a utilitarian rule.

Comparability of levels and differences is not, of course, an either/or. If there are both an ordering of levels and a compatible ordering of utility differences, then we have what Sen (1970a, 1970c) has termed full comparability. If this is to be captured by the use of invariance transforms, then ϕ_i must take the form $\phi_i(u_i) = \alpha + \beta u_i, \beta > 0$, where α and β are independent of i.

We can add more comparability above and beyond full comparability. For instance, it may be possible to compare the level of individual utility with some independent norm that may allow one to make judgments about the value of increasing the population size; for example, a population increase may be desirable if the "new" individuals have a utility above the norm. This is termed ratio-scale comparability. If there is an independent norm, the utility representation can be chosen to ensure that the norm has zero utility and, in terms of invariance transforms, we will have $\phi_i(u_i) = \beta u_i$ where $\beta > 0$ is independent of i. In the limit, we could move to a degree of comparability that implied that each partition consisted of one element. To obtain this from an ordering, it would be necessary to rank outcomes against a set of independent norms or, more concretely, an independent "yardstick." Let us call this total comparability.

5. AGGREGATION POSSIBILITIES

A generally accepted view is that although there is no acceptable method of aggregation based upon the use of individual noncomparable orderings, a wide range of possibilities is opened up when richer informational structures are permitted.

Assume that a reasonable aggregation rule satisfies (U^*), (I^*), (P^*), and (ND^*). If utility functions are cardinal, but not comparable, then utility differences are intrapersonally comparable. However, this information relates to the utility that an individual achieves in at least three states, for example, the difference in utility between x and y and between x and z. By (I^*), this is ruled out as admissible information that can influence the aggregation rule. Thus, cardinality without comparability still gives rise to impossibility, a first (negative) characterization result, proved by Sen (1970a), which moved beyond the Arrow framework.

To make progress, we need to use interpersonally comparable information. If there is comparability of differences, but no more, then the set of aggregation rules satisfying (U^*), (I^*), (P^*), and (ND^*) is the set of weighted utilitarian functions with different individual utility functions being given different weights. This important characterization result is proved by d'Aspremont and Gevers (1977). If there is a desire to treat individuals symmetrically – a condition of anonymity – then the only admissible aggregation rule is the (unweighted) utilitarian rule. These rules apply when the weighted sum of utilities is strictly greater in one state than another; when the sum is the same in the two states, it is possible that the ranking can depend upon nonutility information serving to define social states (Roberts 1980a).

If there is comparability of levels, but no more, then the set of aggregation rules takes the form of associating the welfare of any state with the utility level of one individual in that state, the individual in each state being determined by who the person is and/or the position of the individual in the hierarchy of utilities in that state (Roberts 1980b). If the symmetry condition of anonymity is added, then welfare is associated with the utility level at some position in the utility hierarchy (Gevers 1979). Adding a minimal equity condition, which says that individuals with lower utility should be given at least as much weight as those with higher utility, ensures that the position in the hierarchy on which to focus is the individual with lowest utility (Hammond 1975; Strasnick 1976). We are thus led to the conclusion that interpersonal comparability of levels, but no more than this, leads to a Rawlsian maximin aggregation rule.

Assume that there is both comparability of differences and comparability of levels so we have full comparability, an informational structure that economists, at least, seem to consider rich. With such comparability, there is no information that tells us that we are discussing a society where everybody is subject to abject poverty or to unlimited riches – adding a constant to everybody's utility does not change comparisons of levels or of differences. Any aggregation mechanism must be insensitive to this concern. Relatedly, the aggregation mechanism must be insensitive to the extent of utility inequality as utility differences can be scaled upward or downward.

In particular, aggregation mechanisms cannot be more sensitive to inequality the greater it becomes. For instance, if, in a two-person society, it is determined that the utility vector (10,10) gives as much social welfare as (8,14), then by admissible scaling of utilities, these vectors give the same social welfare as (9,12), using a scaling factor $\beta = 1/2$, or (6,18), using a scaling factor $\beta = 2$.[8] In particular, it can be seen that attitudes to small deviations from equality are fully inherited by the attitudes to large deviations from equality.[9] These considerations are unimportant to a utilitarian or to a welfarist Rawlsian, the utilitarian being unconcerned with utility inequality, the Rawlsian showing maximum concern at all times. But, to implement a rich class of aggregation mechanisms, with attitudes to inequality depending upon the extent of inequality, the informational requirements seem to demand the existence of an independent yardstick. Thus, the use of interpersonal comparisons may allow one to escape from the straitjacket of the Arrow result, but the informational basis approach to social choice points to the restrictiveness of possible aggregation mechanisms, restrictiveness coming from the "technical" limitations of the information on which judgments can be based.

6. UTILITY INFORMATION IN INTERPERSONAL COMPARISONS

The SWFL approach is based upon individual well-being information being captured by a utility function. To economists, the usual use of a utility function is as a way of representing a preference ordering with any meaning to the notion of utility coming entirely from the nature of the preference order being represented. With an ordinal ordering, the utility function is a labeling of states; with cardinal orderings there are restrictions on the orderings that permit representation (Basu 1983; Roberts 1997), and these restrictions are reasonable given that the cardinal ranking relates to a ranking of differences.

---

[8] The class of possible aggregation mechanisms under full comparability is characterized in Roberts (1980a). If one also imposes a separability condition that states that the social ordering over a pair of social states x and y should not be sensitive to utility information of individuals whose well-being is the same in the two states, then the only possible aggregation mechanisms involve a focus on the worst-off, as in a maximin, a focus on the best-off, or a utilitarian focus on total utility. The details of this characterization are in Deschamps and Gevers (1978).

[9] This implies that iso-welfare curves in utility space must be cones emanating from points of full equality. See Roberts (1980a).

We have seen in section 4 that utility information in its primitive form can be captured by an ordering of utility levels and/or utility differences. It may therefore appear more natural to consider SWFLs as a function of these orderings directly rather than through the intermediate step of creating a representative utility function. Here, we show that the use of this intermediate step has some hidden implications.

Consider an example where interpersonal comparability takes the form of difference comparability and, over a pair of states, x and y, a three-individual society exhibits the following difference orderings:

$$u(x, 1) - u(y, 1) > u(y, 2) - u(x, 2) > u(y, 3) - u(x, 3) > 0 \quad (\dagger)$$

Here, the placement of zero is information derivable from the preference ordering of states of each individual. Would a utilitarian prefer x to y or vice versa? Individual 1 gains more in the move from y to x than individuals 2 and 3 each lose, but the "cumulative" loss of 2 and 3 may dominate 1's gain. Thus if we use an SWFL based upon comparability orderings and we invoke an independence condition, which we call (I^{**}), which makes the social ranking over $\{x, y\}$ independent of difference orderings involving states other than $\{x, y\}$, then, in this example, a utilitarian rule would not be implementable.[10] So, if an unrestricted domain condition (U^{**}) is imposed requiring an SWFL to create a social ordering in all cases, then the utilitarian rule is not an admissible SWFL. In fact, we can prove an interesting result for a world where the informational basis is a ranking of utility differences. Let (P^{**}) and (ND^{**}) be the marginally reformulated versions of (P^*) and (ND^*):

Theorem. *The only SWFL that satisfies (U^{**}), (I^{**}), (P^{**}), and (ND^{**}) is a weighted utilitarian rule giving equal weight to two individuals (d_1, and d_2, say) and zero weight to all other individuals.*

PROOF. Any rule satisfying (U^{**}), (I^{**}), (P^{**}), and (ND^{**}) is a rule satisfying (U^*), (I^*), (P^*), and (ND^*) under the invariance transform of difference comparability. From d'Aspremont and Gevers (1977), any such rule must take the form of ranking states according to a weighted sum of utilities. Assume that at least three individuals are given positive weight. Label these three individuals 1, 2, 3, their labeling relating to their weight in the weighted sum of utilities: $\gamma_1 \leq \gamma_2 \leq \gamma_3$. Assume that $u(x, i) = u(y, i)$ for all $i \neq$ 1's, 2's, 3's, and let 1's, 2's, and 3's utility information over

---

[10] See Bossert (1991).

the pair $\{x, y\}$ be as in (†) above. What is the weighted sum of utilities over $\{x, y\}$ in this case? Compatible with (†) is $u(x, 1) - u(y, 1)$ being sufficiently positive (compared to the other utility differences) so that the weighted sum of utilities is higher in state x than y. Thus xPy in scenario (†). However, compatible with (†) is a case where the three utility differences are equal so that, as $w_2 + w_3 > w_1$, then the weighted sum of utilities is higher in state y. We have thus shown that the weighted utilitarian rule with three individuals being given weight cannot be implemented based upon an ordering of utility differences. Now assume that only two individuals, 1 and 2, are given weight and that $\gamma_2 > \gamma_1$. When the ranking of differences is as in (†), the weighted sum of utilities is higher under y when $u(x, 1) - u(y, 1)$ is close to $u(y, 2) - u(x, 2)$ because $\gamma_2 > \gamma_1$, and the weighted sum is higher under x when $u(x, 1) - u(y, 1)$ is large compared to $u(y, 2) - u(x, 2)$. Again, the weighted utilitarian rule is not implementable. If only one individual has positive weight, then (ND^{**}) is directly violated so we are left with the possibility that two individuals, 1 and 2, have equal weight and all others have zero weight. If $sign(u(x, 1) - u(y, 1)) = sign(u(x, 2) - u(y, 2))$, then the weighted sum of utilities is unambiguous. Otherwise, for some labeling of the two individuals and the two states, we have $u(x, 1) - u(y, 1) > u(y, 2) - u(x, 2) > 0$ and the weighted sum of utilities is always higher in state x: thus weighted sum of utilities is implementable in this case, and the proof is completed.

Although an oligarchy of two individuals awards a dictatorship, it is not much of an improvement for a society of perhaps many million!

The theorem above shows the possibilities when the available information is a ranking of utility differences. However, the standard approach to aggregation with information based upon utility differences does not give this result. With an SWFL based upon utility information and this information incorporating difference comparability, that is, with invariance transforms of the form $\phi_i(u_i) = \alpha_i + \beta u_i, \beta > 0$, inducing the invariance partitions of the utility space, we know from d'Aspremont and Gevers (1977) that (U^*), (I^*), (P^*), (ND^*), and $(P\text{-}I^*)$ for this information structure defines the class of admissible SWFLs to be the class of weighted utilitarian functions: the social ordering is determined by the ordering of $\sum_{i \in N} \gamma_i u(., i)$, for appropriate weights γ_i.[11] How is the difference between the two results to be explained? The important source of this difference is that utility information

---

[11] The Pareto condition implies that all the Y_i are nonnegative and at least two must be positive. The weights are otherwise unrestricted.

is created from the ranking of utility differences and utility information relating to a pair of states $\{x, y\}$ can incorporate information about utility differences involving states other than x and y. To see this, consider again the three-person example given in (†). Assume that among all other states, there is a state z such that $u(z, 2) - u(y, 2) = u(y, 3) - u(x, 3)$. Knowing this, it is now possible to compare the sum of utilities over the pair $\{x, y\}$. We have:

$$\sum_{i=1,3} [u(x, 1) - u(y, 1)] = u(x, 1) - u(y, 1) + u(x, 2) - u(y, 2)$$
$$- u(z, 2) + u(y, 2)$$
$$= (u(x, 1) - u(y, 1)) - (u(z, 2) - u(x, 2)).$$

Thus, the ranking of the sum can be computed by information determined by the ordering of utility differences. But, to determine information relating to utility differences over $\{x, y\}$, it is necessary to consider utility differences relating to another state z – the ordering of differences over all pairs of states provides utility information relating to states x and y. If the problem is sufficiently rich, in the sense that states like state z in this example always exist, then, subject to the invariance transform for utility differences, a utility function will be uniquely defined and a weighted utilitarian ranking can always be determined.

In the SWFL approach based upon utility functions, the independence condition is subtly different from an independence condition that only allows information relating to $\{x, y\}$ to determine the social ranking over $\{x, y\}$. Condition (I^*) demands that only utility information over $\{x, y\}$ be used to determine the social ranking over $\{x, y\}$. However, the ranking of utility differences involving states other than $\{x, y\}$ is used to create the utility function over $\{x, y\}$: rankings involving other alternatives are used to *inform* what can be inferred about utilities over $\{x, y\}$. Consequentialism in a strict sense, as captured by (I^{**}) for instance, is foregone, but the motivation for looking at alternative states is fully compatible with the thrust of consequentialism. It is not widely understood that this approach relies upon a degree of nonindependence that permits information relating to "irrelevant" alternatives to be relevant.

7. MEANINGFUL COMPARISONS AND THE INFORMATION FOR COMPARISONS

Robbins (1935) famously asserted the meaninglessness of interpersonal comparisons, and the influence of this idea still casts a shadow over welfare economics. Excluding meaninglessness in a technical sense, which could relate to comparisons that failed a rationality test like transitivity, there still remains a notion of meaninglessness, which relates to how we comprehend statements of comparison. For instance, it may not be difficult to comprehend an ordinal comparison of the form that A is better off than B, whereas to say that A is three times as well off as B lacks such comprehensibility. Part of the problem here relates to the introduction of numerical quantities to compare aspects of well-being. But if, say, an ordering based upon ratio-scale comparisons is accepted, then by using such comparisons over the set of all social states and individuals, this would, through a path similar to that followed in the last section, allow numerical comparisons of relative well-being to be created. However, numerical comparisons, although being an implication of ratio-scale comparisons, could, because they are not part of normal vocabulary, be avoided in the presentation of individual utility information. It is a presentational matter only: if ratio-scale comparisons can be made, then aggregation rules based upon (relative) numerical comparisons of utility can be implemented.

However, despite this, the basic general point remains: it is easier to accept that somebody could find ratio-scale comparisons incomprehensible than that he or she would find interpersonal comparisons of utility differences incomprehensible.

7.1. Informational Bases as Available Information

Another interpretation of alternative information bases is that they relate to the information that is available to be aggregated. Thus, there may be a desire to implement a utilitarian rule, and this requires comparability of differences, but, the information available takes the form of non-interpersonally comparable individual preference orderings. There are at least two approaches that can be taken. First, there is the conservative approach, which gives up on the idea of generating a complete social ordering and, instead, only ranks two states if, with the information available, it is clear that the sum of utilities is at least as high in one state as in the other. In the present example, this would mean that states would be ranked only if they were comparable under the Pareto criterion.

The alternative, more radical, approach is to use available information to estimate a ranking of utility differences. In the present example, one approach is to take each individual's preference ordering and assign a utility of zero to the worst state, a utility of unity to the next worst, two to the next worst, and so on. If a utilitarian rule is applied to this information then the aggregation procedure is the well-known Borda rule of voting. Here, note that condition (I) is violated because information from other states is used to estimate utility information for each pair of states. However, once this is done, the aggregation rule that is utilized is avowedly consequentialist. We note that there are many methods of using preference orderings to estimate difference-comparable information. This contrasts with what was uncovered in the last section, where information from other states enriches the information related to a pair of states but does so nonconjecturally.

The Borda rule is one way of creating interpersonally comparable welfare differences. Without further information beyond preference orderings, the utility difference between two adjacently ranked states is as likely as not to be greater than the utility difference between any two other adjacently ranked states. The expected utility difference in the two circumstances is the same, and so the Borda rule may be viewed as the expression of the judgment of a utilitarian expected welfare maximizer faced with very limited information. Similarly, if level-comparable information is available then a utility of zero can be assigned to the lowest utility level faced by any individual in any state, unity to the second lowest level faced by any individual in any state, and so on (Sen 1977). Here, the utility difference between two adjacently ranked states for some individual will vary, with comparability across individuals being used to estimate the cardinal ranking for the single individual.

As well as using utility information in other states to estimate utility information relating to a pair of states, there is also the possibility of using nonutility information incorporated into the description of social states. For instance, individual income is often used as an indicator of well-being. If the description of states includes individual income information, then this may be combined with available utility information to enhance its quality. However, the reasonableness of this approach is in conflict with the unrestricted domain condition (U^*), which requires that the SWFL determines a social ordering for all utility information. If the description of social states provides information that is useful to enhance the quality of utility information, then it is doubtful, for instance, that all individual orderings of the states can be feasible.[12] Formally, condition (U^*) becomes a condition that one would not wish to impose on aggregation mechanisms.

---

[12] If nonutility information is used to update beliefs, then formally it is possible that utility information and nonutility information are statistically dependent even though the supports of the distribution functions underlying beliefs are independent.

Consider an example where social states include a description of the observable status of individuals, including social variables, for example, health status, and economic variables, like income. Let us accept a restricted domain condition that takes the form that, holding other variables constant, an individual is better off in states where his or her income is higher. Assume that available information is ordinal and noncomparable, captured for individual i by a utility function $u(y_i, s_i, i)$ where y_i is i's income and s_i is a vector of observable nonincome variables. The utility function serves to provide information about the trade-off in well-being for i between income and other variables.

If the domain of the utility function is sufficiently unrestricted then it is possible to discover the income level that, in some benchmark situation s^*, gives i the same utility level as in any particular social state. Define $m(y_i, s_i, i)$ as follows:

$$u(y_i, s_i, i) = u(m(y_i, s_i, i), s^*, i)$$

The function m is an ordinal representation of i's utility – a money-metric utility function. If s^* is fixed, then any welfare function as a function of these money-metric utilities can be implemented. For instance, in a two-person world, consider the welfare function (where m_i is money-metric utility of individual i)

$$W = m_1 + m_2 + m_1^2 + m_2^2.$$

This welfare function would not be implementable if, for instance, the utility functions were provided by utility information based upon ratio-scale comparisons – the ranking between (bm_1, bm_2) and $(b\tilde{m}_1, b\tilde{m}_2)$ is not independent of the scale factor b. Let $m_1 = 1, m_2 = 5, \tilde{m}_1 = 3, \tilde{m}_2 = 4$. Then both (m_1, m_2) and $(\tilde{m}_1, \tilde{m}_2)$ give a welfare of 32. However, if the utilities are scaled by $b = 3/2$, (bm_1, bm_2) gives higher welfare, and if they are scaled by $b = 3$, $(b\tilde{m}_1, b\tilde{m}_2)$ gives higher welfare.

The example demonstrates that nonutility information and, in particular, information from other social states can be used to "create" utility information with none of the measurability and comparability restrictions discussed in section 4 of this chapter.[13] The welfare function described above may be rejected because it is based upon meaningless comparisons,

---

[13] The use of data about income or expenditure and social variables is one route to take when faced with a recognized lack of welfare information (Sen 1999). The example uses information from other states that give the same utility level to individuals as the state under consideration (see Pazner 1979).

but if such comparisons are considered to be meaningful, then nonutility information can be used to estimate the information that is necessary to implement such a function. The money-metric utility function is an example of a created utility function embodying measurability and comparability characteristics different from the original utility information. Again, as with the utilitarian justification for the Borda rule, the created utility function involves a degree of conjecture; in the present example, this relates to a relationship between income and utility.

7.2. Partial Comparability

Once it is accepted that utility information is incomplete, there exists the possibility that available information may be more informative than is implied by being complete with respect to one information base, and incomplete with respect to some richer base. For instance, some, but not all utility differences may be interpersonally comparable with individual preference orderings being complete. As Sen has put it, "We may, for example, have no great difficulty in accepting that Emperor Nero's utility gain from the burning of Rome was smaller than the sum-total of the utility loss of all the other Romans who suffered from the fire" (Sen 1999: 356).

The analysis of this situation has been initiated by Sen (1970a, 1970c), who uses a utility function approach and focuses on the case where comparability of differences would constitute complete information. Thus, if $u(x, i)$ is a utility function representation of available information and

$$u'(x, i) = \alpha_i + \beta u(x, i)$$

for all x, i and for some α_i and $\beta > 0$, u and u' capture equivalent information. As comparability of differences constitutes complete information, wishing to treat all individuals symmetrically would imply that the preferred aggregation mechanism would be utilitarianism.

Sen captures incomplete information by specifying information as a subset L of all utility functions defined over XxN. If $u(.\,,.)$ is a member of L, then, as comparability of differences gives the richest information structure, $u(.,.)$ as defined above will be a member of L. However, L may extend beyond such functions. For instance, it may include all utility functions of the form

$$u''(x, i) = \alpha_i + \beta_i u(x, i)$$

where $b \leq \beta_i / \beta_j$, for all i, j and some $b \leq 1$. If $b = 1$, then the set does not extend beyond the set defined by the u' functions; if b is close to zero, then the set of u'' functions preserves only the cardinality of individuals' utility functions and interpersonal comparability is lost. The subset L can be thought of as being created from a primitive ranking of utility differences that will rank only in some circumstances (recall the Emperor Nero example). Using the (incomplete) ranking, the set L will be determined as the set of all utility functions compatible with the ranking.

Unlike the case of complete information, where the set of all utility functions is partitioned into subsets where any two utility functions in the same partition capture equivalent information, each subset L captures the full extent of incompleteness as well as features of the information base that would be implied by complete information. This means that two different sets L and L' of information can intersect. For instance, an individual may prefer state w to x to y to z. Let L be the set of utility functions capturing this information and the information that the utility difference between w and x is greater than the difference between x and y. Similarly, let L' be the set that captures ordinal information plus the fact that the utility difference between x and y is greater than that between y and z. There are utility functions compatible with the union of this information, which will be members of the intersection of L and L', and there are utility functions compatible with one of the pieces of extra information, but not the other (so L is not a subset of L' and vice versa). Furthermore, if more information is added, then the set of feasible utility functions is restricted, and so L can be a subset of another set L'.

The question arises as to how to aggregate the available information in this environment. If comparability of differences is meaningful then it may be desirable to choose between states based upon the utilitarian sum of utilities. The situation is a variant of the one we investigated in section 7.1. If a social ranking is made only when all utility functions in the set L imply the same ranking in terms of the sum of utilities, the approach adopted by Sen (1970c), then the social ranking will generate an incomplete ordering – a quasi-ordering.

The alternative approach is to use available (partially comparable) information to estimate the expected sum of utility differences between two states and use this to generate a complete social ordering. Again, this will involve a degree of conjecture. This suggests that partial comparability should be captured by a probability distribution over utility functions capturing degrees of belief. This could be a degree of belief over sets of utility functions, each set being a partition of the set of functions that occurs under comparability of differences. In this framework, one extreme is to base aggregate judgments on the expected sum of utilities and create a complete ordering. The other extreme is to be risk averse and rank states only when it is certain that the sum of utilities is higher in one state than another. The intermediate case, with merit, is to rank states only when the probability distribution over the sum of differences is either predominantly in the positive range or predominantly in the negative range. Further development of this sort of approach would be useful.

8. INFORMATIONAL BASES AND WELFARISM

The characterization results under alternative informational bases that were discussed in section 5 all embody the Pareto criterion and lead to rules that can be termed, to generalize Sen's (1979) definition, strict-ranking welfarism – the welfare of each state is evaluated using a function of utilities and the social ranking corresponds to the welfare ranking whenever welfare is not the same in two states. Thus, nonutility information will usually be excluded from the social ranking.

Although it is generally recognized that the Pareto criterion conflicts with the use of nonutility information (Sen 1970b), it is not well recognized that the ability to make judgments incorporating both utility and nonutility information not only requires an abandonment of the Pareto criterion, but also places demands on the richness of utility information that must be available either directly or indirectly through some estimation exercise.

What happens if condition (*P*) is not imposed? In the Arrow setup, Wilson (1972) has shown that conditions (*U*), (*I*), and (*ND*) imply either that a pair of states is ranked independently of preferences or there is a "reverse dictator," where the social ranking is the reverse of the ranking of the individual who is the reverse dictator. In the first case, utility information is ignored; in the second, nonutility information is ignored and individual utilities are viewed as "bad."

To rule out utilities as "bad," a monotonicity condition can be imposed:

(M^*) Monotonicity: For all u, u', and $x, y \in X$ such that

$$u'(z, i) = u(z, i) \quad \text{for all } i \in N, \ \text{ for all } z \neq x, y$$
$$u'(x, i) > u(x, i) \quad \text{for all } i \in N,$$
$$u'(y, i) < u(y, i) \quad \text{for all } i \in N,$$

$$x R y \Rightarrow x P' y \quad \text{where} \quad R = f(<u>) \quad \text{and} \quad R' = f(<u'>).$$

Monotonicity allows for a general bias for some state y over state x, but if utility information is such as to create an aggregate judgment for x over y, then this is reinforced when utilities move further in favor of x and against y. In the Arrow setup, conditions (U), (I), (M^*), and (ND) imply that utility information must be ignored in the social ranking. Thus, strict-ranking welfarism can be avoided by relaxing the condition (P), but at the cost of adopting welfare indifference with no concern for individual utilities!

This striking result is a consequence of the utility informational base in the Arrow problem. To see this, assume that we move to the other extreme – total comparability – where utilities can be evaluated against an independent yardstick. Assume that social states are given some weight $w(x)$, $x \in X$, independently of utilities, and that the social judgment takes the form of ranking x over y if the sum of utilities in state x plus $w(x)$ is greater than the sum of utilities in state y plus $w(y)$. This rule satisfies (U^*), (I^*), (M^*), and (ND^*) and allows a trade-off between utility and nonutility information, for example, the function $w(.)$ may be inversely related to the degree of coercion that exists in any social state.[14]

Now assume that the appropriate informational base is that of full comparability with comparability of utility levels and differences. To begin, let us consider what is possible in a one-person society; full comparability is equivalent to a cardinal utility function for the individual. With condition (I^*), the only relevant utility information to determine the ranking over a pair of states $\{x, y\}$ is the individual's ordinal ranking of the pair. The ranking of x and y will either follow this individual ranking or ignore it; either way, there can be no trade-off between utility and nonutility information.

In a many-person society, nonutility information can interact with utility information only through the trade-off between individual utilities. The full proof of this result will not be presented here.[15] Instead, consider a situation where the set of social states X can be partitioned into subsets $X_1, X_2, \ldots$ such that if $x, y \in X_i$, then these states have the same nonutility characteristics and, to compare x and y, only utility information is used to obtain a ranking. Then the aggregation rule to be applied over X_i will incorporate the Pareto criterion, and as discussed earlier, it must be welfarist. Also, whenever there is a subset of states such that everybody has the same utility level in those states, then a Wilson-type result applies over this subset. Consider $x, y \in X_1$ and $x', y' \in X_2$ such that everybody has the same utility level in state y and everybody has the same level in state y'. The ranking between x and y, and between x' and y', will be welfarist; either

---

[14] But note that there may be restrictions on the measurability of *nonutility* information.
[15] The proof builds upon the characterization of welfarist objectives under full comparability (Roberts 1980a).

the ranking between y and y' will be welfarist, insuring that the ranking between x and x' is essentially welfarist, or the ranking between y and y' will be fixed independently of utilities – in which case all elements of X_1 are always ranked above the elements of X_2 or vice versa.

To give an example of what is achievable, let us focus on the case where weighted utilitarianism is to be applied between states with the same nonutility characteristics. Let the weight on individual i be γ_i^j over X_j. The ranking of states will follow the function

$$W_j = \sum_{i=1,n} \gamma_i^j u(x, i).$$

Now, between two states in different partitions, either the ranking will be dictated by nonutility characteristics or, if utility information is to be relevant, it is necessary that if $u(x, i) = u$ for all i and $u(w, i) = u'$ for all i and $u > u'$, then x will be preferred. This is ensured if the weights satisfy $\sum_i \gamma_i^j = 1$. This serves to characterize the aggregation mechanism – states are to be judged by the weighted average utility level in the state, and nonutility information can determine the weights to be used. Thus, there is no possible trade-off between utility and nonutility information other than that the trade-off between two individuals' utilities can be determined by nonutility information.

If levels of utility are not interpersonally comparable, then this limited possibility of combining utility and nonutility information is not feasible. To see this, note first that comparability of differences only implies that, within each partition, the rule must be weighted utilitarian.[16] If utility information is relevant to rank states in partition j with states in partition k, then the ranking will be based upon weighted utilitarianism with $\sum_i \gamma_i^j = 1$. Assume that $\gamma_1^j > \gamma_1^k$ and $\gamma_2^j < \gamma_2^k$. By adding a large enough constant to 1's utility, states in partition j will be preferred; by adding a large enough constant to 2's utility, states in partition k will be preferred. However, if there is no comparability of levels, then the social choice should be invariant with respect to the addition of constants. Thus, the weights must be equal across a group of partitions where rankings can depend upon welfare information, that is, $\gamma_i^j = \gamma_i^k$.[17]

A variable weighted utilitarian rule, with weights relating to nonutility information, requires comparability of differences and levels to be

---

[16] Recall the characterization result of d'Aspremont and Gevers (1977).
[17] A formal proof is close to the proof of Theorem 9 of Roberts (1980a).

implemented. With only comparability of differences, the weights must be unvarying and nonutility information cannot be combined with utility information to create a social ranking.

On the other hand, if there is comparability of utility levels, but no comparability of differences, then nonutility information can help determine the utility trade-off. For instance, the welfare of each state can be associated with the utility at some position in the utility hierarchy, but, the position chosen can be state-dependent. In coercive states of the world, welfare could be associated with the utility of the worst-off individual; in states where there is considerable freedom, welfare could be associated with the utility of the individual with median utility. Such a rule – a state-dependent positional dictatorship – incorporates a preference for freedom, but only when there is utility inequality, and satisfies (U^*), (I^*), (M^*), and (ND^*) under the informational base of level comparability.

9. CONCLUDING REMARKS

Following Arrow's pioneering formulation of a structure to analyze social choice, Sen has made fundamental contributions to enriching the structure, both with the introduction of social welfare functionals and with insightful analyses of the information on which social welfare functionals can bear.

Arrow's impossibility theorem is commonly viewed as a result of trying to do too much with too little information, and, indeed, with interpersonally comparable information, aggregation mechanisms that satisfy the spirit of his axioms can be formulated. This chapter has examined Sen's informational enrichment approach, this being one part of his overall contribution to the analysis of social choice. It has been shown that whereas the use of interpersonal comparisons permits the implementation of whole classes of aggregation mechanisms, there are still severe restrictions on aspects of these mechanisms. Even with comparability of levels and of differences, aggregation mechanisms are restrictive, both in terms of the way that the distribution of utilities can be assessed, and in terms of the way that utility and nonutility information can interact when welfarist conditions like the Pareto criterion are relaxed. To overcome these problems, rich informational structures are required, and they come from using all available information to estimate interpersonal comparisons with the required degree of richness.

References

Arrow, K. J. (1951). *Social Choice and Individual Values* (New York: Wiley; 2nd ed. 1963).

d'Aspremont, C., and L. Gevers (1977). "Equity and the Informational Base of Collective Choice," *Review of Economic Studies*, 46, 199–210.

Basu, K. (1983). "Cardinal Utility, Utilitarianism, and a Class of Invariance Axioms in Welfare Analysis," *Journal of Mathematical Economics*, 12, 193–206.

Bossert, W. (1991). "On Intra- and Interpersonal Utility Comparisons," *Social Choice and Welfare*, 8, 207–19.

Deschamps, R., and L. Gevers (1978). "Leximin and Utilitarian Rules: A Joint Characterization," *Journal of Economic Theory*, 17, 143–63.

Fleurbaey, M. (2003). "On the Informational Basis of Social Choice," *Social Choice and Welfare*, 21, 347–84.

Gevers, L. (1979). "On Interpersonal Comparability and Social Welfare Orderings," *Econometrica*, 47, 75–90.

Hammond, P. J. (1975). "Equity, Arrow's Conditions and Rawls' Difference Principle," *Econometrica*, 44, 793–804.

Parks, R. P. (1976). "An Impossibility Theorem for Fixed Preferences: A Dictatorial Bergson-Samuelson Welfare Function," *Review of Economic Studies*, 43, 447–50.

Pazner, E. (1979). "Equity, Nonfeasible Alternatives and Social Choice: A Reconsideration of the Concept of Social Welfare," in Laffont (ed.), *Aggregation and Revelation of Preferences* (Amsterdam: North-Holland).

Robbins, L. (1935). *An Essay in the Nature and Significance of Economic Science*, 2nd ed. (London: Macmillan).

Roberts, K. W. S. (1980a). "Interpersonal Comparability and Social Choice Theory," *Review of Economic Studies*, 47, 421–39.

Roberts, K. W. S. (1980b). "Possibility Theorems with Interpersonally Comparable Welfare Levels," *Review of Economic Studies*, 47, 409–20.

Roberts, K. W. S. (1980c). "Social Choice Theory: The Single and Multi-Profile Approaches," *Review of Economic Studies*, 47, 441–50.

Roberts, K. W. S. (1997). "Comment on Suzumura on Interpersonal Comparisons," in Arrow, Sen and Suzumura (eds.), *Social Choice Re-Examined*, Vol. 2 (London: Macmillan).

Sen, A. K. (1966). "A Possibility Theorem on Majority Decisions," *Econometrica*, 34, 481–9.

Sen, A. K. (1970a). *Collective Choice and Social Welfare* (San Francisco: Holden-Day).

Sen, A. K. (1970b). "The Impossibility of a Paretian Liberal," *Journal of Political Economy*, 78, 152–7.

Sen, A. K. (1970c). "Interpersonal Aggregation and Partial Comparability," *Econometrica*, 38, 393–409.

Sen, A. K. (1977). "On Weights and Measures: Informational Constraints in Social Welfare Analysis," *Econometrica*, 45, 1539–72.

Sen, A. K. (1979). "Personal Utilities and Public Judgements or What's Wrong with Welfare Economics," *Economic Journal*, 89, 537–58.

Sen, A. K. (1999). "The Possibility of Social Choice," *American Economic Review*, 89, 349–78.

Sen, A. K., and P. K. Pattanaik (1969). "Necessary and Sufficient Conditions for Rational Choice under Majority Decision," *Journal of Economic Theory*, 1, 178–202.

Strasnick, S. (1976). "Social Choice Theory and the Derivation of Rawls' Difference Principle," *Journal of Philosophy*, 73, 85–99.

Wilson, R. B. (1972). "Social Choice without the Pareto Principle," *Journal of Economic Theory*, 5, 478–86.

6 | Sen on Sufficiency, Priority, and Equality

PETER VALLENTYNE

1. INTRODUCTION

Amartya Sen's contributions to moral philosophy have been enormous. He has made seminal contributions to the measurement of freedom, the measurement of equality, the measurement of poverty, the debate over the kind of equality that is relevant to justice, and the debate over the respective roles of liberty, efficiency, and equality in a theory of justice. I shall here focus on Sen's work on distribution-sensitive principles of justice, and more specifically on his work on (1) sufficientarian principles, which require promoting the adequacy of benefits (nonpoverty), (2) prioritarian principles, which require the promotion of individual benefits, but with some kind of priority for the worse off, and (3) egalitarian principles, which require the promotion of equality of benefits.

Sen's work in this area tends to focus on the development of a framework of investigation rather than an extended defense of any particular principles. My goal here will therefore be to present Sen's work, and related work by others, in an intuitively accessible manner that highlights its importance for existing philosophical debates on the topic. The presentation will mainly be a survey, with critical comments being only suggestive rather than fully defended.

2. BACKGROUND

Justice, as we shall understand it, is concerned with what benefits (net of specified burdens) we owe others. We shall leave open the nature of the relevant benefits (which might be income, wealth, well-being, or anything

For helpful comments and criticisms, I'm indebted to Dick Arneson, Walter Bossert, Ingrid Robeyns, Bertil Tungodden, Paul Weirich, and Andrew Williams.

else). Sen, of course, has argued at length that the equalisandum for justice is capabilities (effective opportunities to function), but here we shall abstract from his commitment to capabilities, as that topic is addressed in another chapter. Below, references to a person being better (or worse, or equally well) off than another should be understood as being assessed with respect to the relevant benefits (and not necessarily in terms of welfare). For simplicity, we shall assume that the value of a given bundle of benefits is fully cardinally measurable and fully interpersonally comparable. This is indeed a simplifying assumption, but, as Sen has emphasized, even if the bundles are not *fully* measurable in this way, they may be at least *partially* so measurable, and this may still generate significant implications.[1]

Sen rightly insists that justice is pluralistic in that there are several distinct considerations that determine what is just.[2] He endorses at least some kind of impartiality condition, some kind of efficiency consideration, and some kind of distributive consideration. He also would endorse some kind of negative rights protecting against certain kinds of interference in one's life, but, we shall ignore this important consideration in what follows, because it is not at the core of his work on distribution-sensitive principles of justice.

In what follows, we shall focus on the ranking relation of being-at-least-as-just. A distribution of benefits is more just than another if and only if it is at least as just as the other, but not vice versa. Two distributions are equally just if and only if each is at least as just as the other is. Except as noted, we shall make the following assumptions, which Sen and other social choice theorists typically make:

Ordering: The relation of being-at-least-as-just is an ordering: (1) It is *reflexive*: each distribution is at least as just as itself. (2) It is *transitive*: for any three distributions, x, y, and, z, if x is at least as just as y, and y is at least as just as z, then x is at least as just as z. (3) It is *complete*: for any two distributions, at least one of them is at least as just as the other.

Reflexivity is entirely uncontroversial, transitivity is somewhat controversial,[3] and completeness is moderately controversial. Nonetheless, for simplicity, we shall here assume them throughout.

---

[1] Sen's general tolerance of indeterminacy reflects an extremely important point. For any given subject matter (and especially when it is normative), many questions may not have completely determinate answers. Furthermore, the mere presence of some indeterminacy does not entail radical indeterminacy. For discussions of this point, see Sen (1985: 205; 1992: 47, 134).

[2] See, for example, Sen (1992: 7–8, 87, 92, 136, 145–6).

[3] See, for example, Temkin (1987, 1996) and Rachels (1998).

A second condition that we shall generally assume is this:

Anonymity: If the pattern of benefits in one distribution is a permutation of the pattern of benefits in another distribution (i.e., the same pattern of benefits but with the benefits reassigned to different people), then the two distributions are equally just.

Anonymity is an impartiality condition. It holds that (assuming, as we shall, that there is a fixed set of individuals) justice is concerned with the patterns of distributions and not with what particular individuals get. The distribution $<2,1>$ (two to the first person and 1 to the second) is equally as just as $<1,2>$. There are, in general, powerful reasons for rejecting Anonymity. One is that justice is sensitive to the past (e.g., what commitments individuals have made or what good or bad deeds they have committed), but Anonymity (at least in its typical crude formulation) makes such information irrelevant. A second problem with Anonymity is that it is incompatible with individuals having differential rights over things (e.g., over their own bodies!). Anonymity holds that if it is just for me to increase my well-being from 5 to 10 units by using my body in a certain way while leaving you with 5 units, then it must also be just for *you* to increase your well-being from 5 to 10 units by using my body, while leaving me with 5 units. Again, this is quite implausible.[4]

Although Anonymity in its crude form is implausible, it may well be plausible as a condition on the distribution of benefits for which agents are in no way accountable (e.g., have no entitlement or desert claims). It is, for example, arguably a plausible condition on the distribution of initial (or brute-luck-generated) nonpersonal resources. In what follows, I shall, as Sen typically does, limit my attention to cases where there are no differential claims to benefits (e.g., from rights or desert). In such contexts, Anonymity is much more plausible. Even here, however, I believe that Anonymity should be rejected, but, once again, it would take us too far astray to examine this issue. Hence, we shall assume it in what follows.

A third condition that we shall generally assume is this:

Strong Pareto: (1) If each person has the same benefits in one distribution as he or she does in another, then the two distributions are equally just. (2) If each person has at least as many benefits in one distribution as he or

---

[4] The need to reject the standard strong form of Anonymity is implicit in Sen's important result on the impossibility of the Paretian liberal. The liberalism condition of this result requires that each person have privileged jurisdiction over certain matters (e.g., when one goes to sleep), which violates Anonymity. See chapters 6 and 6* of Sen (1970).

she does in another, and at least one person has more benefits in the first distribution as in the second, then the first distribution is more just than the second.[5]

The first part of Strong Pareto holds that if, for each person, the benefits of one distribution are the same as those of a second, the two distributions are equally just. This is not plausible in general because justice depends at least in part on the extent to which the *will* (or choices) of people (as opposed to the benefits they get) is respected. The distribution in which I am healthy because I choose not to smoke is not equally just with the one in which I am equally healthy and have the same other overall benefits because you force me not to smoke (and compensate me for the use of force), and no one else is affected. The first part of Strong Pareto rules out adequate sensitivity to choice-protecting rights. In what follows, however, we'll focus on contexts in which there are no relevant rights (or desert claims) at issue. In such contexts, this part of Strong Pareto is plausible.

The second part of Strong Pareto is an efficiency condition. It says that justice is positively sensitive to the benefits people receive. If one distribution is *Pareto superior* to a second – that is, if it gives some people more benefits and no one less – then it is more just. Although this is a relatively weak efficiency requirement (much weaker than the requirement that total benefits be maximized), it has significant implications. It entails that distributive considerations (e.g., equality) never trump efficiency in the sense of Pareto superiority. A Pareto-superior distribution is more just – no matter how bad it is from a distributive viewpoint. For example, <1,99> is deemed more just than <1,1>. Distributive principles, according to this condition, are limited in application at most to assessing the relative justice of *Pareto-incomparable* distributions (i.e., pairs of distributions for which one distribution gives some people more and gives other people less). One positive implication of this limitation is that *leveling down* (reducing the benefits of better-off people) always makes things less just. As such, it is highly plausible. Equality promotion, for example, may well be relevant to justice, but only as a way of making some people's lives better. Making the better-off worse off without benefiting anyone makes things less just, not more just.

---

[5] By way of contrast, Weak Pareto holds that x is more just than y if *everyone* has more benefits in x than in y. It is silent if even just one person has equal benefits. Weak Pareto is incredibly weak and thus highly plausible. Strong Pareto is stronger, but still highly plausible (although of course somewhat less so).

In general, then, Strong Pareto is, it seems, a plausible principle of justice. We shall return to its assessment when we consider certain distributive principles.

The final condition that we shall generally assume appeals to the notion of a *nonreversing downward transfer*, which is a transfer of benefits from a better-off person to a worse-off person, which does not make the originally worse-off person better off than the originally better-off person (i.e., does not reverse their positions in terms of being better off; it can make them equally well off). The move from <8,4> to <6,6>, for example, involves a nonreversing downward transfer of two units. The move from <8,4> to <5,7>, however, is a reversing transfer. Consider this:

Pigou-Dalton: If one distribution can be obtained from another by a nonreversing downward transfer, then it is more just than the other is.[6]

Pigou-Dalton introduces a very weak kind of distribution sensitivity. It says roughly that increasing the benefits of those with fewer benefits by a given amount is morally more important than increasing the benefits of those with greater benefits by the same amount. More exactly, it says that transferring a given amount of benefits from a better-off person to a worse-off person makes things more just when this leaves the originally better-off person at least as well off as the originally worse-off person. For example, it says that <6,6> is more just than <4,8>.

Pigou-Dalton is a very weak, and highly plausible, kind of distribution sensitivity. It holds only where the total is not affected. Most theorists endorse much stronger principles of distribution sensitivity, but we shall start with this one.

In the following sections, we shall examine three distribution-sensitive kinds of principles of justice: sufficientarianism (favoring distributions that better ensure that each person has an adequate amount), prioritarianism (favoring distributions that better benefit those who are worse off), and egalitarianism (favoring more equal distributions).[7]

---

[6] In the context of Transitivity and Anonymity, Pigou-Dalton Transfer is equivalent to a condition known as "strict S-concavity". For discussion, see Sen (1997: 51–6) and Dasgupta et al. (1973).

[7] Other kinds of distribution-sensitive principles include desert principles (favoring distributions that better ensure that people get what they deserve) and entitlement principles (favoring distributions that better ensure that people get what they have a right to get). Although Sen has discussed such principles, his main contribution to the topic of distribution sensitivity concerns sufficientarianism, egalitarianism, and prioritarianism.

3. SUFFICIENTARIANISM

The sufficiency view of justice is concerned with ensuring, to the extent possible, that each person receives an *adequate* amount of the benefits.[8] Obviously, this requires a criterion for how much is adequate. Typically, the criterion of adequacy is something like enough (either in general or for that specific person) to meet basic (e.g., physiological) needs, avoid poverty, or have a minimally decent life (e.g., be able to show oneself in public without shame). Following Sen, we shall not address this important question and simply assume that some particular level of benefits has been selected as the adequacy (poverty) line.

As a theory of justice, (pure) sufficientarianism holds the following:

Sufficientarianism: A distribution is at least as just as another is if and only if it involves less or equal insufficiency.

This, of course, doesn't tell us much until we know how insufficiency of a distribution is measured.

Sen essentially created the framework for poverty (and insufficiency) measurement.[9] All measures of poverty, he claimed, should satisfy the following conditions:

Weak Scale Invariance. Multiplying the poverty line and all the benefit levels by the same positive number does not affect aggregate poverty.

This entails that the chosen unit of measurement (e.g., pennies or dollars) does not affect the measurement of aggregate poverty, which is highly plausible. It also entails, however, that aggregate poverty is *purely relative* to the poverty line, and this is controversial. It requires, for example, that doubling everyone's real benefits while also doubling the poverty line (e.g., because poverty is understood in relative terms) does not affect aggregate poverty. Some might argue, however, that this will reduce aggregate poverty on the grounds, for example, that there is less aggregate poverty when everyone has a $10 shortfall from a poverty line of $100 than when everyone has a $5 shortfall from a poverty line of $50 – because in the former case each person is better off in absolute terms.[10] Weak Scale Invariance,

---

[8] An important statement of sufficientarianism is Frankfurt (1987).

[9] Appendix 7 of Sen (1997) and Sen (1979) are terrific summaries of Sen's work on poverty measurement, as well as that of others. See also Sen (1976a), chapter 7 of Sen (1992), and Foster (1984).

[10] I'm indebted to Walter Bossert for pointing this out to me.

however, requires that aggregate poverty be unaffected. For simplicity, I shall ignore this objection, and accept Weak Scale Invariance.

A second condition imposed by Sen is the following:

Focus: The assessment of poverty (insufficiency) is not affected by changes in benefits above the poverty (adequacy) line, when those changes do not change the poverty line.

This simply ensures that the measure is a measure of poverty. For any fixed poverty line, how well off the nonpoor are is irrelevant to aggregate poverty.[11] Following Sen, we shall focus on the measurement of poverty for a given poverty line.

Focus is indeed a plausible condition for the assessment of poverty (insufficiency), but it is precisely this condition that casts doubt on sufficientarianism as a theory of justice. It ensures that both Strong Pareto and Pigou-Dalton are violated. Strong Pareto is violated because Focus requires that increasing the benefits of a *nonpoor* person not reduce poverty (insufficiency). Sufficientarianism then concludes that such an increase does not make the distribution more just, which seems implausible. Benefits to those below the poverty line matter more for justice than benefits to those above, but – as claimed by Strong Pareto – additional benefits to those above are better, from the viewpoint of justice, than no additional benefits at all. Pigou-Dalton is also violated, as Focus requires that a nonreversing downward transfer from a better-off *nonpoor* person to a worse-off *nonpoor* person does not make things better from the viewpoint of eliminating poverty. Sufficientarianism then concludes that such a transfer does not make the distribution more just, which violates Pigou-Dalton and seems implausible. Such a transfer at least sometimes increases the equality of the distribution of benefits, and this seems to make things more just.

Because of Focus, sufficientarianism is arguably insufficiently demanding.[12] It finds both radical inequality and radical inefficiency morally acceptable as long as everyone has enough. This may be plausible if the benefits to be distributed are benefits the differential production of which is

---

[11] If the criterion of nonpoverty (adequacy) is societally relative and depends on the overall benefits in society, then increasing the benefits of the nonpoor may increase the poverty line and thereby affect the measure of poverty. Focus does not rule this out.

[12] Here, we limit our attention to pure sufficientarian theories. Impure versions can be more demanding. For example, one could hold that sufficientarian concerns are *prior* to all others, but when two distributions are equally good in ensuring that people get adequate benefits, then other concerns (such as efficiency and a stronger distribution sensitivity) apply. See Tungodden (2003) for a defense of this kind of approach.

attributable to the choices of the agents (and not because of differential brute luck in capacities, opportunities, etc.). If, however, the benefits to be distributed are, as we are assuming, only those acquired by brute luck (i.e., because of factors over which the agent had no deliberative influence; e.g., manna from heaven), then the sufficiency view is, I would argue, insufficiently demanding.

Let us continue nonetheless to investigate how aggregative poverty (insufficiency) might be measured in light of the above conditions. One of the simplest measures is the *head count measure*, which simply counts the number of people below the poverty line. A major problem with this measure is that it holds that aggregate poverty is not affected by giving benefits to poor people that do not make them nonpoor. Improving a person's situation from abject poverty to slight poverty does not change the number of poor people and is thus deemed, on this measure, not to affect aggregate poverty. This is implausible.

More generally, any plausible measure of aggregate poverty, Sen rightly holds, should satisfy the following condition:

Monotonicity (below the poverty line): Increasing a *poor* person's benefits reduces aggregate poverty (insufficiency).

This is a kind of restricted Pareto condition applied to poverty measurement rather than justice. Although an increase in a *nonpoor* person's benefits does not affect aggregate poverty (as required by Focus), increasing a *poor* person's benefits does, and it (of course) reduces aggregate poverty. This is a highly plausible condition, and the implausible head count measure violates it.

Consider now a second simple measure of aggregate poverty. The *total gap measure* simply adds up each person's shortfall from the poverty line (where a person's shortfall is zero if he or she is at or above the poverty line). This satisfies Monotonicity, but it suffers from a different problem. Aggregate poverty is surely reduced if one nonreversingly transfers certain benefits from one poor person to a worse-off poor person. The total gap measure, however, fails to generate this judgment. It is insensitive to the distribution of benefits among the poor. It measures only the total shortfall. A distribution-sensitive measure of aggregate poverty is needed.

More generally, Sen rightly imposes the following condition:

Weak Transfer Axiom: Aggregate poverty (insufficiency) is reduced by a nonreversing transfer of benefits from a better-off *poor* person to a worse-off *poor* person.

This is just Pigou-Dalton restricted to transfers below the poverty line. Although downward nonreversing transfers of benefits that occur *above* the poverty line do not affect aggregate poverty (i.e., unrestricted Pigou-Dalton applied to poverty measurement is violated, as required by Focus), such transfers *below* the poverty line reduce poverty. The total gap measure, however, violates this condition (as the total gap is unaffected).

Sen proposes the following measure, S, of aggregate poverty in a given distribution y:

$$S(y) = [HCR(y) \cdot PGR(y)] + [HCR(y) \cdot (1 - PGR(y))] \cdot G_p(y)$$

where $HCR(y)$ is the head count ratio for y (i.e., number of poor divided by population size); $PGR(y)$ is the poverty gap ratio for y (i.e., total poverty gap divided by the product of the poverty line and the number of the poor); and $G_p(y)$ is the inequality in the distribution of benefits among the poor in y as measured by the Gini coefficient (a standard measure of inequality).

Sen (1976a) proves that where large numbers of the poor are involved, roughly this measure follows from two assumptions: (1) For a fixed population size, aggregate poverty is ranked on the basis of the *sum* of the *weighted* poverty gaps, where the weight of a given gap is equal to its ordinal position in the size of such gaps (i.e., if there are n people with poverty gaps, the largest gap has a weight of n, the second largest gap has a weight of $n - 1$, and the smallest gap has a weight of 1). (2) To handle variable population size, the sum of the weighted poverty gaps is normalized by dividing by the population size.[13]

Each of these assumptions is, as Sen clearly recognizes, controversial. The assumption that aggregate poverty is the sum of the weighted poverty gaps, with the ordinal position weights just stated, can be challenged on at least three grounds. One is that aggregate poverty might not ranked on the basis of the sum of weighted poverty gaps. Consider, for example, leximin poverty gap. It holds that there is at least as much aggregate poverty in one distribution as in another if and only if the *largest* poverty gap in the first is at least as great as that in the second, and if they are equally great, the second largest poverty gap in the first is at least as great as that in the second, and so on. This measure satisfies Weak Scale Invariance, Focus, Monotonicity, and the Weak Transfer Axiom, and, as is well known, it is

---

[13] Sen (1976a: 223) states this assumption as follows: When all the poor have the same income (no inequality among the poor), then the poverty ranking is based on the head count ratio multiplied by the poverty gap ratio. In the context of the first assumption (ranking based on the normalized weighted sum of the poverty gaps), this is equivalent to normalizing by dividing by population size.

not based on the sum of (finitely) weighted poverty gaps.[14] Leximin poverty gap is not, however, a very plausible measure of aggregate poverty (because of the absolute priority that it gives to the worse off). Although there are other possibilities, it seems reasonable to grant Sen the assumption that aggregate poverty is ranked on the basis of the sum of (finitely) weighted poverty gaps.

A second challenge to Sen's first assumption is that the particular weights that Sen assumes for weighting poverty gaps seem quite arbitrary. The weights should indeed be greater for greater poverty gaps (as required by the Weak Transfer Axiom), but it's not at all clear why they should correspond precisely to the ordinal position of the poverty gap. More specifically, this weighting scheme seems inappropriately insensitive to the differences in *magnitude* of the poverty gaps beyond those differences reflected in the ordinal rank. For example, suppose that there are only two people in society, the poverty line is 10, and both people are poor in the distributions that we consider. Sen's weighting scheme assigns a weight of 2 to the larger poverty gap and a weight of 1 to the smaller poverty gap – no matter what the size of these poverty gaps. Thus, a weight of 2 is given to the poverty gap of 9 by the first person in <1,9> and is also given to the poverty gap of 2 to the first person in <8,9>. The fact that the former poverty gap is much larger is deemed irrelevant. Only the ordinal position of the poverty gaps matters for the weights. This seems implausible.

A third challenge to Sen's first assumption is that, as he recognizes, it violates the following condition:

Strong Transfer Axiom: Aggregate poverty (insufficiency) is reduced by a nonreversing transfer of benefits from a better-off (poor or nonpoor) person to a worse-off *poor* person.

This is like the Weak Transfer Axiom, except that it does not require that the donor be poor. Given that Sen weights poverty gaps by their ordinal poverty position, his poverty measure violates this condition for certain transfers that move the donor from being nonpoor to being poor. Such transfers increase the number of poor people, and this can have the result of increasing Sen's measure of poverty. (This is so, for example, when there are just two people and the better-off person is initially just barely above

---

[14] More precisely, leximin poverty gap is not representable as a weighted sum of poverty gap, if, as is usual, poverty gaps are measured by standard numbers (e.g., involving no infinitesimals). If nonstandard numbers are used, and I believe this would not be inappropriate, then it is so representable.

the poverty line.) It seems fairly plausible, however, that sufficientarian justice is increased by such a transfer. Even though the number of poor people increases, the total poverty gap does not increase, and the poverty gaps are spread more equally. Thus, the Strong Transfer Axiom seems plausible, and yet it is violated by Sen's assumption about weighted poverty gaps.[15]

Sen's first assumption – that aggregate poverty is based on the sum, suitably normalized for population size, of the weighted poverty gaps, with his ordinal position weighting scheme – thus is implausible for a sufficientarian theory of justice. His second condition – that a suitable normalization for population size is to divide the sum by the population size – is, I shall argue, also implausible.

The general question here is that of whether poverty (sufficiency) is to be understood in (as Sen proposes) population-relative (i.e., per capita) terms or absolute terms. Where 10 is below the poverty line, $<10,100,10,100>$ has twice as much absolute poverty as $<10,100>$ but has the same per capita poverty.

Fortunately, in the present context, we need not resolve this general issue. In the context of Sen's total ordinally weighted poverty gap view, normalizing by dividing by the number of people (i.e., relativization to population size) implausibly has the effect that adding nonpoor people to the population reduces aggregate poverty – because it increases the denominator of his measure (the population size) without increasing the numerator (the sum of the weighted poverty gaps). This, I claim, is an implausible result for a sufficientarian theory of justice.

Another way of stating the above concern is that aggregate poverty should satisfy a strong version of a "focus" (on the poor) condition. Earlier, we noted that Sen's measure satisfies Focus, which states that aggregate poverty is not affected by increasing the *benefits* of the nonpoor. The following Strong Focus condition requires in addition that aggregate poverty not depend on the *number* of the nonpoor.

Strong Focus: The assessment of poverty (insufficiency) is not affected by changes in benefits to those above the poverty (adequacy) line, *nor by the number of nonpoor people*, when this does not change the poverty line.

---

[15] Sen (1997: 176) notes that the following modification, developed by Shorrocks, of Sen's measure satisfies the Strong Transfer Axiom: $S^*(y) = [HCR(y) \cdot PGR(y)] + [1 - HCR(y) \cdot PGR(y)] \cdot G_p(y)$. Sen (2002: 89, n. 40) states that he finds this modified measure more plausible.

Aggregate poverty, that is, should be only about the condition of the poor and not depend in any way on the condition (number or benefit levels) of the nonpoor.

This concludes my discussion of Sen's work on the measurement of poverty. Philosophers have recently begun to give more attention to sufficientarian theories of justice, but few have systematically investigated how aggregate sufficiency is to be measured. When it is feasible to give everyone sufficient amounts of the relevant benefits, there is no need for a theoretical measure of aggregate sufficiency (because any adequate measure will agree that there must be perfect sufficiency). Given, however, that in many contexts it may not be possible to give everyone a sufficient amount, the development of a measure of aggregate sufficiency is indeed important. The work of Sen and other economists thus provides an important framework for the investigation of this issue.[16] I have suggested, however, that neither the rank order weighting system invoked by Sen's measure of poverty nor his relativization to population size are plausible for a sufficientarian theory of justice. This is not a criticism of Sen's work, as he did not intend his measure to be so used.

4. PRIORITARIANISM

The sufficiency view of justice is concerned with increasing the benefits that people have, but only up to an adequate amount. It gives absolute priority to a benefit, no matter how small, to someone whose benefits will remain inadequate, over a benefit, no matter how large, to a person whose benefits are already adequate. Prioritarianism generalizes this idea. It holds that increasing the benefits that people have always matters (and not just below the adequacy level), but a given increase matters more morally when it is given to a person who has a lower initial level of benefits than it does when it is given to someone who has a higher initial level. There is, it is claimed, a kind of decreasing marginal moral importance to marginal increases in benefits.[17]

Because prioritarianism holds that increasing a person's benefits always makes things more just, it (unlike sufficientarianism) satisfies Strong Pareto (and not merely Monotonicity). Furthermore, because it holds that a given

---

[16] Sen (1997) contains references to many other important works on poverty measurement. A particularly important class of measures (satisfying certain additive decomposability and subgroup consistency conditions) has been developed by Foster (1984).

[17] For the classic statements of prioritarianism, see McKerlie (1994) and Parfit (1991).

benefit increase is always more important when it occurs at a lower initial level of benefits, it (unlike sufficientarianism) satisfies Pigou-Dalton. This, I believe, makes it more promising as a theory of justice.

There are several different forms that prioritarianism can take, but the following are the three main ones:

Leximin: One distribution is at least as just as a second if and only if (1) the person with the least benefits in the first distribution has at least as much benefits as the person with the least benefits in the second distribution, and (2) if there is a tie in the previous comparison, then the person with the *second* least benefits in the first distribution has at least as much benefits as the person with the *second* least benefits in the second distribution, and so on for the persons with the third least benefits, and so on.

Strong prioritarian totalism: One distribution is at least as just as a second if and only if its total weighted benefits are at least as great, where the weights for a given increment finitely decrease as the benefits prior to the increment finitely increase.

Weak prioritarian totalism: One distribution is at least as just as a second if and only if (1) it has greater total benefits, or (2) it has the same total benefits and is at least as just according to leximin.

Leximin and weak prioritarian totalism are the polar extremes of prioritarianism. Leximin assigns infinitely greater weight to those who are worse off. It favors a benefit, no matter how small, to a person who remains a worse-off person over a benefit, no matter how large, to a better-off person. Weak prioritarian totalism (of which prioritarian utilitarianism is an example), by contrast, assigns only infinitesimally greater weight to those who are worse off. Where the total benefits are not equal, weak prioritarian totalism agrees with standard totalism, but, where the benefits are equal, it agrees with leximin. Given that, on most conceptions of benefits, the total benefits will typically not be equal, weak prioritarian totalism typically gives a very limited role to leximin. The role it gives, however, is sufficient (just barely!) to ensure that Pigou-Dalton is satisfied. It thus has a claim (just barely) to be a prioritarian theory.

Between these extreme forms of prioritarianism is strong prioritarian totalism. It is like totalism (e.g., total utilitarianism) except that it adds up *weighted* benefits, where the weight assigned to a one-unit increment to a certain level of benefits is *finitely* greater – and not infinitely or infinitesimally greater – than the weight assigned to a one-unit increment to any *higher* level. Thus, for example, the increment from 0 to 1 might have a weight of 1, the increment from 1 to 2 might have a weight of $1/2$, and an increment from 2 to 3 might have a weight of $1/3$. A person with three units of benefits generates 1 5/6 units of weighted benefits, whereas three people, each with one unit, generate 3 units of weighted benefits. The decreasing marginal weights generate extra priority for those who are worse off, but, given that the extra weight is only finite, a sufficiently larger benefit to a better-off person can produce a greater increase in weighted benefits than a given benefit to a worse-off person.

Sen contributed much to our understanding of leximin and weak prioritarian totalism (as well as standard totalism).[18] The following material will bring together some of the results of Sen and others on the topic of prioritarianism.

Leximin, weak prioritarian totalism, and strong prioritarian totalism each satisfy Ordering, Anonymity (our impartiality condition), Strong Pareto (our efficiency condition), and Pigou-Dalton (our distribution sensitivity condition). They each also satisfy the following condition, which, by definition, is satisfied by all prioritarian theories:

Strong Separability (with respect to unaffected individuals): The justice ranking of two distributions, x and y, is fully determined by the benefits of the affected individuals (i.e., the individuals whose benefits are not the same in each distribution) and does not depend on the benefits of the unaffected individuals (i.e., those whose benefits are the same in each distribution).

This condition says that if some set of individuals is unaffected by the choice between x and y (each gets the same benefits in x as in y), then the ranking of x and y does not depend on what their benefits are. For example, the ranking of $<1,4,6,7>$ versus $<2,4,3,7>$ (for which the second and fourth persons are unaffected) must be the same as the ranking of $<1,9,6,2>$ versus $<2,9,3,2>$ (for which the second and fourth persons are unaffected). With respect to affected individuals (the first and third persons), the first pair of distributions is identical to the second pair: $<1,-,6,->$ vs. $<2,-,3,->$ in both cases. Strong separability requires that the first pair be ranked the same way as the second pair. The particular values for the second and fourth persons are deemed irrelevant (given that they are unaffected).

Strong Separability is not uncontroversial. Various forms of egalitarian theory, for example, violate it. All prioritarian views (as well as totalism), however, satisfy it by definition (because they always favor making people

---

[18] See, for example, Sen (1974, 1976b, 1986, 1987).

better off no matter what the situation of those who are unaffected), and so we shall temporarily grant it.[19]

Let us now consider some conditions that distinguish leximin, strong prioritarian totalism, and weak prioritarian totalism from each other. Consider first:

Irrelevance of Cardinality (of benefits):   For any two distributions, transforming each person's benefits by a positive monotonic transformation, the same for all persons, does not affect their relative ranking with respect to justice (if x is at least as just as y before the transformation, then it is also so after the transformation).

A positive monotonic transformation of benefits is a transformation that preserves the relative size of benefits (equal benefits are transformed to equal benefits and larger benefits are transformed to larger benefits). For example, $<1,2,9>$ is a positive monotonic transformation of $<2,4,6>$, but $<3,2,5>$ is not. This condition says that the numbers representing benefits are irrelevant except, perhaps, for the ordinal information they represent (for a given person and perhaps also between people). It does not rule out interpersonal comparability of benefit levels, but it rules out any appeal to cardinality of benefits, and a fortiori any interpersonal comparisons of zero levels or of units.

One way of defending leximin is the following:

Observation 1: If the justice ranking relation satisfies Ordering, Anonymity, Strong Pareto, Pigou-Dalton, Strong Separability, and Irrelevance of Cardinality, then leximin is the justice ranking relation.[20]

---

[19] Fleurbaey (2003) has recently challenged whether there is a principled difference between prioritarianism and impure forms of egalitarianism, which hold that justice is increased by Pareto improvements (even though they decrease equality). He shows that any purported prioritarian theory can be represented by the product of total benefits and a factor that measures equality. This mere representability, I would argue, is not sufficient to show that a theory is egalitarian in any interesting sense. Instead, we should reserve the term "egalitarian" for those theories that satisfy Pigou-Dalton *but violate Strong Separability*. Prioritarian theories, by contrast, are those theories that satisfy Strong Pareto, Pigou-Dalton, and Strong Separability. For excellent discussions of prioritarianism's commitment to Strong Separability, see Tungodden (2003), Jensen (2003), and Broome (2003).

[20] See Sen (1977a: 1549). The result is drawn from the work of Deschamps and Gevers (1978), Gevers (1979), and Roberts (1980). All the results noted here and to follow implicitly assume: (1) Benefitism: The justice ranking relation is defined in the space of benefits (so that nonbenefit features, such as rights violations, are not relevant). (2) Universal Domain: Benefit distributions can take any logically possible shape. (3) Independence of Irrelevant Alternatives: The ranking of two alternatives depends only on their respective distributions of benefits (and not on the features of other distributions). Also, to keep things simple, I

In the context of prioritarian theories, the only controversial condition here is Irrelevance of Cardinality. If benefits are only ordinally measurable (with assessments that one benefit is equal to or greater than another, but with no assessment of how much greater one benefit is), then, of course, Irrelevance of Cardinality is plausible. Here, however, we are abstracting from the specifics of any given conception of benefits, and thus we cannot answer the question of whether the benefits are merely ordinally measurable.

There is, however, a further issue, even if benefits are cardinally measurable: that cardinality may be irrelevant to justice. Justice may depend solely on ordinal information about benefits. If so, then Irrelevance of Cardinality is plausible. Nonetheless, it seems highly plausible that if we can assess, for a given person, not merely that one distribution is better or worse for him or her, but also how much better or worse it is, then surely this is relevant to justice. Hence, Irrelevance of Cardinality is not a very plausible condition, if we assume a conception of benefits for which there is some cardinality. Thus, this condition does not in general (independently of a specific conception of benefits) provide a justification for leximin.

Consider, then, the following condition:

Hammond Equity: If two distributions give everyone, except two individuals, the same benefits, and one of these two individuals has less benefits than the other person under one distribution, and less or equal benefits under the other distribution, then the distribution that gives this worse-off person more benefits is more just than the other distribution.

Consider, for example, <1,5,10> and <2,3,10>. The only difference between these two distributions concerns the benefits that the first and second person get. The first person gets less than the second person does in both distributions (1 vs. 5 in the first distribution, and 2 vs. 3 in the second). Hammond Equity therefore requires that the second distribution (which is better for the worse-off person) be judged more just. Both weak prioritarian totalism and strong prioritarian totalism violate this condition (as both allow that if the loss to the better-off person is sufficiently greater than the

---

invoke Pigou-Dalton rather than the much weaker original condition of Minimal Equity, which requires that for at least two distributions, x and y, in which (1) the best-off person is the same in each distribution, (2) the best-off person is better off in y than in x, and (3) everyone else is better off in x than in y, x is at least as just as y.

benefit to the worse-off person, then the result is less just). Leximin satisfies it. Indeed, an important result is the following:

Observation 2: If the justice ranking relation satisfies Ordering, Anonymity, Strong Pareto, and Hammond Equity, then leximin is the justice ranking relation.[21]

This is an important result for *understanding* leximin, but it fails, I believe, to offer a *justification* of leximin. Hammond Equity is, I claim, implausible. To see this, consider <1,99,100,...100> and <2,3,100,...100>, where the average is slightly less than 100 and where the difference between 3 and 100 units is very significant. Hammond Equity requires that the second distribution be judged more just, because it is better for the worse-off person. This, I claim, is implausible. Benefits to the worse-off person do not have such absolute priority. In particular, when, for two distributions, (1) the two affected individuals are both below average in both, (2) the first distribution, compared with the second distribution, is only *slightly* better for the worse-off person but *very significantly* worse for the better-off person, and (3) the first distribution leaves the worse-off person *only slightly* worse off than the better-off person, then the second distribution is more (not less) just.

It is worth noting that Irrelevance of Cardinality (assuming that benefits are cardinally measurable) and Hammond Equity are, I suggest (without argument), not merely conditions that need not be satisfied, but conditions that a theory *must violate* to be plausible. Any theory that makes available information about cardinality irrelevant, or that always gives absolute priority to a worse-off person, is implausible. Given that leximin satisfies these two conditions, we have, I suggest, reason for rejecting leximin. Again, obviously this is controversial and requires a more careful examination than that given here.

Any plausible theory, I have suggested, will violate Hammond Equity. This thought is roughly captured by the following condition:

Minimal Aggregative Efficiency: At least sometimes, decreasing the benefits of one person and increasing the benefits of a better-off person by a greater amount makes things more just.[22]

---

[21] See Sen (1977a: 1547). The result is based on Hammond (1976) and d'Aspremont and Gevers (1977).

[22] Unlike the other conditions I formulate, this one and Extended Pigou-Dalton are my own inventions and have not, as far as I know, been systematically studied.

This is essentially just the denial that benefits to a worse-off person always have absolute priority. As such, it is extremely weak, and likely to be accepted by a wide range of theorists. Leximin, however, violates this condition.

Let us now turn to weak prioritarian totalism. Consider the following condition:

Irrelevance of External Reference Points: For any two distributions, modifying everyone's benefits by multiplying by a positive constant (perhaps one) and then adding a constant (perhaps zero), the same two constants for all persons, does not affect the ranking of the two distributions with respect to justice (if x is at least as just as y before the modification, then it is also so afterward).[23]

The idea here is that there are no external reference points – for example, natural zero for benefits, level of adequacy for benefits, or upper or lower bounds on benefits – that are relevant to justice. According to this condition, justice is a purely relative matter, and changing everyone's benefits in the same specified way produces a distribution that is equally just with the original. If some external reference point were relevant, then at least sometimes adding a constant benefit to everyone would, for example, make a difference to the justice ranking by changing someone's relationship to the reference point in a relevant way (e.g., moving someone from below to above the adequacy level). The above condition holds, for example, that the ranking of <2,5> and <1,6> must be the same as that of <5,8> and <4,9> (the latter pair is obtained from the former pair by adding three to each person's benefits).

The following result is worth noting:

Observation 3: If the justice ranking relation satisfies Ordering, Anonymity, Strong Pareto, Strong Separability, Pigou-Dalton, Minimal Aggregative Efficiency, and Irrelevance of External Reference Points, then weak prioritarian totalism is the justice ranking relation.[24]

The only theories satisfying Ordering, Anonymity, Strong Pareto, and Strong Separability are leximin, leximax (making the best-off person as well off as possible, etc.), strong prioritarian totalism and related views, totalism,

---

[23] In the social choice literature, this condition is known as Cardinal Full Comparability Invariance.

[24] See Theorem 5 of Sen (1977a: 1549), which is based on Deschamps and Gevers (1978). I have added the conditions of Minimal Aggregative Efficiency and Pigou-Dalton.

and weak prioritarian totalism. Pigou-Dalton rules out totalism and leximax. Minimal Aggregative Efficiency rules out leximin. Irrelevance of External Reference Points rules out (as I'll explain below) strong prioritarian totalism and related views. Weak prioritarian totalism is thus the only theory satisfying all these conditions.

The crucial question here is whether Irrelevance of External Reference Points is plausible. Leximin satisfies this condition. It gives absolute priority to a worse-off person no matter what the benefit levels (e.g., it favors $<2,5>$ over $<1,6>$ and, for any n, favors $<2+n,5+n>$ over $<1+n,6+n>$). Weak prioritarian totalism also invokes no external reference point. If one distribution has a greater total than another does, this remains true if n units are added to everyone's benefits. Furthermore, if one distribution has the same total, but is better according to leximin (e.g., $<2,5>$ vs. $<1,6>$), this remains true if n units are added to everyone's benefits.

Strong prioritarian totalism, however, does require, except under very special circumstances, the relevance of an external reference point. It requires that the weights be anchored in some external reference point and not merely determined in relative terms, which would result in a violation of Strong Separability. More specifically, it requires that for any given interpersonally valid scale for measuring benefits (no matter how the zero point and unit are set), there is a corresponding decreasing positive weighting scale for benefits. If the scale for measuring benefits is changed (by changing the zero point or the unit), the weighting scale must also be correspondingly changed. For example, if the weight for the increase from 4 to 5 units of benefit on a given scale is n, and then the scale is changed by doubling the size of the units, then the weight on this new scale for the increase from 2 (which was 4 on the old scale) to 2.5 (which was 5 on the old scale) must also be n.

Irrelevance of External Reference Points is not, I claim, a very plausible condition. On any plausible conception of benefits, it will be possible to distinguish, for example, cases where a worse-off person is in abject poverty (relative to those benefits) and cases where he or she is relatively prosperous (both of which appeal to an external reference point; benefits are not viewed merely in relative terms). More specifically, it's plausible that the extra weight given by justice to the benefits of a worse-off person compared with those of a person who is n units better off is greater when the worse-off person is abjectly poor than when he or she is very affluent. Irrelevance of External Reference Points, however, rules out these appeals to absolute poverty and affluence, and is thus not very plausible.

We should then, I suggest, reject Irrelevance of External Reference Points. Indeed, a theory of justice is plausible only if it violates this condition. Thus, we have some reason for rejecting weak prioritarian totalism (as well as totalism) and leximin.

Let us turn now to strong prioritarian totalism, and consider the following condition:

Continuity: For any two distributions, x and y, if there is an infinite sequence of distributions such that (1) the sequence converges (at the limit) to x (i.e., for each person, the benefits to him or her in the sequence converge to his or her benefits in x), and (2) each distribution in the sequence is at least as just as y, then x is at least as just as y.

The core idea here is twofold: (1) If all the distributions in the sequence that converges to x are *equally as just* as y, then x should also be judged equally as just. (2) If all the distributions in the sequence that converges to x are *more just* than y, then x either should also be judged as more just than y or should be judged equally as just. Distribution x should not be judged as less just, because this would involve a kind of gap (x is less just, but all the members of the sequence that converges to x are more just).

We can note the following conjecture (suggested to me by Bertil Tungodden):

Observation 4: If the justice ranking relation satisfies Ordering, Anonymity, Strong Pareto, Pigou-Dalton, Strong Separability, and Continuity, then strong prioritarian totalism is the justice ranking relation.[25]

Continuity is violated by leximin and weak prioritarian totalism, but is satisfied by strong prioritarian totalism. To see that leximin violates Continuity, consider a two-person case with an infinite sequence of distributions starting with <2,2> that approaches (but never reaches) <1,1> at the limit (e.g., <2,2>, <1.5,1.5>, <1.25,1.25>, etc.). Each member of this sequence will be judged better off than <1,3> by leximin (because the first person is the worst off and is better off), but <1,1> is judged worse than <1,3> (because both people are worst-off persons and each is worse off). This violates Continuity. To see that weak prioritarian totalism violates Continuity, consider an infinite sequence of distributions starting with <3,1> that approaches (but never reaches) <2,0> at the limit (e.g., <3,1>, <2.5,0.5>, <2.25,0.25>, etc.). Each member of this sequence will be judged better off than <1,1> by weak prioritarian totalism (because each member has a greater total), but <2,0> is judged worse off (because it has the same total,

---

[25] This result is from Blackorby et al. (2002) and assumes that there are at least three individuals. They call strong prioritarian totalism "generalized utilitarianism."

but is leximin inferior). This violates Continuity. Strong prioritarian totalism, on the other hand, satisfies Continuity, roughly because it gives only
finitely (and not infinitesimally or infinitely) extra weight to the worse off.

Strong prioritarian totalism, it turns out, is the *only* theory satisfying
Continuity and the conditions above. Continuity thus provides support,
in the prioritarian context, for strong prioritarian totalism. It's doubtful,
however, that we should accept Continuity as a condition for justice. It
would be formally nice for justice to behave in a continuous fashion, but it's
far from clear that justice must do so. It may, for example, be implausible
for leximin to give absolute priority to the worse off, but this implausibility
stems from the *substantive* implausibility of such a judgment and not, it
seems, from the formal requirement of Continuity. Continuity rules out
treating some considerations as lexically posterior to others, but there is
nothing incoherent, or even obviously implausible, about such treatment.

Let us consider one final condition that supports strong prioritarian
totalism:

Extended Pigou-Dalton: At least sometimes, decreasing one person's
benefits and increasing a worse-off person's benefits by less, when this
still leaves the originally worse-off person no better off than the originally
better-off person, makes things more just.

Like Pigou-Dalton, this requires that, under certain conditions, justice
be increased by certain nonreversing downward transfers. Unlike Pigou-
Dalton, which deals with "even" ("fixed amount") downward transfers,
Extended Pigou-Dalton deals with "inefficient" downward transfers, which
are downward transfers where the benefit to the recipient is less than the cost
to the donor. Some benefits are lost. Furthermore, unlike Pigou-Dalton,
which holds that "even" nonreversing downward transfers *always* increase
justice, Extended Pigou-Dalton only requires that "inefficient" nonreversing downward transfers *sometimes* increase justice.

Extended Pigou-Dalton is a very weak condition, and is likely to be
endorsed by a wide range of theorists. It is satisfied by leximin and by strong
prioritarian totalism, but it is violated by weak prioritarian totalism. The
latter always favors a distribution with a greater total, and thus (like standard
totalism) never favors inefficient transfers, whereas Extended Pigou-Dalton
requires that sometimes inefficient nonreversing downward transfers make
things more just.

Consider, then, the following observation:

Observation 5: Strong prioritarian totalism satisfies Ordering, Anonymity, Strong Pareto, Pigou-Dalton, Strong Separability, Minimal

Aggregative Efficiency, and Extended Pigou-Dalton, but leximin violates Minimal Aggregative Efficiency and weak prioritarian totalism violates Extended Pigou-Dalton.

Imposing Minimal Aggregative Efficiency and Extended Pigou-Dalton is thus sufficient to rule out leximin and weak prioritarian totalism, and leave standing strong prioritarian totalism. The above conditions, however, do not fully characterize the latter view, for there are other related theories that satisfy all these conditions (see example in note 26). Thus, adding Extended Pigou-Dalton brings us closer to fully characterizing strong prioritarian totalism, but does not suffice. I do not know whether anyone has fully characterized strong prioritarian totalism without appealing to Continuity.[26]

Strong prioritarian totalism is, I believe, the most plausible prioritarian view. Even it, however, is subject to a powerful objection – at least where the benefits being distributed are generated by brute luck. Suppose that there are just two people: a person with no benefits and a person with enormous levels of benefits. Suppose that you can give either a large benefit to the rich person or a much smaller benefit to the poor person. The Finitely Weighted Total View says that, if the larger benefit to the rich person is sufficiently larger, then it is more just to give that benefit to the rich person than to give the much smaller benefit to the poor person. This is because, no matter how finitely much greater weight is given to the benefits of the poor person, the increased weighted benefits for the rich person will be greater, if the increase in benefits is sufficiently greater. This seems, however, to be mistaken. In a context in which everyone has an equal claim to benefits (e.g., the distribution of brute-luck benefits), justice gives *absolute priority* to benefits to a person who remains with no more than an average share over those to individuals who already have at least an average share. Leximin is at least right about this kind of case.

This objection gives a special role to the benchmark of an average benefit, and it will be raised by certain kinds of egalitarian theorists. Let us therefore now consider egalitarianism, our third distribution-sensitive theory of justice.

---

[26] The following theory satisfies all the above conditions: a distribution is at least as just as another if and only if (1) the total of weighted benefits received by the poor (given a specified poverty line) is greater, or (2) the total of weighted benefits received by the poor is the same, and the total of weighted benefits received by the nonpoor is at least as great. This theory is just like strong prioritarian totalism except that it gives lexical priority to benefits to the poor over the nonpoor. I'm indebted to Bertil Tungodden for this example.

5. EGALITARIANISM

Pure egalitarian theories – which make justice depend solely on how equal the distribution of benefits is – satisfy Ordering, Anonymity, and Pigou-Dalton, but violate Strong Pareto. They violate the latter because they view perfect equality as more just than a Pareto improvement thereto (e.g., <2,2> is more just than <8,9>). This reflects the fact that pure egalitarianism is not in any way concerned with increasing the benefits that people receive. It is only concerned with how equally they are distributed. Following Sen, I have suggested that a plausible theory of justice (understood as concerned with what we owe others) will be both distribution sensitive (satisfy at least Pigou-Dalton) and sensitive to some kind of efficiency consideration (satisfy at least Strong Pareto). Hence, pure egalitarianism is not, I believe, a plausible theory of justice.

In what follows, we shall be concerned with impure forms of egalitarianism. More specifically, we shall assume that a plausible version of egalitarianism may only satisfy the following weak egalitarian condition. The condition appeals to the notion of *anonymous Pareto incomparability*, which holds between two distributions if and only if the first distribution, *and each of its permutations* (i.e., same pattern of distribution but perhaps with individuals occupying different positions), is Pareto incomparable with the second (i.e., better for some people, but worse for others). For example, <3,5> is Pareto incomparable with <4,3>, but it is not anonymously Pareto incomparable, as <3,4> is a permutation of <4,3> and is Pareto inferior to <3,5>. Distribution <3,5> is, however, anonymously Pareto incomparable with <6,2>, because it and its only distinct permutation, <5,3>, are each Pareto incomparable with <6,2>. Anonymous Pareto incomparability entails Pareto incomparability, but not vice versa.

Consider, then, the following condition:

Weak Egalitarianism: If two distributions are anonymously Pareto incomparable, and one is more equal than the other is, then it is more just than the other is.

This is a very weak egalitarian condition. Not only is it silent when one distribution is Pareto superior to the other, it is also silent when one distribution is Pareto incomparable to the other but is not anonymously Pareto incomparable. Some egalitarians may want equality to be determinative whenever distributions are Pareto incomparable (even if not anonymously Pareto incomparable), but we shall start with this weak condition.

Weak Egalitarianism requires justice to be based partly on the promotion of equality, but it is compatible with Strong Pareto and our other background conditions (Ordering, Anonymity, and Pigou-Dalton). Its content, however, is not clear until we know how equality is measured. The rest of this section will be primarily concerned with the measurement of equality, a topic on which Sen has been extremely influential.[27]

The concept of equality also satisfies Ordering (or at least reflexivity and transitivity), Anonymity, and Pigou-Dalton, as defined in the background section, but now understood as applying to the relation of being-at-least-as-*equal* rather than to the relation of being-at-least-as-*just*.

An obvious condition on equality is the following:

Perfect Equality: Perfect equality obtains when everyone has the same benefit level.

There are other conditions that the concept of equality satisfies, but these will suffice for our purposes. These conditions, as Sen and others have noted, entail that, where the population size and mean are fixed, *Lorenz domination*, as defined shortly, is sufficient for being more equal. One distribution Lorenz dominates another if and only if (1) for any real number, n, inclusively between 0 and 100, the percentage of total benefits allocated to the poorest (in terms of the benefits) n percent of the population is at least as great for the first distribution as it is for the second, and (2) for some real number, n, between 0 and 100, that percentage is greater. For example, for <1,2,3,4>, the Lorenz values for 25 percent, 50 percent, 75 percent, and 100 percent of the population are 10 percent, 30 percent, 60 percent, and 100 percent respectively, and for <2,2,2,4> the corresponding Lorenz values are 20 percent, 40 percent, 60 percent, and 100 percent respectively. Thus, the second distribution Lorenz dominates the first. (For example, it gives 20 percent, rather than 10 percent, of the total benefits to the poorest 25 percent.) By contrast, for <1,3,3,3> the corresponding Lorenz values are 10 percent, 40 percent, 70 percent, and 100 percent respectively. It neither Lorenz dominates nor is Lorenz dominated by <2,2,2,4>, as it gives a smaller share of the benefits (10 percent vs. 20 percent) to the poorest 25 percent, but gives a larger share (70 percent vs. 60 percent) to the poorest 75 percent.

---

[27] See, for example, Sen (1978, 1992, and especially 1997) and Dasgupta et al. (1973). See also Temkin (1993) for an excellent philosophical discussion of the issues in equality measurement.

The interesting result, connecting the concept of equality and Lorenz domination, is this:

Observation 1: Given that the equality relation satisfies Ordering (more minimally: transitivity), Anonymity, and Pigou-Dalton, for any two distributions having the same population size and the same mean (i.e., average), if one distribution Lorenz dominates the other, then it is more equal.[28]

For a fixed population size and fixed mean benefit, Lorenz domination provides the core of the equality relation. This leaves open three issues for the measurement of equality for egalitarian theories of justice: (1) For a fixed population size and fixed mean benefits, what determines whether one distribution is more equal than another when neither Lorenz dominates the other? (2) How are judgments of equality affected when the size of the mean benefit is varied? (3) How are judgments of equality affected when the population size is varied? Because of space limitations, I shall address only the first two questions.

With respect to extension of the equality relation beyond Lorenz domination, for a fixed population size and mean, a common condition is the following:

Diminishing Transfers: Equality is increased by the combination of (1) a strictly nonreversing *downward* transfer of m units ($m > 0$) from a person j to a person who has n units fewer of benefits ($n > 2m$), and (2) a strictly nonreversing *upward* transfer of m units from a person k, who is more than m units better off than j, to a person who has n units more benefits than k.

The idea of this principle is that the impact on equality of a nonreversing transfer of a given amount to a person whose benefit level is lower by a given amount is greater when it is between people with lower levels of benefits (e.g., among poor people) than when it is between people with higher levels of benefits (e.g., among rich people). That is, there is a decreasing marginal impact on equality for a fixed transfer amount and a fixed transfer distance. Thus, for a fixed transfer amount and distance, if a downward transfer is combined with an upward transfer, the net result should increase equality

---

[28] See, for example, Sen (1997: 54) and Dasgupta et al. (1973). Note that for a fixed mean and population size of n, Lorenz dominance is equivalent to second-order dominance: for all integers i between 1 and n, the total of benefits for the poorest i people is at least as great, and for some such i it is greater. The result is based on a result of Hardy, Littlewood, and Polya in the 1930s.

as long as the transferor of the upward transfer is better off after the transfer than the transferee of the downward transfer was before the transfer.

This principle has a fair amount of plausibility. I believe, however, that it is slightly too strong. For it requires that $<10,10,30,70,100>$ (mean of 44) be judged as *more equal* than $<0,20,40,60,100>$ (mean of 44) – even though it gives fewer benefits to those below the mean (50 vs. 60). The former distribution is obtainable from the latter by transferring 10 units from the person with 20 to the person with 0, and transferring 10 units from the person with 40 (slightly below the mean of 44) to the person with 60 (already above the mean). Diminishing Transfers does not take into account that some upward transfers are from people below the mean to people above the mean. Such transfers, I claim, can decrease equality when coupled with a nonreversing downward transfer of an equal amount and an equal distance. A slight weakening of Diminishing Transfers, however, is plausible:

Non-Upward-Crossing Diminishing Transfers: Equality is increased by the combination of (1) an even strictly nonreversing downward transfer of m units ($m > 0$) from a person j to a person who has n units fewer of benefits ($n > 2m$), and (2) an even strictly nonreversing upward transfer of m units from a person k, who is more than m units better off than j, to a person who has n units more benefits than k, *where the transferor and the transferee of this upward transfer are on the same side of the mean (both above or both below).*[29]

This condition is exactly like the original except that it does not apply where the upward transferor is below the mean and the upward transferee is above the mean. Non-Upward-Crossing Diminishing Transfers is, I believe, a plausible principle. Even if it (or the original Diminishing Transfers) is accepted, that does not completely determine how equality is measured – even in the case of fixed population size and mean. Sen discusses various measures, but space limitations prevent me from addressing this issue further.[30]

Let us turn now to the main question of how changes in the mean benefit (for a fixed population size) affect equality. More specifically, we can ask what the impact on equality is of (1) increasing everyone's benefit by the

---

[29] I introduce this condition in Vallentyne (2000), in which I defend a particular conception of equality. There, I defend a strengthening of this condition, which drops the requirement that the distance between the donor and recipient be the same for the upward transfer as for the downward transfer.

[30] It is worth noting, however, that the Gini coefficient, a common measure of inequality, violates the weakened diminishing transfer condition.

same amount, or (2) multiplying everyone's benefit by the same positive factor. The following are the main answers that have been given to this question.

Constant Additions Invariance: Equality is unaffected by increasing each person's benefits by the same amount.

This is the standard condition for an absolute conception of equality. It holds that equality is based on the absolute magnitude of the differences in people's benefits. Increasing everyone's benefits by the same amount does not affect these differences and thus does not affect the level of equality. Distribution <1,2> is equally equal with <2,3>.

Constant Additions Improvements: Equality is increased by increasing each person's benefits by the same amount.

This is a standard condition for conceptions of equality that are at least partially relative to the mean. The idea here is that although constant additions do not affect the differences between individuals, they do make those differences a smaller percentage of the benefits that people have (since everyone has more). Hence, equality is increased.

Proportionate Increases Invariance: Equality is unaffected by multiplying each person's benefits by the same positive factor.[31]

This is the standard condition for a purely mean-relative view of benefits. It holds that equality is based on the proportionate shares rather than the absolute benefit levels. Thus, increasing everyone's benefits by the same proportion does not affect the level of equality. Distribution <1,2> is equally equal with <2,4>. In both cases, the first person has one third of the benefits.

Proportionate Increases Worsening: When some inequality is present, equality is decreased by multiplying each person's benefits by the same factor greater than one.

This is the standard condition for views that are at least partially absolute. It holds that <2,4> is less equal than <1,2>, on the ground that in absolute terms there is a greater difference in benefits in <2,4>.

For the purposes of egalitarian theories of justice, Proportionate Increases Invariance (and any purely relative view of equality) is, I would

---

[31] A more careful statement of this condition would make it conditional on there being a natural zero for benefits and on all benefits being nonnegative or all being nonpositive.

argue, implausible. There is much less relevant inequality in <1,2> than there is in <100,200>. Indeed, Proportionate Increases Worsening seems highly plausible. The assessment of Constant Additions Invariance and Constant Additions Improvements is more difficult, and here I leave that issue open.

We have seen, then, that there are many controversial issues concerning the measurement of equality. Before concluding, we shall note a recent striking result, which shows that, if certain seemingly plausible conditions on justice and on equality are satisfied, then the justice relation must hold that a distribution is more just if it is maximin better (i.e., makes the worst-off person better off). This is a striking result, because it seems to show that a plausible egalitarian theory must overlap very significantly with the prioritarian theory of leximin.

The result rests on one further condition concerning the measurement of equality. It concerns the effect on equality of increasing the benefits of all the worst-off persons, whereas decreasing the benefits of all the best-off persons. If there is only one worst-off and only one best-off person (i.e., if there are no ties for worst off or for best off), then the condition concerns changes in only those two people. If, however, there is a tie for worst off, or for best off, then the condition concerns the same change for *all* the worst off, and *all* the best off. Consider, then, the following:

Strong Conditional Contracting Extremes: Equality is increased by the combined effect of (1) increasing the benefits of all the worst-off individuals without causing any of them to cease to be a worst-off person, and (2) decreasing the benefits of all the best-off individuals without causing any of them to cease to be a best-off person.

The rough idea is that equality is increased by contracting the extremes of a distribution (reducing the benefits for those at the very top, but still leaving them at the top, and increasing the benefits at the very bottom, but still leaving them at the bottom, without any changes to anyone else). This condition judges <2,2,5,8,8,8> to be more equal than <1,1,5,9,9,9>.

This condition is highly plausible. Indeed, it seems to be part of the concept of equality – and not merely part of a plausible, but debatable, conception of equality for the theory of justice.

Bertil Tungodden has established the following:

Observation 2: If (1) the justice relation satisfies Ordering (more minimally: transitivity and reflexivity), Strong Pareto, Anonymity, and Weak Egalitarianism, and (2) the equality relation satisfies Strong Conditional

Contracting Extremes, then x is more just than y if it is *maximin* better (i.e., makes the worst-off person better off).[32]

This result doesn't establish that leximin is the only plausible form of Paretian egalitarianism, but it yields something very close. If the conditions of the theorem are satisfied, then (as with leximin) making the worst-off person better off always makes things more just. The result leaves open how two distributions are ranked by justice in the case where the worst-off person is equally well off in each distribution (whereas leximin then requires the ranking to be based on how well off the second worst-off person is, etc.).

The main problem with leximin – its near monomaniacal concern for the worst off – arises with its maximin core as well. Hence, this maximin result is troubling for egalitarians who want to avoid this feature. It appears that Weak Egalitarianism (which holds that equality prevails between anonymously Pareto-incomparable distributions) cannot plausibly be combined with Strong Pareto (a weak efficiency condition) without (given the other seemingly plausible assumptions) being committed to maximin betterness being sufficient for greater justice.

I cannot here examine this troubling result. I shall simply state my (very tentative) belief that some of the underlying conditions are not as plausible as they seem. In particular, Anonymity for justice may not be (rather surprisingly) plausible (although it is a plausible condition for equality). In the presence of the plausible Strong Pareto, which gives priority to a weak kind of efficiency, Anonymity radically increases the kind of efficiency that is given priority, and thus radically decreases the role for equality. The role of equality is limited, not merely to cases where one distribution is Pareto incomparable to another, but more generally to cases where one distribution is *anonymously* Pareto incomparable to the other. For example, Strong Pareto entails that $<1,3,9>$ is more just than $<1,3,4>$, and then Anonymity adds that it is also more just than $<4,1,3>$. This latter distribution is Pareto incomparable with $<1,3,4>$ and more equal. Some egalitarians may want to hold that it is more just (or at least not less just). Anonymity in this context, however, rules out this judgment. Hence, I believe, this strong form of anonymity may be rejected for some weaker form that leaves more room for egalitarian considerations.

The rejection of Anonymity, however, may not be sufficient to avoid this troubling result. A second way of challenging the result is to challenge

---

[32] See Tungodden (2000). He does not explicitly appeal to Weak Egalitarianism as a condition of justice or to Strong Conditional Contracting Extremes as a condition on equality. Instead, he combines them into one condition on justice.

the framework in which it is formulated. It assumes that justice can be articulated in terms of a transitive binary relationship (of being-at-least-as-just-as), but this is not obviously so. A weaker conception of justice would only require that justice determine, for any given feasible set of distributions, which distributions are just. This approach does not require a general transitive ranking of distributions in terms of justice; it only requires the selection of just alternatives for a given feasible set. Of course, it may be that this second approach, once various plausible assumptions are made, will also produce the maximin result. Further investigation is needed.[33]

In summary, until a clear case can be made for rejecting one or more of the crucial conditions in Tungodden's result (e.g., Anonymity and transitivity), it appears that it may not be possible to have a Paretian egalitarian theory of justice that is radically different from the leximin prioritarian theory of justice. This is an important issue that needs to be resolved.

6. CONCLUSION

Three of the main theories of justice are sufficientarianism, prioritarianism, and egalitarianism. Sen's work in this area has vastly increased our understanding of the key issues by identifying key conditions that underlie each approach. In presenting a survey of these issues, I have given indications of which approaches seem plausible. Obviously, this is all very controversial, and my brief assessment should be understood solely as the beginning of a more careful examination.

References

Blackorby, C., W. Bossert, and D. Donaldson (2002). "Utilitarianism and the Theory of Justice," in Arrow, Sen, and Suzumura (eds.), *Handbook of Social Choice and Welfare*, Vol. 1 (Amsterdam: North-Holland).

Broome, J. (2003). "Equality vs. Priority: A Useful Distinction," in Wikler and Murray (eds.), *'Goodness' and 'Fairness': Ethical Issues in Health Resource Allocation* (unpublished).

Dasgupta, P., A. Sen, and D. Starrett (1973). "Notes on the Measurement of Inequality," *Journal of Economic Theory*, 6, 180–7.

---

[33] The general issue of whether social choice (e.g., justice) should be understood as based on a binary ranking relation or on a choice function (that selects from the feasible set) has been extensively studied by economists. In particular, it is well known that if certain expansion and contraction consistency properties are accepted, then the choice function approach will reduce to the binary relation approach. See, for example, Sen (1977b). In Tungodden and Vallentyne (2005), we examine whether these properties should be accepted.

d'Aspremont, C., and L. Gevers (1977). "Equity and the Informational Basis of Collective Choice," *Review of Economic Studies*, 44, 199–210.

Deschamps, R., and L. Gevers (1978). "Leximin and Totalism: A Joint Characterization," *Journal of Economic Theory*, 17, 143–63.

Fleurbaey, M. (2003). "Equality versus Priority: How Relevant is the Distinction?" in Wikler and Murray (eds.), *'Goodness' and 'Fairness': Ethical Issues in Health Resource Allocation* (unpublished).

Foster, J. (1984). "On Economic Poverty: A Survey of Aggregate Measures," in Basmann and Rhodes, Jr. (eds.), *Advances in Econometrics*, Vol. 3 (Greenwich, CT: JAI Press).

Foster, J., J. Greer, and E. Thorbecke (1984). "A Class of Decomposable Poverty Measures," *Econometrica*, 52, 761–6.

Frankfurt, H. (1987). "Equality as a Moral Idea," *Ethics*, 98, 21–43.

Gevers, L. (1979). "On Interpersonal Comparability and Social Welfare Orderings," *Econometrica*, 47, 75–89.

Hammond, P. J. (1976). "Equity, Arrow's Conditions, and Rawls' Difference Principle," *Econometrica*, 44, 793–804.

Jensen, K. K. (2003). "What is the Difference between (Moderate) Egalitarianism and Prioritarianism?" *Economics and Philosophy*, 19, 89–109.

McKerlie, D. (1994). "Egalitarianism," *Dialogue*, 23, 223–38.

Parfit, D. (1991). "Equality or Priority?" (1991 Lindley lecture), in Clayton and Williams (eds.), *The Ideal of Equality* (New York: St. Martin's Press).

Rachels, S. (1998). "Counterexamples to the Transitivity of *Better Than*," *Australasian Journal of Philosophy*, 76, 71–83.

Roberts, K. (1980). "Possibility Theorems with Interpersonally Comparable Welfare Levels," *Review of Economic Studies*, 47, 409–20.

Sen, A. (1970). *Collective Choice and Social Welfare* (San Francisco: Holden-Day).

Sen, A. (1974). "Rawls versus Bentham: An Axiomatic Examination of the Pure Distribution Problem," *Theory and Decision*, 4, 301–10. Reprinted with slight revisions in Daniels (ed.), *Reading Rawls* (New York: Basic Books, 1975).

Sen, A. (1976a). "Poverty: An Ordinal Approach to Measurement," *Econometrica*, 44, 219–31. Reprinted in Sen, *Choice, Welfare, and Measurement* (Oxford: Basil Blackwell, 1982), 373–87.

Sen, A. (1976b). "Welfare Inequalities and Rawlsian Axiomatics," *Theory and Decision*, 7, 243–62. Reprinted in Butts and Hintikka (eds.), *Logic, Methodology, and Philosophy of Science* (Dordrecht: D. Reidel, 1977).

Sen, A. (1977a). "On Weights and Measurements: Informational Constraints in Social Welfare Analysis," *Econometrica*, 45, 1539–72. Reprinted in Sen, *Choice, Welfare, and Measurement* (Oxford: Basil Blackwell, 1982).

Sen, A. (1977b). "Social Choice Theory: A Re-Examination," *Econometrica*, 45, 53–89. Reprinted in Sen, *Choice, Welfare, and Measurement* (Oxford: Basil Blackwell, 1982).

Sen, A. (1978). "Ethical Measurement of Inequality: Some Difficulties," in Kreller and Shorrocks (eds.), *Personal Income Distribution* (Amsterdam: North-Holland).

Reprinted in Sen, *Choice, Welfare, and Measurement* (Oxford: Basil Blackwell, 1982).

Sen, A. (1979). "Issues in the Measurement of Poverty," *Scandinavian Journal of Economics*, 81, 285–307.

Sen, A. (1985). *Commodities and Capabilities* (Amsterdam: North-Holland).

Sen, A. (1986). "Social Choice Theory," in Arrow and Intriligator (eds.), *Handbook of Mathematical Economics*, Vol. 3 (Amsterdam: North-Holland).

Sen, A. (1987). *On Ethics and Economics* (Oxford: Basil Blackwell).

Sen, A. (1992). *Inequality Reexamined* (Cambridge, MA: Harvard University Press).

Sen, A. (1997). *On Economic Inequality*, enlarged ed. (Oxford: Oxford University Press). Original edition published in 1973.

Sen, A. (2002). *Rationality and Freedom* (Cambridge, MA: Harvard University Press).

Temkin, L. (1987). "Intransitivity, and the Mere Addition Paradox," *Philosophy and Public Affairs*, 16, 138–87.

Temkin, L. (1993). *Inequality* (Oxford: Oxford University Press).

Temkin, L. (1996). "A Continuum Argument for Intransitivity," *Philosophy and Public Affairs*, 25, 175–210.

Tungodden, B. (2000). "Egalitarianism: Is Leximin the Only Option?" *Economics and Philosophy*, 16, 229–46.

Tungodden, B. (2003). "The Value of Equality," *Economics and Philosophy*, 19, 1–44.

Tungodden, B., and P. Vallentyne (2005). "On the Possibility of Paretian Egalitarianism," *Journal of Philosophy*, 102, 126–54.

Vallentyne, P. (2000). "Equality, Efficiency, and Priority for the Worse Off," *Economics and Philosophy*, 16, 1–19.

7 | Famine, Poverty, and Property Rights

STEVEN SCALET AND DAVID SCHMIDTZ

What causes famine? President Robert Mugabe of Zimbabwe blames drought.[1] Amartya Sen observes,

> Blaming nature can, of course, be very consoling and comforting. It can be of great use especially to those in positions of power and responsibility. Comfortable inaction is, however, typically purchased at a very heavy price – a price that is paid by others, often with their lives.... The points of overriding importance are: that there is no real evidence to doubt that all famines in the modern world are preventable by human action; that many countries – even some very poor ones – manage consistently to prevent them; that when people die of starvation there is almost inevitably some massive social failure (whether or not a natural phenomenon had an initiating role in the causal process); and that the responsibilities for that failure deserve explicit attention and analysis, not evasion. There is, of course, much more to be said, but we have to say the first things first. (Drèze and Sen 1989: 4)

Of course, Mugabe has his reasons for wanting to blame nature rather than his own policies. If Amartya Sen's analysis of causes of famine is right, though, we should suspect that the real problem lies in a collapse of Zimbabwe's system of property rights. This chapter explains and evaluates Sen's analysis.

THE TRADITION SEN CHALLENGED

One fact about famines seems plain enough: people starve because there is not enough food. For example, a cyclone and torrential rains led to a

---

[1] "Eyewitness: Zimbabwe in Turmoil," *BBC*, 11 July 2002.

We thank Christopher Morris for his patience in bringing this project to fruition, and we thank Montgomery Brown, Ingrid Gregg, and David Kennedy of the Earhart Foundation for generously supporting us on both this and other projects over the years.

shortage of rice in the Great Bengal Famine of 1943. The Famine Inquiry Commission in 1945 concluded that the primary cause of the famine was this shortage of rice, killing over 1.5 million people (Sen 1981: 57). In Ethiopia, a drought led to crop failure causing the famine of 1972–4, killing between 50,000 and 200,000 Ethiopians. In the Sahel, low rainfalls led to food shortages and famine from 1968–73. In Bangladesh, the famine of 1974 follows the same basic story: "First the floods; then the famine. So runs the capsule story of the Bangladesh Famine of 1974" (Sen 1981: 131). In all these cases, it seems, the cause of famine is food shortages, initiated by some natural event.

These facts suggest a thesis that Sen calls food availability decline (FAD). The thesis states that "famines occur if and only if there is a sharp decline in average food availability per head" (Sen 1981: 118). Proponents of FAD measure and understand famines by gathering aggregate statistics that document declines or expected declines in food output within some regional population.

FAD is what Sen rejects in his *Poverty and Famines: An Essay on Entitlement and Deprivation* (Sen 1981). He studied food output statistics for each of the famines mentioned above and found no evidence that food output declined significantly in three of these cases (Bengal, Ethiopia, Bangladesh). In some cases, food output *increased* and included exports from famine-stricken regions (Sen 1981: 161). And, in the one case where famine did correlate with food availability decline – the Sahel famine – Sen argues that understanding *who* starved and *why* has little to do with aggregate statistics about food decline. Millions died of starvation in the last century. People continue to die of starvation in this century – and food shortage, Sen argues, is not the real cause.

SEN'S ENTITLEMENT APPROACH

In Sen's words, there is a difference between a person not *having* enough food and there not *being* enough food (Sen 1981: 1). People starve because they lack command or entitlements over food, and all sorts of reasons beyond overall food supply explain why people lack this command. There may be times and places where individuals cannot get enough food because there is not enough food. This is not necessarily the root of the problem, though, and Sen doubts it is even typically so.

Persons are exposed to starvation, Sen argues, if they are unable to convert what they own (through production or trade) into a bundle that includes enough food to sustain them. To understand why such inability would be prevalent in a given time and place, Sen holds, the thing we need to understand about that time and place is not its food supply so much as its entitlement system. The food shortage thesis, which Sen rejects, recommends a macro analysis that collects aggregate statistics about food supply. Sen's entitlement approach is a micro analysis that studies property relations among occupational sectors. The advantage of Sen's approach is that it draws our attention to a plurality of causes beyond food shortage, enabling us to understand why particular sectors of society endure famine, whereas others do not.

Another difference is conceptual. We can understand famine as a lack of food. In this sense, we understand property as a thing: food. Alternatively, we can understand famine as failed relationships among people regarding food.[2] Now we think of property as a relationship among persons – the rules governing how people create, exchange, and come to be rightful possessors of particular things. Sen's analysis is essentially about the legal rules regarding food rather than food itself.[3] If and when there is a problem with legal rules, people may not be able to do much about their inadequate access to the thing, and external efforts to increase aggregate supply will be unlikely to improve long-run access for people most in need, and may not help much even in the short run.

Boom Famine

We can return to the Great Bengal Famine of 1943 to illustrate Sen's analysis. Sen found that the famine year of 1943 had food output only 5 percent less than the average crop yield of the preceding five years. The crop yield was 13 percent *higher* than in 1941, a nonfamine year.[4] Yet, at least 1.5 million people died of starvation. General food shortages did not cause this famine.

Sen sought a property rights explanation. For Sen, the critical questions are, Who became unemployed? Who lost their ability to produce their own food? Did food prices fluctuate? What government benefits could people collect? What taxes were they required to pay?

---

[2] Stephen Munzer discusses this distinction (Munzer 1990).
[3] He writes, for example, "The focus on entitlement has the effect of emphasizing legal rights. . . . Starvation deaths can reflect legality with a vengeance" (Sen 1981: 166).
[4] Sen considers various data corrections, but all support his conclusion that the famine was not accompanied by a significant decline in overall food output in the Bengal region.

Despite the many deaths, only a fraction of the population was exposed to starvation. Victims generally lived in rural areas. Rural farmers and pastoralists were the hardest hit. Why? Sen found that the price of rice skyrocketed and incomes of agricultural workers did not keep pace. The initial rise in prices was caused by wartime inflationary pressures from military and civil expenditures, the first inflation to occur after twenty-five years of unchanged prices. Spiraling prices left agricultural workers destitute. Sen writes, "Those involved in military and civil defense works, in the army, in industries and commerce stimulated by war activities, and almost the entire normal population of Calcutta covered by distribution arrangements at subsidized prices could exercise strong demand pressures on food, while others excluded from this expansion or protection had to take the consequences of the rise in food prices" (Sen 1981: 77). Agricultural workers were more vulnerable than sharecroppers, too. Why? Because the stagnant wages of the former decreased their food entitlement (that is, their purchasing power). By contrast, the sharecroppers' direct payments in rice entitled them to enough food to survive. Sen describes the Great Bengal Famine as a "boom famine," because those who starved lacked the purchasing power to buy food that soared in price because of an economic expansion.[5]

Of course, this "expansion" had little to do with any genuine increase in productivity, but was instead an expansion of the money supply. Putting more money into circulation means that, other things being equal, the purchasing power of each unit of currency has to decrease. Thus, workers paid in units of the currency will have the same nominal after-tax income, but some of (in this case a lot of) the real buying power of the currency has been transferred away. By expanding the money supply, a government can transfer real wealth from agricultural workers, or other holders of its currency, and use it to finance military and civil expenditures, without officially raising taxes.[6]

Consider the Bangladesh famine of 1974 and the data on food availability shown in Table 7.1.

A famine occurred in 1974, but we would never have guessed this from data on average food availability. There was flooding in 1974, but it did not affect food availability much, and Sen says it did not affect food availability at all until the famine was already over. So, what happened? Sen says people anticipated that the floods would cause a food shortage, which led to frantic

---

[5] Sen considered other factors as well.
[6] Sen writes, "Bengal saw military and civil construction at a totally unprecedented scale, and the war expenditures were financed to a great extent by printing notes" (Sen 1981: 75).

Table 7.1 Food Availability in
Bangladesh

Year	Per head availability of grain (ounces per day)
1967	15.0
1968	15.7
1969	16.6
1970	17.1
1971	14.9
1972	15.3
1973	15.3
1974	15.9
1975	14.9
1976	14.8

Source: Drèze and Sen 1989: 27, Table 2.1.

buying, which led grain prices to explode, which led to famine. The problem
was not flooding per se, but anticipation of flooding in a market where, for
whatever reason, sellers of food (local and otherwise) were not attracted to
the area by the rising prices. Food normally exhibits a considerable elasticity
of supply that works to moderate price increases. (Indeed, famine relief
efforts sometimes send enough food to an area to drive local prices into
the ground, bankrupting local farmers, leaving them with no choice but to
migrate to the city, where they become additional mouths to feed rather
than people who would in time have helped to put the local economy back
on its feet.)

The wrong way to understand famine, argues Sen, is to document
declines in food availability and treat the poor as a homogenous group, the
members of which are equally affected by changing economic conditions.
The government of India was committed to the wrong way. They calculated (correctly, according to Sen) that there was no significant problem
regarding average food availability. Their theoretical approach left them
no choice but to deny that a famine existed even as people were dying in
the streets.[7] The right way is to examine how shifting entitlements deprive
particular occupational groups of access to food. For Sen, what matters most
are the legal rules that define how people may acquire and command food.

---

[7] Sen calls this Malthusian optimism.

Direct and Trade Entitlement Failures

Sen examines the basic legal rights of ownership, including production and exchange. He defines a person's *endowment set* as the combination of all resources the person owns, and a person's *entitlement set* as the combination of all resources a person could own, given the person's endowment set. In a market economy, the entitlement set depends on the person's ability to produce and trade for various goods and services, which may be either enhanced or diminished by government transfers such as social security provisions and taxation. Persons are at risk of starvation if their entitlement set (which Sen defines as any entitlement set people could work toward) does not enable them to satisfy their minimum food requirement.

For Sen, the study of famine is the study of factors that determine what a person owns and what a person can obtain given this ownership. A *direct entitlement failure* is starvation caused by a decline in one's direct food production. Historically, it may be reasonable to suppose that direct entitlement failures explain the onset of many famines throughout history. As opportunities for exchange have increased, however, fewer people independently produce everything they need even in the best of times, so in the contemporary world, famine almost always involves some form of *trade entitlement failure* as well – starvation caused by a loss of trade opportunities. This can occur if one's endowment set collapses, such as through loss of livestock from disease, or if food prices increase relative to the value of one's endowment, such as in the case of the Bengal boom famine. Sen's distinctive contribution within his property rights approach was to emphasize the significance of trade entitlement failures for understanding contemporary famines.

Consider Sen's explanation of the Ethiopian famine of 1972–4. This famine coincided with a modest *increase* in agricultural output across Ethiopia as a whole, according to the National Bank of Ethiopia. But, the province of Wollo was hit with mass starvation. Sen argued that this famine occurred because Wollo farmers suffered a direct entitlement failure, in which they were unable to produce enough food for themselves, and trade entitlement failures, where individuals and families lacked the purchasing power to attract food into their region.[8]

---

[8] We note in passing that although Sen sometimes talks about attracting food *to a region*, he presumably would agree that the solution from his own analysis is to attract food *to the household* and not to a region. The latter is a "macro" idea, at odds with Sen's overall analysis. As Sen says elsewhere, if a household or group is starving, attracting food to the region may or may not help.

Sen analyzed various occupational groups in the region to pinpoint the source of failure for each group. The pastoralists, for example, reached a desperate situation because distress circumstances caused a general shift in demand away from animal products. Animal products were a luxury item relative to grains. The quantity of livestock dropped (as animals died from drought) *and* the price of livestock fell (as people shifted their trade to grains).[9] The dual collapse of their endowment set and the market value of livestock caused a severe drop in the pastoralists' purchasing power for buying grains, a necessary part of their diet.

Unlike the Bengali famine, the Ethiopian famine occurred without any significant price increases in grains. Rural Wollo was in a bind. Residents could not produce enough food for themselves, and they could not afford to buy grains at market prices. Overall output levels do not tell this story.

Sen does not argue that droughts and floods are irrelevant for understanding famine, only that the property rights system provides the more fundamental explanation. Property rights prompt an analysis intermediate between the starving person and aggregate statistics about food supply (Sen 1981: 154). Television images of starving people can prompt international intervention, but it will be too late for many. This aid can take months to reach an area when the window is a few days. And more to the point, understanding that people are starving does not explain famine – it just shows us the tragedy, the effect rather than the cause.

The link between some natural event and declines in food supply distracts from the more proximate causes and what ultimately is the real issue: the property rights scheme that defines opportunities for production and exchange. Moreover, when famine is *not* associated with declines in food supply, as in Bengal and Ethiopia, the entitlement approach recognizes what is a mystery for the food availability decline theory: that people can starve from entitlement failures without serious food shortages. "Just moving food into such an area," Sen says, "will not help the affected population when what is required is the generation of food entitlement" (Sen 1981: 165). Sen is referring to the generation of a practically effective ability

---

[9] Sen draws on a variety of factors for explaining this unusual outcome (Sen 1981: 105–11). Apparently, under normal circumstances, the relative price of animal products is held up by aesthetic and protein factors, but, in the face of drought, the effective currency becomes caloric value and everything else falls by the wayside. This does not imply a total collapse of animal prices, though, because animal prices will fall only to the point where cash per calorie comes into equilibrium for plant and animal sources.

on the part of individuals to feed themselves and their families, and he is strikingly open minded about the sorts of packages (of market reforms, cultural reforms, reforms in government programs, and restructurings of legal rules for acquiring and transferring property) that would serve to nurture and secure that ability in a given time and place. There is no single cause of famine, but examining the network of property relations, Sen argues, is the best way to investigate these causes.[10]

PUBLIC ACTION

In his later writings, after *Poverty and Famines* (1981), Sen shifts and broadens his analysis in at least three respects. First, he shifts from explaining the causes of famine to suggesting both short-run and long-run policy responses to famine. Second, he extends his analysis to issues of persistent hunger and poverty beyond the short-term crisis of famine. Third, Sen develops a moral theory to explain what's wrong with poverty and hunger. Combining these three, perhaps we could summarize his views with the following. For Sen, poverty is a moral wrong because it prevents people from developing basic capabilities necessary for living a minimally decent life. Solving these problems requires that citizens take public action to create changes in the entitlement system.[11] Because legal entitlements are a means for persons to realize their capabilities, and many factors contribute to developing one's capabilities, public action must also target policy issues beyond entitlements. Influencing how people utilize what they are entitled to – through education, for example – can also significantly increase a person's capabilities for living a meaningful and adequately nourished life (Drèze and Sen 1989: 261–2).

We would do well not to interpret "public action" too narrowly, as if we were talking only about the actions of public officials, or about our

---

[10] "What emerges irresistably from the preceding analysis is the danger of concentrating only on the aggregative issues, overlooking the details of the entitlement system.... The focus on population and food supply would have been innocuous but for what it does to hide the realities that determine who can command how much food" (Sen 1981: 150). Overall, Sen's property rights approach leads him to emphasize purchasing power failures for specific occupational groups, direct production failures, and failures of social security networks in rural areas.

[11] "Since property rights over food are derived from property rights over other goods and resources (through production and trade), the entire system of rights of acquisition and transfer is implicated in the emergence and survival of hunger and starvation" (Sen 1988: 64).

actions only insofar as we are trying to influence public officials. Indeed, the actions actually called for in a given context often involve more initiative and entrepreneurship than any narrow conception of public action would include. As an example of public action at a community rather than overtly political level, V. Rukmini Rao discusses the plight of landless and uneducated women of the dalit class on the Deccan Plateau. She describes how people set up a microbank called the Deccan Development Society in 1983 to help men, but today the bank works exclusively with women (partly because the women are in a worse situation to begin with, and partly because women are more willing to cooperate). Rao reports that "over the past 15 years, more than 5000 women have been organized into self-help groups who are on the path to sustainable development" (Rao 2002: 256). The groups borrow small amounts of money, use it to lease land, and then plant borrowed native seed that will not serve as a cash crop (and thus is of no interest to the men) that but will feed their families without degrading the soil or depleting the water table. Within a year, clients return half the money and twice the seed (the rest is subsidized by governmental and nongovernmental organizations). Rao concludes:

> With a little outside financial and organizational help, poor women have formed groups dedicated to norms of equality and respect for each other, irrespective of caste. They have established local seed banks, brought fallow land back into production, and promoted sustainable, organic agriculture. In accomplishing these, they have begun to incrementally acquire the power needed to change cultural norms that have held them down. (Rao 2002: 260)

Rao's experience is in keeping with Sen's theory, and also with that of Hernando de Soto (discussed later in this chapter). Sen resists any simple "pro-market" or "pro-state" response. He believes that markets and governments each have assets and liabilities. In the poorest countries, Sen advocates economic growth through diversified production, enhanced medical care, direct food distribution for the most vulnerable, improved education and literacy rates, a free press, and reduced gender-based inequalities (Sen 2001: 185). He emphasizes the need for a free press as an early warning system for preventing famines, noting that famines have never occurred in a democracy (Drèze and Sen 1989: 264; Sen 2001: 188–9). He emphasizes the need for literacy, health care, stable property rights, and attitudes of trust and cooperation – ingredients for creating the economic growth that is fundamental to a reduction of poverty. For Sen, public action is about creating the right incentives, through competitive markets and through democratic political and civil institutions that permit its citizens to make, or demand, changes.[12]

Rao's account of the emergence of a microbank catering to dalit women illustrates only one of the ways in which the empowerment of women has been an ecological and economic boon, helping families in developing countries to feed themselves. It is a little-noted fact that far fewer people are starving today than a generation ago. In fact, Elizabeth Willott reports, not only are fewer people starving on a percentage basis, but amazingly, even "in absolute numbers, fewer people were undernourished in 1999 than in 1970. In 1970, roughly 900 million out of a population of 3.7 billion – 1 in 4 people – were undernourished. In 1999, despite a population of 6 billion, roughly 800 million – or fewer than 1 in 7 people – were undernourished."[13]

What accounts for this? The change occurred not because the weather has gotten better over the past thirty years, nor because international famine relief organizations radically increased the scale or efficiency of their efforts. The real reason is in keeping with Sen's analysis: namely, people in developing countries are generally in a better position to produce what they need, and above all to retain title to what they produce. People are in a better position to produce what they need partly because birth rates are declining virtually everywhere, partly because women are more able to trust that their rights as citizens will be respected in practice as well as in theory. Birth rates are declining because women have access to birth control technologies and because they have access to educational opportunities (along with the whole range of socioeconomic changes of which increasing educational opportunities are a part), which give them alternatives beyond being mothers and housewives.[14]

---

[12] "Incentives are, in fact, central to the logic of public action. But the incentives that must be considered are not only those that offer profits in the market, but also those that motivate governments to implement well-planned public policies, induce families to reject intra-household discrimination, encourage political parties and the news media to make reasoned demands, and inspire the public at large to cooperate, criticize and coordinate" (Drèze and Sen 1989: 259). Drèze and Sen explicitly wish to counterbalance the "privatization" perspective by reemphasizing the functions of public action. They include "employment creation" programs: government-provided public works programs to get money into the pockets of the desperate. Rather than trying to provide food directly, with all the attendant delays, the idea is to place money in the hands of those who need and let market incentive respond.

[13] Willott 2002: 276. Willott's data is from the United Nations Food and Agriculture Organization.

[14] Garrett Hardin (1974) and Paul Ehrlich (1968) made notorious claims that the world soon would be drowning in a sea of human overpopulation; only a draconian police state such as China's could prevent the common tragedy that would occur if people were free to have as many children as they pleased. Liberal optimists claimed the key to reproductive

APPLYING THE PROPERTY RIGHTS APPROACH

Zimbabwe

Some people continue to place nature in the foreground of famine analysis. African dictators are especially interested in blaming nature. When the cause is traced to bad governance and poorly conceived property rights, says Dr. Wilfred Mlay of Africa of World Vision, "there's not the same kind of [international] sympathy as when the crisis is attributed to natural factors."[15] But Zimbabwe's President Robert Mugabe has gone further, interfering with the distribution of international aid to punish areas that did not vote for him (Ferrett 2002).

The issues in Zimbabwe are complicated, like all real examples. White farmers seized huge tracts of fertile land years ago. We might say the land should be redistributed to those who are entitled to it: people from whom the white settlers took it, or perhaps people from whom previous occupants in turn took it. (We have to stop somewhere.) As his popular support waned, Mugabe began a high-profile campaign to redistribute these property rights not to previous occupants or descendants thereof, but to people who helped him in his various military campaigns. (There are rumors that Mugabe also wants to get HIV-positive males, of which there are huge numbers, out of the cities.) Once-productive farms sit idle as politicians wrestle over who gets the land. They also have to figure out how to help new landowners, some of whom had never seen a farm prior to being dumped off the back of a truck and told they now owned the land they were standing on.[16]

---

responsibility was to liberate women from traditional stereotypical roles by offering them educational opportunities and career alternatives, and by equipping them with the latest birth control technology. It turns out the liberals were correct, although as Willott (2002) elaborates, in the 1960s when these debates began it was not so clear which side was right.

[15] Dr. Wilfred Mlay, vice president for Africa of World Vision, quoted in Itano (2002).

[16] *WorldNetDaily* reporter Anthony C. LoBaido (2002a) reports an interview (7 May) with evicted farmer Cathy Buckle regarding the confiscation of her land by someone who called himself Wind. "I have lost the farm it took a decade to pay for and establish and the rent I was getting, which was my only income. In an article I wrote for a local newspaper about the events of last weekend I pointed out the immediate results of Wind's actions: 63 people are now homeless, 28 adults and 35 children. Because of these evictions, Zimbabwe is immediately deprived of 110 dozen eggs a week, 1,500 liters of milk a week and 1,000 kilograms of beef a week." Buckle said that Wind and his cronies had only a few comfortable days on her farm. "They had nice hot baths and listened to their radio at a very loud volume until Wednesday when they ran the borehole dry and burnt out the electric motor. They sent a message to me saying that as I was still the owner of the farm I should pay for the borehole motor to be repaired, as they could not survive without water." In a follow-up (28 July) interview (LoBaido 2002b), Buckle said, "As on our property, Zimbabwe's new farmers are concentrated in camps near the roadside and are living in appalling conditions.

Mugabe's program has brought food production nearly to a halt. The people of Zimbabwe are now very much at risk of starving.

What should be the role of property rights in a political and economic system? Consider two models. The first model begins with an idea of markets, with assigned and stable property rights that enable people to cooperate to mutual advantage. Ownership changes hands through voluntary exchange. Secure and stable legal rights form the background for market exchange. Citizens exercise these rights within a civil society whose voluntary associations reinforce social norms of trust and cooperation. These civil institutions provide stability and confidence in the marketplace as the source for generating wealth. Property rights form the background for a smoothly functioning market system. At its best, this model promises cooperation and economic development against the backdrop of a stable set of rules. Markets and civil society are the foreground of a flourishing community, and government is the background (Scalet and Schmidtz 2002).

A second model begins with an idea of politics, where property rights are under political control. Democratic governance becomes the heart of a flourishing community and markets the background. Citizens exercise political rights by participating in a political process that confers legitimacy over the ground rules of society, including property rights. At its best, this model promises a spirited citizenry where all have a stake in deliberation and the choice of the most basic ground rules.

In practice, the most successful societies integrate both markets and democracy, balancing these visions through a constitutionally limited democracy that allows for a free flow of capital. These models are in tension with each other to some degree – the first looks to buffer property rights from politics, whereas the second vision celebrates the direct control. If property rights are buffered from politics, who should resolve injustices and disagreements as they occur over time? But, if the answer is politics, then how can the process create a cooperative game rather than pit citizens against each other in a destructive contest of winner takes all? The best system will acknowledge that politics are unavoidable and yet recognize how politics can be a terrible impediment to production and cooperation. (When politics begins to colonize decisions better left to individual initiative, we refer to it as bureaucratic red tape.)

Their houses are tatty little shacks covered with thatching grass or old plastic. Their complexes are surrounded by felled trees, and the men sit around in groups near the edge of the road. There was no sign of any production at all."

When people own land without legitimacy, what should be done? Government can redistribute this land based on principles of justice. But what if a government redistributes for purposes of its own that may have nothing to do with principles of justice? What if such redistribution takes land out of the hands of those who know how to put it to productive use? (Perhaps their forefathers acquired the land illegitimately, but still, the question remains.) What if redistribution causes famine, as is now occurring in Zimbabwe? In the best of circumstances, a democratic society would need to make choices, and outcomes would be messy. Zimbabwe is not the best of circumstances. Government is not even approximately democratic. Due process and a basic rule of law are missing. We cannot assume that restoring land to previous owners will necessarily solve hunger problems, or that solving hunger problems has anything to do with restoring land to those previous owners. We also cannot assume that understanding famines is related to understanding reparations issues. Every real example of poverty and hunger raises many questions at once; the causes are many, and the histories are long.

The question we want to ask is, what kind of property rights are best at averting conditions of extreme poverty and famine? We can treat these tragedies like crimes against humanity, but that suggests we solve the problem by putting bad guys in jail. Often, though, the problem lies in a system that produced them, and so putting them in jail only treats a symptom. In the end, as Sen says, empirical arguments are central to moral philosophy. The issue is which institutions help make impoverished people better off. Some institutions induce cooperation and production, whereas others undermine the long-term prosperity of a people. In the rest of this chapter, we address several aspects of property rights as they relate to poverty and famine.

Government Help, Government Hindrance

Government can be understood as the provider of last resort, as the vehicle for disaster relief.[17] In this role, the idea is to put food in the hands of the

---

[17] Sen explains famines in large part by dramatic shifts in purchasing power that leaves some occupational groups unable to feed themselves through market purchases. Market mechanisms can fail, Sen says, and government must fulfill an obligation to get food to those who need it. He emphasizes the need for an effective domestic social security system and cautions that emergency international aid is not a long-term solution. But, he also recognizes that government can also be the cause of as much as the solution to famine, implementing ineffective and counterproductive public policies. He writes, "The focus on entitlement has

starving. Alternatively, without rejecting the previous idea, government can be understood to support a property rights scheme and a rule of law for people to create their own solutions. Sen's analysis suggests as much: if food shortage per se isn't the problem, then sending food isn't necessarily the solution. The long-run solution requires a different understanding of what a government realistically can do to help prevent famine – in particular, how it can establish the rules of a cooperative game that will be played primarily in the arena of civil society. There is no single blueprint for guaranteed prosperity. It depends on what people do.

One way to destroy this ideal is to create totalitarian governments that stifle and control citizens who are trying to forge a life together. Markets need a healthy civil society, and the long-run function of government should be to support its development.

De Soto on Social Capital

In his massive study of developing countries, Hernando de Soto found that governments often work against the best efforts of citizens to improve their own lives. They work against what de Soto calls the "extralegal" sector of society, stifling productive activity in a maze of regulation. Citizens are left with no choice but to pursue their lives and run their businesses outside the boundaries of formal law.

As an experiment, de Soto's research team tried to establish a small garment shop with one employee in Peru. It took them 289 days, spending on average six hours a day, to register the business according to formal law. The cost of registration was $1,231, thirty-one times the monthly minimum wage (de Soto 2000: 12). When de Soto and his colleagues began to study the extralegal sector in Peru, they "found that people who could not operate within the law also could not hold property efficiently or enforce contracts through the courts; nor could they reduce uncertainty through limited liability systems and insurance policies or create stock companies to attract additional capital and share risk" (de Soto 2000: 8).

de Soto's team found that the obstacles were no less and sometimes more formidable in other developing countries around the world. The lesson to take away from this, de Soto believes, is that an important obstacle to the development of local economies has nothing to do with free trade or

---

the effect of emphasizing legal rights. Other relevant factors, for example market forces, can be seen as operating *through* a system of legal relations. ... Starvation deaths can reflect legality with a vengeance" (Sen 1981: 166).

globalization. If de Soto is right, an important obstacle to the emergence and flourishing of local business is local bureaucracy. Further, a prerequisite of an expanding economy, if de Soto is right, is an institutional framework than gives entrepreneurs access to low-cost loans, so they can expand successful businesses.

de Soto analyzes emerging economics as follows:

> The migration and extralegality plaguing cities in the developing and former communist world closely resemble what the advanced nations of the West went through during their own industrial revolution. They too focused on trying to solve their problems one by one. The lesson of the West is that piecemeal solutions and stopgap measures to alleviate poverty were not enough. Living standards rose only when governments reformed the law and the property system to facilitate the division of labor. With the ability to increase their productivity through the beneficial effects of integrated property systems, ordinary people were able to specialize in ever-widening markets and to increase capital formation. (de Soto 2000: 75)

For the most part, de Soto's analysis complements rather than competes with Sen's. In a nutshell, Sen says that hunger tends to be caused neither by lack of food per se, nor by ecological catastrophe, but rather by bad economic infrastructure. de Soto examines the differences between good and bad infrastructure. He offers many details of the ways in which the former is able to unleash human productivity, whereas the latter stifles it.

Trading, negotiating, buying, selling – market activity in developing countries is everywhere. The energy is tremendous. The widespread poverty is startling. The problem is not that people lack a sense of business. The problem is not that impoverished people lack assets. They have assets. Turning shanties, crops, and fledgling businesses into economic development requires leveraging these assets to get loans and lines of credit. But getting these loans requires titles, deeds, and statutes of incorporation. de Soto estimates that the total value of real estate held by the poor in developing countries amounts to $9.3 trillion (de Soto 2000: 35). Unfortunately, this real estate is not held in a form that allows it to be used as collateral and thereby injected into an economy. According to de Soto's estimate, 50 to 80 percent of the population in developing countries reside in homes that lack clear formal titles. When the poor live and conduct business outside the formal property rights system, they can trade and lend only within local circles of people who know and trust each other. They are unable to participate in a system that creates sustained economic growth because the legal property rights system does not include them. The most impoverished people live where homegrown rules regulate property and commerce and no formal property system exists for turning assets into capital growth.

Sen presumably would agree with de Soto that "a modern government and a market economy are unviable without an integrated formal property system. Many of the problems of non-Western markets today mainly result from the fragmentation of their property arrangements and the unavailability of standard norms that allow assets and economic agents to interact and governments to rule by law" (de Soto 2000: 72). de Soto draws an interesting analogy: "Like computer networks, which had existed for years before anyone thought to link them, property systems become tremendously powerful when they are interconnected in a larger network. Only then is the potential of a particular property right not limited to the imagination of its owner, his neighbors, or his acquaintances, but subject to a larger network of other imaginations" (de Soto 2000: 72). There are many dimensions to poverty, but poverty can be alleviated in the long run only if the majority of the population works within an integrated formal property rights system.

A formal property rights system is not simply about establishing who owns what. It's about creating institutional rules that enable people to see the potential for creating new production, leveraging what they already have, and then providing a practical means for realizing this production.

One of de Soto's key claims is that part of the explanation of gigantic differences in life prospects between the highest and lowest classes (dwarfing anything seen in the developed world) is that developing countries characteristically exhibit a dearth of institutions offering affordable credit. Indeed, in de Soto's analysis, this is no coincidence: middle classes are nonexistent in developing countries precisely because poor people cannot get mortgages or loans that they would use to start small businesses and eventually achieve a measure of security and prosperity. Rao's (Rao 2002) experience on the Deccan Plateau illustrates de Soto's point that the institution of affordable credit is one of the main keys to getting economies going. And, people in developing economies tend not to own property in a form that makes it useful as collateral that would secure affordable loans. Where there is useful collateral, interest rates can drop as the risk premium for being a lender goes down.

Norms and Law

Formal property law exists in every country. The problem is the enormous gap between formal law and the expansive extralegal norms that govern so much economic activity in developing societies. Citizens carve out such norms in an attempt to lead peaceful and cooperative lives. These norms can and often do compete against rules designed by local bureaucracies. They often compete against or supplant formal property law as people devise practical means for dealing with one another. These norms form initially from the ground up without legal sanction. They are fragmented and disjointed across even small geographical areas. Helping the poor requires that a unified formal property rights system mesh with these local traditions.[18] This can happen only by absorbing local norms into the formal property system.

At their best, legal property rights are an effective intermediary between government and individuals. The government secures and enforces a unified property system, creating a stable rule of law that gives people access to and participation in productive activities. Individuals develop their own cooperative norms alongside and beyond the rules of government. A formal property rights system must constantly evolve to link these rules of government with the informal norms of individuals (Scalet 2003). Laws and regulations that adapt alongside local traditions allow individuals to view law as an enabling force for cooperative activity rather than as an impediment and a foreign invasion.

Absorbing these norms into law gives legitimacy to the norms and to the law. The norms become publicly recognized beyond local circles. They become integrated into a larger network of imaginations, as de Soto puts it, where everyone has access to a rule of law for securing and enforcing agreements that arise through these norms. The law also gains legitimacy as it becomes responsive to traditions that already claim citizens' allegiance. Citizens will be more likely to accept the system and use formal law for their own development rather than feel victim to a system that would not otherwise recognize them. Property rights that evolve in this way will change local traditions to some degree and formal law to some degree. The point is to offer a means for impoverished people to pursue economic development through a formal system that they can understand and utilize.

A system of evolving property rights can also mediate between markets and democracy. As we just discussed, markets and democracy share somewhat different visions about the role of property rights. Markets are a response to needs at the local level. Markets need stable property rights. A

---

[18] About western democracies, de Soto writes, "The integration of all property systems under one formal property law shifted the legitimacy of the rights of owners from the politicized context of local communities to the impersonal context of law" (de Soto 2002: 54).

state that allows or demands radical change as politics change can undermine this stability and undermine capital growth. Democracies control property rights. Constitutional protections offer one mechanism for balance. Beyond this, a formal property rights system linked to local traditions offers another mechanism for balance. Property rights can both connect law with stable traditions that have stood the test of time and connect law with democratic institutions that shape these property rights over time. The goal is a mix of market and democratic institutions that empower people, including poor people, to find new ways to create and retain wealth.

CONCLUSION

Sen is right that the fundamental problem is one of institutional design. Famine is not about drought, or even food supply. Climate and soil quality are issues in certain times and places, but even those tend to implicate institutional designs that lead people to try to grow crops that do not belong in that climate or to use faulty farming techniques, outdated technologies, and so on.

Sen says there is enough food, but the trouble is that the wrong people own it. The lesson, though, is not that proper redistributive mechanisms are not in place. We suspect there has never been a society that succeeded in feeding its people mainly by getting them to play zero-sum games. Societies need to empower the currently powerless not so they can seize other people's assets but so they can produce their own, and so they can be securely entitled to what they produce.

Some say that the problem in developing countries is not that there is too little food, but that it is improperly distributed. Although we do not disagree, we would suggest, inspired by Sen's own analysis, that the nation is not the proper unit of analysis. The proper unit of analysis is the individual consumer and, perhaps even more important, the individual producer. What would result in the food being well distributed? One clear answer is that food would be well distributed if the opportunity to produce were well distributed.

When a family has too little food, this does not imply that there is too little food in the country but rather that there is too little in that household. That particular family lacks adequate ability or opportunity to produce enough to feed itself, or lacks adequate *control* over whatever the family can produce. "Teaching a person to fish" is not enough. After teaching a person to fish – and giving him or her a fishing rod and whatever other tools he or she needs – we also have to provide a social system in which the person can know that if he or she catches a fish, it will not be taken away. The solution to the maldistribution problem typically does not lie in tweaking the tax rates of his or her country, or ours. Rather, what is needed is social capital in a general way, where "social capital" describes all those social assets that help people initiate and further productive activity. The poor lack access to the means of production. They lack access to affordable credit. Women, in many places the primary producers of agricultural products, often can participate in the market only in limited and relatively ineffective ways, because they are not treated as rights-bearing citizens.

It would be misleading to say enough has already been produced and it just has not been distributed properly. That conclusion is implied by the sort of macro analysis that Sen rejects, whereas a better way to look at it would be to say that not enough food is being produced by the people who most need an opportunity to produce it. There is famine in Zimbabwe because the people who know how to grow food and who previously had been largely responsible for (and successful at) supplying the country with food no longer have the right to produce in peace. (It is literally forbidden in Zimbabwe today for a white farmer to plant a crop.) This is a case where there is not enough food, but Sen's analysis is still right. Although there is not enough food, the fundamental problem is not that there is insufficient food, but that people have insufficient opportunity to produce and market food in peace. The same thing is true among India's dalit women. They have plenty of capability. What they need is an infrastructure that respects their right to produce in peace, and does not presume a right to redistribute what their husbands or others deem to be improperly distributed.

There is no single cure-all for famine. Societies that prosper do so for many reasons. They pursue education, build basic infrastructures, and create decent health care. These are crucial issues. But, if we care about the poor, understanding the role of property rights is fundamental. Law that absorbs the informal property rules of local communities respects how people relate to each other at the local level. At the same time, these rules must be integrated within one unified property system that provides the means for economic development.

Most Americans can expect to buy a home (and, indeed, to do so long before they could afford to pay for it in cash, using the instrument of mortgage financing). They can expect those property rights to be respected as a matter of routine, and not only by their next-door neighbors. They can expect to sell the home and benefit from increasing property values. They can take a second mortgage to start a small business or invest in home improvements. These experiences are unimaginable in many parts of the world.[19]

We may sometimes need government as a provider of last resort. Yet, governments and international agencies rushing to the scene to save those who have not yet died from a famine is more than tragedy; it is the failure to help develop formal property rights systems of the sort that can grow economies and make famines a historical relic.

References

Drèze, J., and A. Sen (eds.) (1989). *Hunger and Public Action* (Oxford: Clarendon Press).

Ehrlich, P. R. (1968). *The Population Bomb* (Cutchogue, NY: Buccaneer Books).

Ferrett, G. (2002). "Mugabe Supporters 'Starving Enemies,'" *BBC News*, 30 July. http://news.bbc.co.uk/2/hi/africa/2157949.stm.

Hardin, G. (1974). "Living on a Lifeboat," *BioScience*, 24, 561–8.

Itano, N. (2002). "Why Donors Hesitate to Give," *Christian Science Monitor*, 16 July. http://www.csmonitor.com/2002/0716/p06s01-woaf.html?rl.

LoBaido, A. C. (2002a). "Zimbabwe Officially in Famine Condition," *WorldNet-Daily*, 7 May. http://www.worldnetdaily.com/index.php?pageId=13805.

LoBaido, A. (2002b). "An Eyewitness to Zimbabwe's Famine," *WorldNetDaily*, 28 July. http://www.worldnetdaily.com/index.php?pageId=14698.

Munzer, S. (1990). *A Theory of Property* (Cambridge: Cambridge University Press).

Rao, V. R. (2002). "Women Farmers of India's Deccan Plateau: Ecofeminists Challenge World Elites," in Schmidtz and Willott (eds.), *Environmental Ethics: What Really Matters, What Really Works* (New York: Oxford University Press).

Scalet, S. (2003). "Fitting the People They Are Meant to Serve: Reasonableness in the American Legal System," *Law and Philosophy*, 22, 75–110.

Scalet, S., and D. Schmidtz (2002). "State, Civil Society and Classical Liberalism," in Post and Rosenblum (eds.), *Civil Society and Government* (Princeton, NJ: Princeton University Press).

Schmidtz, D., and J. Brennan (2009). *A Brief History of Liberty* (Oxford: Blackwell).

Sen, A. (1977). "Starvation and Exchange Entitlements: A General Approach and Its Application to the Great Bengal Famine," *Cambridge Journal of Economics*, 1, 33–59.

---

[19] We wrote this before the mortgage crisis, which certainly raises questions about what happens when both borrowers and lenders are accustomed to thinking of the government as obliged to bail them out if they should become overextended. We acknowledge that being able to buy on credit is a dangerous servant and a terrible master, but we do not (yet) see any reason to doubt that institutions of credit are massively liberating. For more discussion, see Schmidtz and Brennan (2009).

Sen, A. (1981). *Poverty and Famines: An Essay on Entitlement and Deprivation* (Oxford: Clarendon Press).

Sen, A. (1988). "Property and Hunger," *Economics and Philosophy*, 4, 1, 57–68.

Sen, A. (2001). "Economic Development and Capability Expansion in Historical Perspective," *Pacific Economic Review*, 6, 2, 179–91.

de Soto, H. (2000). *The Mystery of Capital: Why Capitalism Triumphs in the West and Fails Everywhere Else* (New York: Basic Books).

Willott, E. (2002). "Population Trends," in Schmidtz and Willott (eds.), *Environmental Ethics: What Really Matters, What Really Works* (New York: Oxford University Press).

8 Development

"A Misconceived Theory Can Kill"

SABINA ALKIRE

Human capabilities are partly created or undermined by development policies, markets, and other social arrangements. Put differently, human freedom is partly "human"-made. Sen's philosophical writings propose the expansion of human capabilities and freedoms as an objective for social arrangements, and argue that this objective satisfies certain considerations better than Rawlsian primary goods or utility measures. In approaching development, the chain of exploration can also be reversed. The policies, practices, analyses, and measures that guide development institutions can be scrutinized to uncover which truly aim at human freedoms, and how true their aim might be. Much of Sen's development writings engage or draw on investigations of this form. By such inspection, the oversights of development theories might be uncovered and corrected. Such work is terribly salient, for lives are at stake. In development, Sen observes, "a misconceived theory can kill" (Sen 1999a: 209).

Sen's writings on development include nine books, eight coauthored books, and more than 100 articles addressing economic development, poverty measurement, famines and hunger, gender inequalities, education, health, employment, population and the environment, written over more than forty years. His best-selling *Development as Freedom* (1999a) synthesizes previous work and provides an introduction to this approach. Sen has also presented his approach in overview articles, as have others (Sen 1980a, 1983a, 1984, 1985a, 1985b, 1987, 1988, 1989, 1990a; Crocker 1992, 1995; Qizilbash 1996; Alkire 2005; Clark 2005; Robeyns 2005). Given the abundance of writings, this chapter can only synthesize a few key insights regarding concrete actions to expand people's capabilities, and the method of analysis. Here, attention is paid to capability expansion, not primarily as a criterion of justice (although of course reflections on justice can be informed by this analysis), but as evidence that development has occurred.

I am grateful for the comments of Séverine Deneulin, John Hammock, and Christopher Morris on this chapter and to Afsan Bhadelia for research assistance. Errors remain my own.

191

Development thus defined can be investigated independently of whether governments and institutions articulate their objectives in terms of expanding capabilities, or increasing economic growth, or any other possible sets of social goals.

The first section of this chapter orients the reader to the relationship between development and freedoms. The second section demonstrates how Sen uses aspects of the capability approach in relation to poverty measurement, the market, education, gender, population and reason, health, and hunger.

The trouble with overviews is that instead of distilling an essence, they tend merely to shed all charms of style, and lose not only the playfulness of the conversation, but a chorus of counterarguments and subtleties as well. So, although I can see no way around this predicament, let me at least acknowledge what has been lost, and urge readers to rush out to fetch the original texts – which tend to be far juicier reading than this chapter lets on.

I. TERMS

Sen's "capability approach" has developed over twenty-five years. It has employed core terms of capabilities, functionings, well-being, and agency. More recent writings emphasize the terminology of freedoms, particularly opportunity freedoms and process freedoms (which may be personal or systemic) (Sen 1999a; 2002b: chapters 19–21). The key terms are as follows:

Capabilities "represent the various combinations of functionings (beings and doings) that the person can achieve. Capability is, thus, a set of vectors of functionings, reflecting the person's freedom to lead one type of life or another . . . to choose from possible livings" (Sen 1992a: 40). Capabilities are "the substantive freedoms he or she enjoys to lead the kind of life he or she has reason to value" (Sen 1999a: 87).

Freedom, when used to describe a social or economic objective – in the title *Development as Freedom* for example – is an "irreducibly plural concept" (Sen 2002b: 585). Two overlapping kinds of freedom are of particular note. *Process freedom* relates to "freedom of action and decisions" (Sen 1999a: 17) and other procedural considerations, and may be considered at the personal level or at the systemic level. *Opportunity freedom* relates to the opportunities that are available to people and that they value and have reason to value – their freedom to achieve valued outcomes. Although the terms are not synonymous, opportunity freedoms are closely related to capabilities, and process freedoms are related to agency and the conditions in which people and groups can exert agency.

Development pertains to positive processes of social, economic, and political change that expand valued capabilities (Sen 2003a). Although development is most often associated with poorer countries, Sen's capability approach and the related human development approach apply equally to rich countries. Indeed *Development as Freedom* is replete with examples from such "developed" countries as the United Kingdom, Japan, the United States, and Italy.

Beyond Economic Development

"So act as to treat humanity, whether in thine own person or in that of any other, in every case as an end withal, never as means only."[1] It is with this sentence from Immanuel Kant's work that Sen begins an exposition of development. The status of human beings as "ends" of development must be reiterated, Sen argues, because human beings "also happen to be – directly or indirectly – the primary means of all production" (Sen 1990a: 41). In fact, the dominant approach to economic development regards people *principally* as means. For example, the economic planning and policy making by which development advances largely appreciates "production and prosperity as the essence of progress" and hence considers "the expansion of real income and . . . economic growth as the characteristics of successful development" (Sen 1990a: 41). People are valued insofar as they advance growth and prosperity.

In contrast, Sen's approach to development firmly places economic growth and real income in the category of means. So Sen often cites with approval Aristotle's observation that "wealth is evidently not the good we are seeking; for it is merely useful and for the sake of something else" (Sen 1990a: 44, citing Aristotle 1984: book 1, sec. 5). Rather than aiming only for economic growth or the expansion of markets or real income or wealth, Sen argues that the objective of development should be the expansion of people's capabilities – of their real freedoms, their opportunities to achieve and enjoy states of affairs that they value and have reason to value. Income, market expansion, and growth are useful to the extent that they promote these intrinsically valuable ends. Given this emphasis, Sen's and related

---

[1] Sen 1990a: 41, citing Kant 1785: sect. II; Kant 1909: 47. Note that Sen's understanding of well-being and, it would seem, of "humanity" is broader than Kant's.

approaches to development are often referred to as "human development" to distinguish them from growth-oriented development.

To wrest the orientation of development away from income and economic growth alone might seem an elementary move. It is certainly preliminary, and the work of Sen and others further specifies this move conceptually as well as methodologically. Empirical studies demonstrate the difference this change in orientation makes. But, it is worth pausing to study why Sen's writings on development often begin with a forceful clarification of the relationship between means and ends. It seems arguable that several significant features follow from the shift in objective: First, the *focal variable* shifts. Traditionally, development focused on income or consumption; here the focal variables are people's capabilities – which constitute a wider set of dimensions, not all of which are necessarily the subject of public policy. Second, considerably greater attention is given to the role of *human agency*, public debates, and social movements in making social choices and advancing development goals. Third, *procedural* considerations such as human rights, democracy, equity, and sustainability supplement the traditional focus on efficiency.

The following sections address these items in order.

Focal Variables

When development is defined by economic growth, and a healthy economy is one that is growing strongly, then the unit of analysis is evident: the economy. This may be the national economy, or the economy of a particular region or sector. The currency of assessment is likewise clear: growth in income per capita. In contrast, if development is defined by real freedoms, and a healthy economy is one that contributes to the expansion or growth in diverse people's real freedoms, then the analysis shifts to each person affected by the economy, and the currency of assessment becomes their capabilities. Questions of how to prioritize and weight, aggregate, and evaluate distributions of different capabilities, the capabilities of different people, and people's capabilities in different time periods must be addressed explicitly.

Sen's writings on capability undergird this shift to a "people-centered" approach by providing a conceptual substructure. This conceptual framework could support not only Sen's writings but also a range of related broader approaches including the basic human needs approach (Ghai and International Labour Office 1977; Streeten and World Bank 1981; Stewart 1985) and some approaches based on human rights or ubuntu. Indeed,

Sen carefully distinguished this approach from utilitarianism and revealed preference theories, which underlie support for economic growth, as well as from resource-based approaches.

By shifting the objective of development from a unitary, tangible measure that can be aggregated (income) to diverse human capabilities, which vary across people and across time, and are to some degree incommensurable, Sen's approach shifts "development" onto ethical ground. The term "human development" is often used to signal this shift. The objective now relates to "what life we lead and what we can or cannot do, can or cannot be" (Sen et al. 1987: 16) – topics on which people's reasoned views differ. The information that is morally relevant to the assessment of social arrangements also expands quite significantly, and can include noneconomic and nonmaterial aspects of life such as cultural activities, dignity, self-respect, and other meaningful activities and states (Sen 1979, 1985b, 1999a).

It may be worth underlining this last point explicitly, if only to counter potential misunderstandings. Human development is *not* defined by the inclusion of health and education in development analyses. It is more than this. Deprivations with respect to health and education are indeed core elements of development and have been recognized by participatory, social exclusion, capability, and income approaches, among others. Furthermore, as we shall see, the Human Development Index and the Human Poverty Index give prominence to health and education, and were developed by a team including Sen to contrast human development with income-based evaluations of development. However, the indices were also shaped by feasibility considerations, including data constraints on internationally comparable data, and the need to have a terribly simple and compelling public message. Health and education do not exhaust the kinds of capabilities that are relevant to development analyses. In fact, a growing body of research demonstrates that people, including people who are "absolutely poor" in material terms, value dimensions such as safety from violence, livelihoods, agency, and relationships fundamentally. The 2004 *Human Development Report* also proposed cultural liberties (a term that encompasses social, cultural, and religious freedoms) as a fourth "pillar" of human development.

The focal variables of development differ from income, not only in their plurality, but also in the fact that the freedoms that constitute the "objective" of development in any given context depend in part upon the values of the referent population. Capabilities are freedoms that people *value and have reason to value*. Value judgments are entailed in the identification of freedoms at the individual and collective level, in the prioritization among capabilities that can be created or undermined by development processes, and in the distribution of widely valued capabilities among different people and groups. Furthermore, as these judgments may evolve – for example, with new information or because the referent population has changed – existing priorities should, Sen argues, be the subject of explicit scrutiny and ongoing public discussion.[2]

Agency and Public Engagement

In this approach to development, people are to be considered and involved not merely as self-interested utility maximizers, but as agents who contribute to social choices and value judgments, as well as to development activities. An agent is "someone who acts and brings about change, and whose achievements can be judged in terms of her own values and objectives, whether or not we assess them in terms of some external criteria as well" (Sen 1999a: 19). Although agency may be used to further activities that expand the actor's own utility function (what Adam Smith called *sympathy*), in other situations people's agency (*commitment*) may drive "a wedge between personal choice and personal welfare, and much of traditional economic theory relies on the identity of the two" (Sen 1977: 329). The capability approach innovates beyond development theory in introducing – and indeed emphasizing – commitment-based agency (Sen 1977).

When Drèze and Sen apply the capabilities approach to the Indian situation in their book *India: Development and Participation*, agency figures centrally.

> The approach used in this book is much concerned with the opportunities that people have to improve the quality of their lives. It is essentially a 'people-centred' approach, which puts human agency (rather than organizations such as markets or governments) at the centre of the stage. The crucial role of social opportunities is to expand the realm of human agency and freedom, both as an end in itself and as a means of further expansion of freedom. (Drèze and Sen 2002: 6)

It may be useful to observe a few characteristics of agency. First, agency is not limited to decision-making control; it also includes situations of effective power, in which decisions are "exercised in line with what we would have

---

[2] The kinds of value judgments under discussion are noncompulsive; see Sen 1967.

chosen and because of it" (Sen 1985b: 211; Alkire 2008). Second, effective power is often held by groups rather than individuals: "Given the interdependences of social living, many liberties are not separately exercisable, and effective power may have to be seen in terms of what all, or nearly all, members of the group would have chosen" (Sen 1985b: 211). Third, agency may be exercised to advance the well-being of the agent and the agent's family or community, but it might equally well be exercised to advance some other-regarding aims the person values and has reason to value, such as to comfort victims of a disaster, or to protect an endangered species. Fourth, a fully worked-out account of agency might also include some assessment of the responsibility of an agent – based on his or her role in creating the situation, and on his or her effective power and imperfect obligations toward others (Sen 1983b, 1985b).

This account of human agency differs significantly from *homo economicus*. For example, the assumption that a single self-interested motivation will adequately predict human behavior is no longer either sufficient or required (Sen 1977; Alkire and Deneulin 2002). Individuals are viewed, not only as centers of their own well-being (which they aim to optimize), but also as actors and agents, whose activities (including but not limited to buying and selling) advance or constrain development. Furthermore, agents can act as *means* for reducing their own poverty directly, or for confronting poverty in their society. Sen writes, "Individual agency is, ultimately, central to addressing these deprivations. On the other hand, the freedom of agency that we individually have is inescapably qualified and constrained by the social, political and economic opportunities that are available to us" (Sen 1999a: xvi–xvii). Thus a central objective of development, alongside the expansion of capabilities, is the cultivation and support of agency as an end and as a means: "Greater freedom enhances the ability of people to help themselves and also to influence the world, and these matters are central to the process of development" (Sen 1999a: 18).

In sum, there is a two-way relationship between people as agents, and development – which is partly created by human agency. Freedoms and capabilities "can be enhanced by public policy, but also, on the other side, the direction of public policy can be influenced by the effective use of participatory capabilities by the public" (Sen 1999a: 18). Thus people's agency, values, and reflections form an integral and active part of the development process. Indeed the interrelationship between development and freedom – the ways in which more freedoms create a means to development as well as shaping its end – provides a distinctive core in Sen's approach.

Plural Principles and Justice Comparisons

Sen's approach to development subordinates economic growth and market expansion within the larger framework of human freedom, which entails a wider informational basis and, as we shall briefly observe, a substantially wider rationality. The capability approach identifies a space for the evaluation of social welfare and development that is, it argues, superior to utility or commodities. To advance *development* requires more than merely the identification of a space, however. It requires the comparison of different states of affairs, even if these are incomplete or only generate partial orderings. Traditional economics employs efficiency as the primary criterion, embodied in the principle of Pareto optimality. Comparisons may also employ considerations such as the equity of their capability distributions across class, or gender, or social groups; or the extent to which certain fundamental rights are respected; or the extent to which a political process is transparent and can be influenced by vigorous public debate. Sen argues that plural principles such as these – which are components of a wider ethical rationality – can be introduced into a "consequential evaluation" (focused, at least in part, on expanding people's capabilities; see Sen 2000).

For example, human rights – including social, cultural, economic, political, and civil rights – can be incorporated into the evaluation of states of affairs, which allows rights (or the infringement of rights) to be considered in comparing alternative courses of action (Sen 1982: 5–39; 1983b: 113–32; 2004). Equity is also to be included, as we shall see in the section on missing women. Another principle, which might be considered, is the prevention of capability contractions – which might be called human security. Earlier we noted that the objective of human development is to expand human capabilities. As laudable as this buoyant and progressive objective is, Sen also observes that it "is far too upbeat to focus on rearguard actions needed to secure what has to be safeguarded" (Sen 2003c: 8). In other situations, including war and conflict or financial crisis or an epidemic, "the notion of human security becomes particularly relevant" (Sen 2003c: 8).

Principles such as human rights, equity, protection from downside risk, and others thus complement the principle of efficiency and capability expansion in this approach.

Development, then, is concerned with expanding people's freedoms and capabilities, with treating people as agents, and with plural principles of assessment. These considerations might be brought together by a different approach to justice, which Sen refers to as "comparative." A comparative approach to justice functions by undertaking pairwise comparison and ranking of alternative societal arrangements in terms of justice (whether some arrangement is 'less just' or 'more just' than another). A comparative approach also allows "systematic room for incompleteness" (Sen 2006: 223) – because some principles may conflict, some data may be missing, and people will differ in their assessment of the appropriate principles. Despite these limitations, a maximizing yet incomplete comparative approach could be used to identify and reject options that are clearly inferior to others according to multiple principles or considerations.

II. DEVELOPMENT WRITINGS

This section surveys some of Sen's empirical contributions to different topics that fall, broadly, within development as sketched in the previous section. The development framework just sketched indicates the *direction* toward which these contributions extend development analyses that were current at the different times of writing (they are not presented chronologically), but in some cases, such as the Sen Index, which we address next, the particular contribution is an initial contribution to an ongoing literature that involved many other authors. The purpose of this section is to provide readers with a guide to well-known insights found in Sen's development writings – regarding poverty measurement, markets, the market, basic education, cooperative conflicts, missing women, population and reason, health, and hunger – rather than to give a more general overview of each topic.

Poverty Measurement I – Sen Index

The simplest and most pervasive poverty measure – still – is the "head-count" ratio, which reports the percentage of the population who fall below an income poverty line (e.g., "34 percent of the population are poor"). When this measure is used to guide policy, however, several flaws appear. Sen's initial work on poverty measurement did not focus on measuring capabilities but rather on income-based poverty measures. In particular, he drew attention to the insensitivity of the head-count index to the depth of poverty. Assume there are gradations of poverty among those who live beneath the poverty line. When poverty is measured only by a head-count ratio, it appears to be as much of a triumph to lift one person who was $3 below the poverty line above it as it is to lift above the line one person who was $300 below it. Thus, policy makers will naturally try to reduce poverty "the most" by focusing their efforts on the people who are nearest to the poverty line or whose condition is easiest to alleviate. A related problem is that if some of those living beneath the poverty line are further impoverished while the poverty of a few near to the poverty line is reduced, this would count, again, as a victory because the measure is insensitive to the "distribution" of poverty below the poverty line.

In response, a second class of poverty measures were developed that focus on the depth of poverty – usually by measuring the "gap" between the person's income (for example – other indicators could be used) and the (income) poverty line. The measure, which averages the poverty gap for all of the poor persons, is indeed sensitive to the "depth" of poverty.

The Sen Index is a measure of income poverty that reflects the distribution of poverty among the poor (Sen 1973, 1976; Sen and Foster 1997). The Sen Index combines three measures into one: the head-count ratio, the poverty-gap measure, and a measure of distribution of income among the poor (the Gini coefficient). The measure gave rise to a considerable literature,[3] which applied and also modified and improved the Sen Index so that it could satisfy some properties that the original measure could not – in particular "subgroup decomposability," which is relevant in some – but not all – contexts.

Poverty Measurement

Sen has argued since the 1980s that poverty should be conceived not as lowness of income, but rather in terms of capability deprivation. "What the capability perspective does in poverty analysis is to enhance the understanding of the nature and causes of poverty and deprivation by shifting primary attention away from *means* to *ends* that people have reason to pursue, and, correspondingly, to the *freedoms* to be able to satisfy these ends" (Sen 1999a: 90). Clearly income is a key feature of poverty and is correlated with other kinds of impoverishment. However, the statistical connection is imperfect, and policies may be better crafted by considering their contribution to human freedoms.[4]

---

[3] References to the secondary literature are also in Sen and Foster 1997: 171, n. 86. More recent measurement work has extended these considerations in multidimensional space. See Alkire and Foster 2007; Kakwani and Silber 2008a, 2008b.

[4] In *Development as Freedom* Sen cites a study by Sudhir Anand and Martin Ravallion. Their study first documented a correlation between life expectancy and income – a common observation – but then went on to show that the correlation worked through the incomes of the poor and public expenditure, especially expenditures related to basic health. These variables explained all of the relevant correlation (Sen 1999a: 44).

Considerable evidence can be brought to bear showing the imperfections of a statistical relationship between income and capabilities. For example, "the relationship between income and capability would be strongly affected by the age of the person..., by gender and social roles (e.g., through special responsibilities of maternity and also custom-determined family obligations), by location (e.g., by proneness to flooding or drought, or by insecurity and violence...), by epidemiological atmosphere... and by other variations over which a person may have no – or only limited – control" (Sen 1999a: 88). Another example of the inadequacy of income as a proxy for freedom is that measures of income per household will obscure inequalities of distribution within the household – such as discrimination against girl children – that direct measures of nutrition and health would reveal.

> The important point to note is that the valuation of income is entirely as a means to other ends and also that it is one means among others.... Income is, of course, a crucially important means, but its importance lies in the fact that it helps the person to do the things that she values doing and to achieve states of being that she has reasons to desire. The worth of incomes cannot stand separated from these deeper concerns, and a society that respects individual well-being and freedom must take note of these concerns in making interpersonal comparisons as well as social evaluations. (Sen 1997: 384–401)

Furthermore, persons who are capability deprived – disabled or ill for example – both may have greater difficulty in earning an income and may require more income than others. On the positive side, however, persons with greater capabilities – for example in health and education – not only enjoy these direct benefits, but have also been shown to be, on the whole, more productive economically as well. For these reasons, Sen argues that policies of poverty reduction, even if they employ income measures for certain approximations, should aim at capability expansion.

In a similar way, Sen argues that policies to reduce inequality should be framed with respect to capabilities rather than income alone. For example, European income inequality is relatively low, but this obscures very high rates of unemployment. In contrast, U.S. income inequality is high, but unemployment rates are far lower (implying a lower inequality in the opportunity to be employed). Thus, to focus only on reducing income inequality would be to overlook the European unemployment problem altogether. Similarly, the income inequality between African American men and women and other U.S. citizens is considerable, although African Americans are still better off, in terms of income, than citizens in developing countries.

However, the life expectancy of African American men is *lower* than that of people in China, Kerala, Sri Lanka, Costa Rica, Jamaica, and many other countries. A policy merely to reduce income inequality in the United States would overlook this intense health deprivation. Comparing inequalities in other spaces – for example, undernourishment, infant mortality, or adult literacy in select states of India or countries in Africa – similarly brings to light stark and distinct patterns that income comparisons would overlook but that are relevant for policy.

Thus, the application of Sen's framework to issues of poverty requires a reframing of the means and ends involved. "Policy debates have indeed been distorted by over-emphasis on income poverty and income inequality, to the neglect of deprivations that relate to other variables, such as unemployment, ill health, lack of education, and social exclusion" (Sen 1999a: 108). When a broader range of capabilities are considered, then of course policies will embody value judgments as to the relative importance of diverse capabilities. Here, too, Sen's approach brings a distinctive view in advocating public participation and discussion of the priorities embodied by public policy.

The pioneering measure designed to provoke such debates is the Human Development Index (HDI) released in 1990. The HDI combines three components: measures of basic education, longevity, and income. The index was created as a summary measure of development to contrast with the dominant measure, GNP per capita, and to raise questions at a popular level about the objectives of development. Mahbub ul Haq, the director of the newly created Human Development Report Office of the United Nations Development Programme (UNDP), called for an index "of the same level of vulgarity as the GNP – just one number – but a measure that is not as blind to social aspect of human lives as the GNP is" (Sen 1998). The index was crafted by a group including Sudhir Anand and Sen (Anand and Sen 1994). In 1997 a Human Poverty Index was released to catalyze a similar discussion on the meaning of poverty.

The Market

Sen views the market as "a basic arrangement through which people can interact with each other and undertake mutually advantageous activities" (Sen 1999a: 142).

Sen contrasts his view with an approach in which the market expansion is promoted almost without qualifications. His first contrast is positive toward the market and addresses the *reasons* that markets are worthwhile. Although the dominant view values markets because of the results they produce, Sen argues that the freedoms to buy, sell, exchange, seek employment, and transact have value themselves, quite separately from valued market outcomes. Bonded labor, feudalism, the prohibition of female employment in some areas, and the denial of economic freedom under communism all represent violations of the very freedoms that markets introduce.

A second characteristic of the perfect market is Pareto optimality, which is a type of efficiency in which no person's utility can be increased without someone else's utility being reduced. This efficiency result, Sen demonstrates, can also be reached if persons' well-being is considered in the space of valuable capabilities. But, as is well-known, Pareto optimality is a limited notion even of efficiency, and is blind to the distribution of utilities or goods or freedoms. Sen argues that markets' outcomes should be considered according to *both* efficiency and equity (and at times according to other principles as well) (Sen 2000). That way, any conflicts or trade-offs between efficiency and equity (for example) can be deliberated together, and social priorities can be set in full view of all relevant considerations.

Considerations of capability equity are particularly important because vested interests with much to gain will try to skew markets in their own favor (and often succeed in doing so): "Political influence in search of economic gain is a very real phenomenon in the world in which we live" (Sen 1999a: 122). Because of these power imbalances, a sufficient response to inequities (and other shortcomings of the market), and the introduction of certain market restrictions, are important components underlying well-functioning markets themselves. Sen thus advocates public discussion, not only to deliberate equity-efficiency trade-offs, but also to protect markets against special interests. "In the test of open democracy, public interest may well have excellent prospects of winning against the spirited advocacy of the small coterie of vested interests . . . the remedy has to lie in more freedom – including that of public discussion and participatory political decisions" (Sen 1999a: 123).

Finally, although much of economic development rightly focuses on market expansion, markets are by no means sufficient institutions for advancing human freedoms. Vigorous, well-supported nonmarket institutions are required for the provision of public goods such as public health, defense, police, and in many cases basic education. Many low-income countries have managed to invest in strong social systems, and indeed these provide a strong foundation for equitable growth – which shows again the interconnections between these institutions and markets. A feature of this

approach, coming back again to the perspective of freedom, is "to see people – even beneficiaries – as agents rather than as motionless patients" (Sen
1999a: 137).

Education

Education can have intrinsic value, as a capability people deeply enjoy –
the ability to read a new poem, to satisfy their curiosity on some subject, or
to deepen their understanding of history and of world affairs, for example.
It is also astoundingly useful. Literacy, for example, enables people better
to navigate in society – they can become aware of their legal rights, take
out a bank loan, catch the right bus, secure better employment, write to
family and loved ones, and engage with new technologies. Education can
also be a "catalyst of social change" (Drèze and Sen 2002: 143) – enabling
people to overcome historical inequalities due to class, gender, caste, race,
disability, and so on. Indeed, disadvantaged groups in India widely per-
ceive education to be "the most promising means of upward mobility for
their children" (Drèze and Sen 2002: 144). Furthermore, an educated populace can be empowered to undertake public action, lobby, vote, organize
campaigns, and make their values and demands heard effectively. As the
title of Sen's article "To Build a Country, Build a Schoolhouse" might suggest, Drèze and Sen repeatedly and emphatically underline the fundamental
importance of education. "It is hard to overstate the need for unequivocal
rejection of . . . dismissive views of the value of education. A firm commitment to the widespread and equitable provision of basic education is the
first requirement of rapid progress in eradicating educational deprivation
in India" (Drèze and Sen 2002: 146; see Sen 2002c).

A clear reason for emphasizing education lies in the educational deprivations that so many face. Taking the example of India, Drèze and Sen (2002)
observe that half of the adult population are unable to read and write. Further, literacy is unequally spread by gender and geography, with 86 percent
female literacy in the Indian state of Kerala compared with 20 percent in
Rajasthan. Illiteracy rises sharply in rural areas, and among certain castes
and tribes. Further, although school attendance increased significantly in
the 1990s, the progress did not benefit all of these groups equally. Moreover, in some areas teachers are often absent; the quality of education is, in
other cases, extremely poor.

Having established that educational capabilities should be expanded,
the question is how? The analysis in Drèze and Sen (2002) demonstrates
the thorough, many-faceted kind of analysis that explores connections

between development actions and human capabilities. Here are some of the footprints of that exploration. One possible cause of low education was that education is not a valued capability in the eyes of the parents and the communities. However, a parent survey found keen interest among parents in children's education and indeed in girls' education also. Another possibility was that the need for child labor prohibited deprived families from sending children to school; again this was not substantiated empirically. Rather, the barriers appeared to be the affordability of books and uniforms, the distance to schools, and the anticipated returns on education – which were stronger for boys than for girls. Perhaps the strongest barrier was the low quality of education – ramshackle schools, large class sizes, a complex curriculum structure, and unmotivated teachers. Further analysis showed that a significant contribution to the low quality of education was weak motivation and accountability of government teachers – either to school inspectors or to the parents and local community.

Drèze and Sen's analysis then turns to observe that the Indian constitution (Article 45) urges states to provide free and compulsory education for children up to fourteen years old. Political parties have reiterated this commitment, promising to increase educational expenditure. Instead, government of India figures show that expenditure declined from 4.4 percent of GDP in 1989 to 3.6 percent in 1997 (Drèze and Sen 2002: 166). The analysis implies there might be reason for parents and others to demand political responses to the ramshackle schools and missing teachers.

To deepen this consideration of proactive public action by parents, the positive experience of one state – Himachal Pradesh – in furthering basic education was analyzed. Between 1961 and 1991, girls' literacy improved from 61 percent to 86 percent, and by 1998–9, school attendance was above 97 percent for both girls and boys – a rate higher than that in Kerala. This advance took place against considerable odds: Himachal Pradesh has many remote areas that are difficult to access, has been overlooked by private or religious schools, and relied economically on child labor. Although it is one of the wealthier Indian states, its educational advances were not mirrored in other states of a similar economic level such as Punjab or Harayana. Drèze and Sen trace the "virtuous circle" that developed in Himachal Pradesh. By drawing on and mobilizing a strong tradition of local cooperation and collaboration for shared ends, groups created a politically salient impetus to invest in education. A relatively egalitarian economic structure assured that the expansion of education occurred relatively evenly, and that teachers and students were of similar status. Furthermore, because women in Himachal Pradesh do regularly work outside the home, education increased their economic capacity, which provided a balanced incentive for girls and boys to attend school and, similarly, to teach school.

On the basis of this analysis of the educational shortcomings, Drèze and Sen advocate a political mobilization in support of basic education that would work locally as well as through formal political and economic channels:

> What is perhaps most striking of all is that the failures of government policy over an extended period have provoked so little political challenge.... The fact that the government was able to get away with so much in the field of elementary education relates to the lack of political power of the illiterate masses.... It also reflects the fact ... that the social value of basic education has been neglected not only by government authorities but also in social and political movements. (Drèze and Sen 2002: 187)

This account of education and development gives the flavor of Sen's method of investigating a development priority. It considers the possible *value* of education – intrinsically as well as instrumentally – and the *deprivations* that many experience in education, and examines the reasons for these. Is it that basic education is not *valued* by the relevant group (parents and students)? Are they blocked from taking advantage of it, thus lacking the *real* freedom to be educated although they may have formal access? Or are there institutional reasons for nonattendance – in this case deep flaws in the public education system itself? Having diagnosed, as it were, core issues, the analysis turns to actions that people (parents, students, and teachers as well as public institutions, in this example) could undertake as *agents* in order to redress the situation. In this case, drawing on the example of Himachal Pradesh, these include political action and direct involvement.

Gender I: Cooperative Conflict

Sen describes himself "in part, as a feminist economist" (Sen et al. 2003: 322), and gender recurs throughout his writings on many themes. Drawing on various empirical studies, Sen regularly consolidates for readers the evidence from other studies that women's agency and work affect the lives of all family members – men and children as well as others in the public. Women's empowerment, often generated by an improvement in women's education and employment and property rights, leads to important changes. For example, repeated empirical studies show that empowering women increases the proportion of resources within a family that women control, decreases fertility, and increases child survival and health.

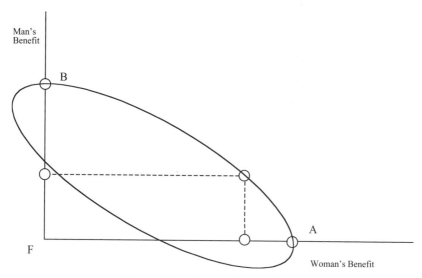

Figure 8.1 Cooperative Conflicts.

In addition to building on previous studies, Sen develops a distinct theoretical insight on cooperative conflicts. Sen first clarified cooperative conflicts with respect to the relationship between women and men within the
household, and subsequently has used this as the basis on which to scruti-
nize globalization. The insight is this: consider a woman, Lila, and a man,
Milo, who join together and form a cooperative household. It is likely that
their cooperation enables a higher standard of living than they could attain
separately. At the same time, they could divide the "gains" that arise from
their cooperation in many ways. In some possible scenarios, Milo would be
a great deal better off with respect to his former bachelordom and Lila only
marginally better; in others, Lila would excel. In all situations, we presume,
each person's position is better than it would be if they split up. In such
situations, Sen argues, it is important to recognize the particular nature
of bargaining, which he terms "cooperative conflicts" – how the gains of
cooperation are divided among cooperating partners. Unlike other sorts of
conflicts, these are likely to be largely implicit, and occur under the guise
of cooperation that defines the relationship.

In Figure 8.1, position F (the origin) represents the fallback position of
being single. The vertical axis represents the man's benefits from the relationship; the horizontal, the woman's benefits. The oval traces the feasible
outcomes for their relationship. Obviously the lower curves are dominated
by the upper, so the couple is likely to choose some point along the upper

curve AB. However, as is readily apparent, the point they choose may well be *far* better for the man than for the woman or vice versa. It is in the man's interest to go as far left as possible along the curve; in the woman's, to go as far right. As Sen observes, "The choice over AB is one of pure *conflict* and that between any given point on AB and the fall-back position F is one of pure *co-operation*" (Sen 1985c: 201).

Cooperative conflicts can occur not only between men and women, but between members of many groups. To detect and consider the disparities in members' benefits from belonging to a group or collective enterprise, Sen focuses attention on the capability of individual people rather than only considering the sum total of the household or group. This curiosity regarding people's actual welfare within the boundary of a group recurs in many other settings, for example in considering issues of intrahousehold distribution of food.

Gender II: Missing Women

Another significant finding on gender equality was publicized famously under the title of 100 million "missing women."[5] The problem arose from the following sequence of empirical observations:

- In the natural state, 5 percent more boys than girls are born (Sen 1992b).
- "But women are hardier than men, and, given similar care, survive better at all ages" (Sen 1992b: 587).
- Not only in Europe and America, but also in Sub-Saharan Africa, women outnumber men (Sen 1992b).
- In some parts of Asia and North Africa, the gender ratio was reversed. Instead of the ratio of women to men being 1.05 (as in Europe) or 1.02 (as in sub-Saharan Africa), it was between 0.90 (Pakistan) and 0.95 (Egypt) (data in Sen 1992b).
- Closer examination of this inequality in 1992 suggested that women and particularly young girls were being systematically deprived of nutritional and health requirements in the countries, which increased their mortality (Sen 1992b).

---

[5] This finding was first published in *Hunger and Public Action* (Drèze and Sen 1989: 51f) and subsequently in the *British Medical Journal* (Sen 1992c), and was revisited in Sen 2003b. See also Sen 1999a: 104f, 319n; Sen 1990b; Klasen 1994; Klasen and Wink 2002, 2003; Croll 2001; Hicks 2003.

To highlight the magnitude of this problem, Sen calculated the number of girls and women whose premature deaths underlay the skewed male-female ratios, using the sub-Saharan ratio as "normal." The evidence showed that more than 100 million women were missing from the planet. This eye-catching finding generated further empirical work on the calculation itself as well as on the underlying gender inequalities it advertised.

Recently Sen returned to the issue of differential mortality, noting that while girls' survival rates had improved tremendously "this has been counterbalanced by a new female disadvantage – that in natality – through sex specific abortions aimed against the female fetus" (Sen 2003b: 1297). Because of sex-specific abortions in the north and west of India, for example, sex ratios at birth have become alarmingly low – between 79.3 and 89.7 girls to 100 boys in four states. Sex-selective abortion – like the under-nourishment of girls – is a concrete symptom of a deeper gender bias. The empirical 100 million headline does much to publicize the new problem and encourage further examination of it.

This work explicitly introduces the principle of equity into considerations of development, alongside capability expansion. For, if one were interested solely in equalizing the capability to live a long life, for example (which would not be an unreasonable position if basal equality is to be considered in capability space) (Sen 1992a), medical attention might be given preferentially to men – at least above a certain age – to prolong their lives, and so on. Equity introduces a more balanced framework for evaluation.

Population and Reason

Sen argues that the problem of increasing population requires "more freedom, not less" (Sen 1999a: 216). In the analysis of population control, attention is steadily directed to parents as agents. The view of persons that Sen's approach draws upon is consistent with the approach just outlined for education. Parents are seen as agents whose values can be informed, and who can be engaged to act on their values; they are not seen as unreasonable and in need of sharp coercive control from above.

With respect to population growth, Sen presents data showing that there is still no world food crisis. Rather, food production per head has been increasing in every world region except Africa since 1974, and it has been increasing the most in Asia, the most populous region. Food availability has increased despite a drop in food prices, hence a reduction of economic incentives to produce food. Thus the "population problem" is not that there is an impending lack of food (although it is often scarily framed that way). The real problem is that world population has ballooned, causing overcrowding and environmental strains, so in many countries fertility reduction would be desirable. This is particularly the case given the accelerating nature of population growth: "It took the world population millions of years to reach the first billion [human beings], then 123 years to get to the second, followed by 33 years to the third, 14 years to the fourth, and 13 years to the fifth billion" (Sen 1999a: 210).

But, by what strategies or policies can and should population growth be slowed? Sen explores two alternative sets of policies, both of which have contemporary advocates. The first, traced to Malthus, relies on coercive practices of threats, sterilization, or the restriction of benefits to multi-children families. These policies arise from a distrust in the power of reason and planning among the wider population. In contrast, "Condorcet anticipated a voluntary reduction in fertility rates and predicted the emergence of new norms of small family size based on 'the progress of reason'" (Sen 1999a: 214). Using comparative studies from states in China and India, it is possible to explore how quickly coercive policies – which have been used in China and some parts of India – reduced total fertility rates, in comparison with a second stream of strategies, which offer women education and empowerment, and make affordable contraceptives available (investment in family planning is necessary, but, as Sen discusses in relation to Bangladesh, is insufficient without other investment in women's empowerment). Sen concludes, "There is no imminent emergency that calls for a breathless response. What is called for is systematic support for people's own decisions to reduce family size through expanding education and health care, and through economic and social development" (Sen 1994).

In the issue of population, like education, the structure of the analysis is similarly multifaceted, tracing people's values and knowledge, drawing on empirical evidence, but consistently and steadily proposing policies that have the dual characteristics of promising instrumental success (actual reduction of fertility) and advancing freedom and respecting people as agents.

Health

In analyses of health, considerations span the value of health to people, the indicators of good health, instrumental arrangements that best secure health as well as other capabilities, and the role of people as agents in securing their own health capabilities.

Sen takes as a starting point "the ubiquity of health as a social consideration" (Sen 2002d: 659). His observation that health appears to be deeply valued by people across cultures and generations, and thus is integral to development, is hardly controversial. Pointing out the empirical connections between health and many other freedoms such as education, employment, democratic participation, and so on, Sen argues that health capabilities are also instrumentally powerful for promoting development. A range of articles also address complex issues of health equity – the distribution of health-related capabilities across a population (Sen 1999b, 1999c, 2002a, 2002d; Klasen and Wink 2002;Williams 2003; Anand, Peter, and Sen 2004).

But, how to establish good public health outcomes? Again, in answering this question Sen scrutinizes different historical paths by which communities have achieved these expansions in such basic health capabilities as the ability to live long. Drèze and Sen identified two paths: those used in countries that have succeeded in increasing the length and quality of life *and* enjoying economic growth (growth-mediated strategies – e.g., South Korea and Taiwan), and those used in countries that have done so without growth (support-led strategies, such as Sri Lanka and pre-reform China) (Drèze and Sen 1989). They observe that in a low-growth situation, poor countries can still provide basic health care because of the lower relative costs: "A poor economy may *have* less money to spend on health care and education, but it also *needs* less money to spend to provide the same services, which would cost much more in the richer countries" (Drèze and Sen 2002: 48). Analyzing the reduction of mortality in twentieth-century Britain, for example, Sen draws attention to the striking result that the reduction of mortality and undernourishment was steepest *during* the two World Wars, when Britain adopted support-led strategies (Drèze and Sen 2002: 50). Of course – and this is important to note – it may be deeply preferable for nations *also* to experience economic growth, because this would expand other capabilities that would not be nurtured under support-led strategies. Yet, in the absence of such growth, public health can still be promoted.

On the basis of such empirical studies, Sen advocates public investment in health care. At the same time, the role for positive public engagement by people seen as agents, not merely as beneficiaries of public health programs, never slips from view. Here the example is China. China's pre-reform public health arrangements are legendary – in preventative health, barefoot doctors, collective health insurance, and medical infrastructure. Yet, overnight, in 1979, in the enthusiasm of liberalization, China dismantled its public health system. According to some estimates this swift action has left

70 percent of Chinese citizens without health insurance. Such action could not have been undertaken in a democracy – at least not without outcry and vigorous public debate and the possibility of reinstatement. Subsequent to the reform, the pace of China's health advances has slowed, leaving its infant mortality rate of thirty per thousand, for example, still significantly above that of the Indian state of Kerala – which is ten. Life expectancy gains also slowed. From 1979 to 1999, China's life expectancy rose from sixty-eight to just over seventy years; in the same period India's life expectancy rose six years from fifty-four to sixty. Although in China's case democratic practices were not required to create the public health system, in the absence of such practices the 1979 reforms showed how vulnerable even the much-admired health system was to a lightning-swift decline (Sen 1999a).

This conclusion is unambiguously summarized in the closing sentences of a keynote address Sen gave to the World Health Assembly in 1999: "Ultimately, there is nothing as important as informed public discussion and the participation of the people in pressing for changes that can protect our lives and liberties. The public has to see itself not merely as a patient, but also as an agent of change. The penalty of inaction and apathy can be illness and death" (Sen 1999c).

Hunger

Poverty and Famines opens by observing: "There is no law against dying of hunger" (Sen 1981). Yet, people's action and protests of injustice can effectively prevent famines. Sen's writings politicized famine, giving rise to a new approach to the problem.[6] The insight is often expressed this way: "No famine has ever taken place in the history of the world in a functioning democracy" (Sen 1999a: 16).

This body of famine studies is central to consider because it was the first to frame hunger as a political problem rather than a lack of food availability or the result of a market failure or other natural causes.

> Hunger is ... intolerable in the modern world in a way it could not have been in the past. This is not so much because it is more intense, but because widespread hunger is so unnecessary and unwarranted in the modern world. ... If politics is 'the art of the possible', then conquering world

---

[6] Sen's work on famine in particular is found in Sen 1980b, 1981, 1991, and Drèze and Sen 1989, 1990. For other work, see, for example, Devereux 2001; de Waal 2004.

hunger has become a political issue in a way it could not have been in the past. (Drèze and Sen 1989: 5–6)

How did this politicization – in which political action was identified as a lever for change and a source for hope – emerge?

The argument was initially built put forward in Sen's *Poverty and Famines*, later expanded into three volumes of studies, which examined physiological, market-based, economic, weather-related, and political aspects of famine as well as endemic hunger in different countries (Sen 1981; Drèze and Sen 1989, 1990). Three observations across these studies support the politicization of famine as an issue of structural injustice.

One key *independence* that Sen established empirically and early was the independence of famine from food production and availability. For example, the famines in Bengal in 1943, Ethiopia in 1973, and Bangladesh in 1974, all occurred in the absence of a decline in food availability (Drèze and Sen 1989: 27).

Another observation was that famine had an impact on different sections of the population unequally: "Different groups typically do have very different commanding powers over food, and an over-all shortage brings out the contrasting powers in stark clarity" (Sen 1981: 43). This gave further evidence of injustice: that some weathered the famine intact – or even with economic gain – whereas others perished.

A third observation related to the feasibility of a public response. Having studied successful experiences in avoiding famine, especially in India and many African countries, Drèze and Sen observe that

> these experiences firmly demonstrate how easy it is to exterminate famines if public support . . . is well planned on a regular basis to protect the entitlements of vulnerable groups. . . . It is also clear that the eradication of famines need not *await* a major breakthrough in raising the per-capita availability of food, or in radically reducing its variance (even though these goals are important in themselves and can be – and must be – promoted in the long run by well-organized public policy). Public action can decisively eliminate famines *now*. (Drèze and Sen 1989: 257–8)

These observations about the injustice of famine and the potential for human response (however fallible and imperfect) enabled famine to be framed as a political issue, in the sense that action by the public at large could catalyze the necessary public and economic actions that might not arise in the absence of public outcry.

Public Action

What is evident in many of the preceding analyses is not only the tremendous breadth of analysis, but also the steady appeal to people as agents: to public deliberation and debate, to protests, democratic practices, social movements, and other forms of participation that balance and complete development processes. "The case for relating public policy to a close scrutiny of its actual effects is certainly very strong, but the need to protest – to rage, to holler – is not any weaker" (Sen 2001).

Sen's insistent focus on people as agents – whose values must be engaged in setting development objectives, whose energies will help to propel these objectives – has the effect of shifting the borders of development out from a narrowly economic space to include aspects of political engagement, which are broadly titled public action.

> By public action we mean not merely the activities of the state, but also social actions taken by members of the public – both 'collaborative' (through civil cooperation) and 'adversarial' (through social criticism and political opposition. The . . . reach of public action goes well beyond the doings of the state, and involves what is done *by* the public – not merely *for* the public. We also argue that the nature and effectiveness of the activities of the state can deteriorate very easily in the absence of public vigilance and activism. (Drèze and Sen 1989: vii)

Thus, the reach of public action permeates well beyond participation in formal political procedures. It gestures to participation within families, community groups, informal organizations, press and the media, and other forums.

Sen's account of the substantive value of political freedom and democratic practice demonstrates the prominence given to public action. Those who are skeptical of political freedom often ask, "Why bother about the finesse of political freedoms given the overpowering grossness of intense economic needs?" (Sen 1999a: 147). The view that economic development should precede the procuring of political liberties and civil rights for the poor is a common thesis, which Sen challenges both at the individual and at the collective level. As we have seen, Sen defends the direct value of human agency and thus of social and political arrangements that support its exercise. Whereas people's actual views on democratic practice may be difficult to test in repressive situations, evidence such as the protest against Indira Gandhi's 1970s "emergency" as well as "the struggle for democratic freedoms in South Korea, Thailand, Bangladesh, Pakistan, Burma (or Myanmar) and elsewhere in Asia" (Sen 1999a: 151) suggests a value for it, even among the poor. Further, scrutiny of the evidence does not support the view that authoritarianism is a more efficient midwife of economic growth and prosperity than democratic practice. The evidence is ambiguous and varied, with no consistent results either of conflict or of synergy between the economic output and the political system (Sen 1999a: 122). Given this situation, Sen advocates that both economic and political freedoms be pursued simultaneously.

I will not try to summarize this chapter, but instead close with one observation on public action that applies also to the other topics that have been discussed. A number of authors have observed that Sen's account of agency, although inspiring, is incomplete. For example, it defines agency such that it relates to people's values and the common good, but in so doing excludes by definition actions that undermine the common good for personal or group gain, or express prejudice or exact vengeance, so it is an important, but incomplete account of human action (Stewart 2005; Deneulin 2006; Crocker 2008). This observation is developed in many engagements with Sen's writings in the subsequent literature. Yet, however incomplete Sen's interventions have been, across many crucial areas of development theory, they identify directions of inquiry that are considerably less misconceived than existing theories, and suggest how concrete policies, practices, analyses, and measures might aim more accurately and realistically at justice and human freedoms.

References

Alkire, S. (2005). "Why the Capability Approach?" *Journal of Human Development*, 6, 115–33.

Alkire, S. (2008). "The Capability Approach: Mapping Measurement Issues and Choosing Dimensions," in Kakwani and Silber (eds), *The Many Dimension of Poverty* (Basingstoke: Palgrave-Macmillan).

Alkire, S., and S. Deneulin (2002). "Individual Motivation, Its Nature, Determinants and Consequences for within Group Behaviour," in Heyer, Stewart, and Thorp (eds.), *Group Motivation and Development: Is the Market Destroying Cooperation?* (Oxford: Oxford University Press).

Alkire, S., and J. Foster (2007). "Counting and Multidimensional Poverty Measures," OPHI working paper series.

Anand, S., F. Peter, and A. Sen. (2004). *Public Health, Ethics, and Equity* (Oxford: Oxford University Press).

Anand, S., and A. K. Sen (1994). *Human Development Index: Methodology and Measurement* (New York: Human Development Report Office, United Nations Development Programme).

Aristotle (1984). *The Nicomachean Ethics*, trans. D. Ross (Oxford: Oxford University Press).

Clark, D. A. (2005). "Sen's Capability Approach and the Many Spaces of Human Well-Being," *Journal of Development Studies*, 41, 1339–68.

Crocker, D. (1992). "Functioning and Capabilities: The Foundation of Sen's and Nussbaum's Development Ethic," *Political Theory*, 20, 584–612.

Crocker, D. (1995). "Functioning and Capability: The Foundation of Sen's and Nussbaum's Development Ethic, Part II," in Nussbaum and Glover (eds.), *Women, Culture, and Development* (Oxford: Clarendon Press).

Crocker, D. (2008). *Ethics of Global Development: Agency, Capability, and Deliberative Democracy* (Cambridge: Cambridge University Press).

Croll, E. J. (2001). "Amartya Sen's 100 Million Missing Women," *Oxford Development Studies*, 29, 225–44.

Deneulin, S. (2006). *The Capability Approach and the Praxis of Development* (Basingstoke: Palgrave Macmillan).

Devereux, S. (2001). "Sen's Entitlement Approach: Critiques and Counter-Critiques," *Oxford Journal of Development Studies*, 29, 245–63.

de Waal, A. (2004). *Famine That Kills* (Oxford: Oxford University Press).

Drèze, J., and A. K. Sen (1989). *Hunger and Public Action* (Oxford: Clarendon Press).

Drèze, J., and A. K. Sen (1990). *The Political Economy of Hunger* (Oxford: Clarendon Press; New York: Oxford University Press).

Drèze, J., and A. K. Sen (2002). *India, Development and Participation* (New Delhi: Oxford University Press).

Ghai, D. P., and International Labour Office (1977). *The Basic-Needs Approach to Development: Some Issues Regarding Concepts and Methodology* (Geneva: International Labour Office).

Hicks, D. (2003). "Gender, Discrimination, and Capability," *Journal of Religious Ethics*, 30, 1, 140–53.

Kakwani, N., and J. Silber (2008a). *The Many Dimensions of Poverty* (Basingstoke: Palgrave Macmillan).

Kakwani, N., and J. Silber (2008b). *Quantitative Approaches to Multidimensional Poverty Measurement* (Basingstoke: Palgrave Macmillan).

Kant, I. (1785). *Grundlegung Zur Metaphysik De Sitten*.

Kant, I. (1909). "Fundamental Principles of the Metaphysics of Morals," in Abbot (ed.), *Critique of Practical Reason and Other Works on the Theory of Ethics* (London: Longmans).

Klasen, S. (1994). "Missing Women Reconsidered," *World Development*, 1022, 61–71.

Klasen, S., and C. Wink (2002). "A Turning Point in Gender Bias in Mortality? An Update on the Number of Missing Women," *Population & Development Review*, 28, 285–312.

Klasen, S., and C. Wink (2003). "'Missing Women': Revisiting the Debate," *Feminist Economics*, 9, 263–99.

Qizilbash, M. (1996). "Capabilities, Well-Being and Human Development: A Survey," *Journal of Development Studies*, 33, 143–62.

Robeyns, I. (2005). "The Capability Approach: A Theoretical Survey," *Journal of Human Development*, 6, 93–114.

Sen, A. K. (1967). "The Nature and Classes of Prescriptive Judgments," *Philosophical Quarterly*, 17, 46–62.

Sen, A. K. (1973). *On Economic Inequality* (Oxford: Clarendon Press).

Sen, A. K. (1976). "Poverty: An Ordinal Approach to Measurement," *Econometrica*, 44, 219–31.

Sen, A. K. (1977). "Rational Fools: A Critique of the Behavioral Foundations of Economic Theory," *Philosophy and Public Affairs*, 6, 317–44.

Sen, A. K. (1979). "Informational Analysis of Moral Principles," in Harrison (ed.), *Rational Action* (Cambridge: Cambridge University Press).

Sen, A. K. (1980a). "Equality of What?" in McMurrin (ed.), *The Tanner Lectures on Human Values* 1 (Salt Lake City: University of Utah Press).

Sen, A. K. (1980b). "Famines," *World Development*, 8, 613–21.

Sen, A. K. (1981). *Poverty and Famines: An Essay on Entitlement and Deprivation* (Oxford: Clarendon Press; New York: Oxford University Press).

Sen, A. K. (1982). "Rights and Agency," *Philosophy and Public Affairs*, 11, 3–39.

Sen, A. K. (1983a). "Development: Which Way Now?" *The Economic Journal*, 93, 745.

Sen, A. K. (1983b). "Evaluator Relativity and Consequential Evaluation," *Philosophy and Public Affairs*, 12, 113–32.

Sen, A. K. (1984). "The Living Standard," *Oxford Economic Papers*, 36, 74–90.

Sen, A. K. (1985a). *Commodities and Capabilities*(Amsterdam: North-Holland; New York: Elsevier Science).

Sen, A. K. (1985b). "Well-Being, Agency and Freedom: The Dewey Lectures 1984," *Journal of Philosophy*, 82, 169–221.

Sen, A. K. (1985c). "Women, Technology and Sexual Divisions," *Trade and Development*, 6, 195–223.

Sen, A. K. (1987). "The Standard of Living," in Hawthorn (ed.), *The Standard of Living* (Cambridge: Cambridge University Press).

Sen, A. K. (1988). "The Concept of Development," in Chenery and Srinivasan (eds.), *Handbook of Development Economics* (Amsterdam: North-Holland; New York: Elsevier Science).

Sen, A. K. (1989). "Development as Capability Expansion," *Journal of Development Planning*, 19, 41–58.

Sen, A. K. (1990a). "Development as Capability Expansion," in Griffin and Knight (eds.), *Human Development and the International Development Strategy for the 1990s* (London: Macmillan).

Sen, A. K. (1990b). "More Than 100 Million Women Are Missing," *New York Review of Books*, 37, 20 (20 December).

Sen, A. K. (1991). "Wars and Famines: On Divisions and Incentives," Suntory-Toyota International Centre Discussion Paper No. 33 (London School of Economics, Development Economics Research Program).

Sen, A. K. (1992a). *Inequality Reexamined* (Cambridge, MA: Harvard University Press).

Sen, A. K. (1992b). "Missing Women," *British Medical Journal*, 304, 6827, 587–8.

Sen, A. K. (1994). "Population: Delusion and Reality," *New York Review of Books*, 41, 15 (22 September).

Sen, A. K. (1997). "From Income Inequality to Economic Inequality," *Southern Economic Journal*, 64, 384.

Sen, A. K. (1998). "Mahbub Ul Haq: The Courage and Creativity of His Ideas," text of speech at the Memorial Meeting for Mahbub ul Haq at the United Nations, New York, October 15, 1998.

Sen, A. K. (1999a). *Development as Freedom* (New York: Anchor Books).

Sen, A. K. (1999b). "Economics and Health," *Lancet (North American Edition)*, 354, SIV20.

Sen, A. K. (1999c). "Health in Development," *Bulletin of the World Health Organization*, 77, 619.

Sen, A. K. (2000). "Consequential Evaluation and Practical Reason," *Journal of Philosophy*, 97, 477.

Sen, A. K. (2001). "Hunger: Old Torments and New Blunders," *The Little Magazine*, 2, 9–13.

Sen, A. K. (2002a). "Health: Perception Versus Observation," *British Medical Journal*, 324, 860–1.

Sen, A. K. (2002b). *Rationality and Freedom* (Cambridge, MA: Belknap Press).

Sen, A. K. (2002c). "To Build a Country, Build a Schoolhouse," *New York Times*, 27 May.

Sen, A. K. (2002d). "Why Health Equity?" *Health Economics*, 11, 659–66.

Sen, A. K. (2003a). "Development as Capability Expansion," in Fukuda-Parr (ed.), *Readings in Human Development* (New Delhi: Oxford University Press).

Sen, A. K. (2003b). "Missing Women Revisited," *British Medical Journal*, 327, 1297–8.

Sen, A. K. (2003c). "Development, Rights and Human Security," Box 1.3, pp. 8–9 in *Human Security Now* (Report of the Commission on Human Security) (New York: United Nations).

Sen, A. K. (2004). "Elements of a Theory of Human Rights," *Philosophy and Public Affairs*, 234, 315–56.

Sen, A. K. (2006). "What Do We Want from a Theory of Justice," *Journal of Philosophy*, 53, 5, 215–38.

Sen, A. K., B. Agarwal, J. Humphries, and I. Robeyns (2003). "Continuing the Conversation," *Feminist Economics*, 9, 319–32.

Sen, A. K., and J. E. Foster (1997). *On Economic Inequality* (Oxford: Clarendon Press; New York: Oxford University Press).

Sen, A. K., J. Muellbauer, et al. (1987). Hawthorn (ed.), *The Standard of Living* (Cambridge: Cambridge University Press).

Stewart, F. (1985). *Basic Needs in Developing Countries* (Baltimore: Johns Hopkins University Press).

Stewart, F. (2005). "Groups and Capabilities," *Journal of Human Development*, 6, 185–204.

Streeten, P., and World Bank (1981). *First Things First: Meeting Basic Human Needs in the Developing Countries* (New York: Oxford University Press for the World Bank).

United Nations Development Programme (2004). *Human Development Report 2004: Cultural Liberty in Today's Diverse World* (New York: United Nations Development Programme).

Williams, A. (2003). "Comment on Amartya Sen's 'Why Health Equity,'" *Health Economics*, 12, 65.

Selected Bibliography

A complete list of Sen's writings is available at http://www.economics.harvard.
edu/faculty/sen. This bibliography is meant to guide those who are not already
familiar with Sen's work. Additional references are to be found at the end of each
chapter.

Collective Choice and Social Welfare (San Francisco: Holden-Day, 1970; Edinburgh:
Oliver and Boyd, 1971; Amsterdam: North-Holland, 1979).

> Still one of the best introductions to social or collective choice theory. The book
> is divided into formal and informal chapters, attempting "to cater to two distinct
> groups of readers, viz., those who are primarily interested in the relevance of
> the results rather than in their formal statement and technical derivation, and
> those who are also concerned with the latter."

Poverty and Famines: An Essay on Entitlement and Deprivation (Oxford: Clarendon
Press, 1981).

> A good statement of Sen's research on famine, with some technical appendixes.

Choice, Welfare, and Measurement (Oxford: Basil Blackwell, 1982; Cambridge, MA:
Harvard University Press, 1997).

> The first of three major collections of Sen's essays. It contains many well-known
> and influential papers, including "Rational Fools: A Critique of the Behavioral
> Foundations of Economic Theory" (1977), "The Impossibility of a Paretian
> Liberal" (1970), and "Equality of What?" (1980). Two others (chapters 8 and
> 11) are important accounts of social choice theory that are good follow-ups to
> *Collective Choice and Social Welfare*.

Resources, Values and Development (Oxford: Basil Blackwell; 1984; Cambridge, MA:
Harvard University Press, 1984).

> The essays in this collection may be of interest primarily to economists, devel-
> opment theorists, and students of public policy.

Commodities and Capabilities (Amsterdam: North-Holland, 1985).

> A good statement of Sen's capabilities approach to welfare economics and policy.

On Ethics and Economics (Oxford: Basil Blackwell, 1987).

A short book, based on lectures given at Berkeley in 1986, arguing that economics is impoverished by its distance from ethics.

Inequality Reexamined (Oxford: Clarendon Press; New York: Russell Sage Foundation; Cambridge, MA: Harvard University Press, 1992).

An accessible presentation of Sen's view on equality, capabilities, and freedom.

Development as Freedom (New York: Knopf, 1999; paperback, New York: Anchor Books, 2000).

Based on a series of lectures presented to the World Bank in 1996 and 1997, this book defends the thesis that the expansion of freedom is both the primary end and the principal means of development. It is also recommended as a good statement of many of Sen's views about political and social organization.

Rationality and Freedom (Cambridge, MA: Harvard University Press, 2002).

The third collection of essays, with a useful introduction, Sen's Nobel Prize lecture (1998), some important papers on rationality, liberty, and markets, and the Arrow lectures on freedom and social choice (1991).

Identity and Violence: The Illusion of Destiny (New York: Norton, 2006).

Sen's reflections on identity, its importance, and the ways in which it can kill.

Index